Acts of Violence
in the School Setting

THEORY AND PRACTICE
IN CRIMINAL JUSTICE SERIES

Series Editor
Kimberly A. McCabe, University of Lynchburg, mccabe@lynchburg.edu

Theory and Practice in Criminal Justice provides professors with textbooks that cover popular criminal justice topics. This series of textbooks are comprehensible to students, while also having direct coverage and case examples. Each textbook in the series includes both core textbooks and supplemental textbooks, with complementing formats to allow instructors to utilize them together for the same course. Finally, the authorship of this series incorporates an academic and practitioner perspective that brings scholarship and real-life experiences to the student for a better preparation in the classroom and to the field.

Books in the Series
Child Abuse, Child Exploitation, and Criminal Justice Responses, by Daniel G. Murphy and April G. Rasmussen
Acts of Violence in the School Setting: National and International Responses, by Kimberly A. McCabe with Brianna Egan and Toy D. Eagle
Sex Crimes and Offenders: Exploring Questions of Character and Culture, by Mary Clifford and Alison Feigh

Acts of Violence in the School Setting

National and International Responses

By Kimberly McCabe

With Brianna Egan and Toy Eagle

ROWMAN & LITTLEFIELD
Lanham • Boulder • New York • London

Executive Editor: Kathryn Knigge
Editorial Assistant: Charlotte Gosnell
Channel Manager: Jonathan Raeder
Interior Designer: by Ilze Lemesis

Credits and acknowledgments for material borrowed from other sources, and reproduced with permission, appear on the appropriate pages within the text.

Published by Rowman & Littlefield
An imprint of The Rowman & Littlefield Publishing Group, Inc.
4501 Forbes Boulevard, Suite 200, Lanham, Maryland 20706
www.rowman.com

6 Tinworth Street, London SE11 5AL, United Kingdom

British Library Cataloguing in Publication Information Available

Library of Congress Cataloging-in-Publication Data Available

Library of Congress Control Number: 2019952495

ISBN 978-1-5381-2534-2 (cloth)
ISBN 978-1-5381-2535-9 (pbk.)
ISBN 978-1-5381-2536-6 (electronic)

For children across the globe

For Jesse and Mac—KM
For my parents and brother—BE
For Kevin, Amanda, Jansen, and Ryker—TE

Contents

Foreword

Acts of Violence in the School Setting: National and International Responses, written by Kimberly McCabe, Brianna Egan, and Toy Eagle, is a wonderful addition to the required textbooks often reserved for courses focusing on child abuse, juvenile justice, and victims. With its international attention to school violence, this book is also applicable to comparative criminal justice courses that provide students the opportunity to evaluate criminal justice efforts to reduce crime and criminal behavior across the world.

The authors, all knowledgeable in the subject of school violence, victims, and child abuse through their work or research, provide the reader a *real-world* approach to discussions on school violence and explanations of the behavioral characteristics that may proceed an incident of violence within the school setting.

Within this book, crimes such as shootings, bullying, gang violence, and sexual assaults are discussed within the context of a school setting. Unique to this book is its section on violence in higher education, adult perpetrators, and mental illness. Lastly, this book integrates discussion on technology-assisted crimes as related to school violence.

As the global community focuses on school violence related to shootings such as Columbine, this book brings to light the historical research missteps in attempts to profile school shootings based upon Columbine. In addition, this book expands the discussion on school violence beyond those discussions on shootings.

Central to the themes of this book are insights into identifying the dynamics that exist in a school setting prior to an incident of violence and preventive measures that have been established globally in response to school violence. This book is recommended for anyone wishing to further understand the violence that may exist within a school.

Preface

As a parent of two children, I understand the worries of a mother when she sends her children to school, Will they be bullied? Will they have friends? Will they be safe? Even while my children are now attending universities, I am still concerned. Unfortunately, sometimes, being a criminologist has its disadvantages. By discipline, criminologists see the worst of human actions and, as a result, we are even more cautious when attempting to determine the causal factors to such tragedies as an incident of violence within a school. My coauthors, both embedded in the areas of victims' services, help to provide the balance in this book.

This book attempts to address school violence not only from the perspective of crime and punishment but also from the perspective of assisting victims and addressing mental illness. It is my desire that this book will provide you the information on school violence to better your understanding of this complex issue. For it is through the understanding of school violence that we are better able to adequately address school violence.

Kimberly McCabe

Chapter One

A History of School Violence

KEY WORDS

1870 Education Act (British)
Apprenticeships
Catholic schools
Central Parental Schools
Common School Era

Disciplinary class-rooms
Education Act of 1918
Horace Mann
Massachusetts Act of 1647

Progressive School Era
Public school system
School violence
Second Chance (Last Chance) Schools
Traditional actions of violence

KEY ACRONYMS

(EPRS) European Parliamentary Research Service
(EU) European Union
(NCES) National Center for Education Statistics
(SRO) School Resource Officer
(UNICEF) United Nations International Children's Emergency Fund

On February 14, 2018, an expelled student from a Florida high school (USA) killed seventeen individuals in another US school shooting. On October 17 of the same year, a student attending Kerch Polytechnic College (Russia) killed twenty individuals in a school shooting. In August of 2018, only a few days after the start of the school year, a nine-year-old Colorado boy (USA) committed suicide after being bullied regarding his sexual orientation.[1] These accounts of school violence are too common in today's world.

One of the greatest concerns for parents across the globe is the safety of their children. The news of an incident of school violence, particularly a school shooting, produces a fear unlike no other. Parents are not aware of their child's situation, they are unable to contact their children, and they are often at the mercy of the media and first responders for any news about the event. The school environment was once one of the safest locations for children—this remains the case even though this may not be the public's perception. However, although children are still less likely to be victimized in school than at home or at the hands of a family member, the victimization of children within the school environment is a reality.[2]

In the United States on an annual basis, approximately 2 percent of students ages twelve to eighteen report being a victim of a violent act while within the school environment.[3] Internationally, in Denmark, approximately 7 percent of students report being victims of acts of violence within the school environment. In Switzerland, approximately 10 percent of students report being victimized at school, and in Ireland, approximately 15 percent of students report being a victim of an act of violence while at school.[4]

In addition, these actions of victimization within the school or by peers may lead a student to choose to engage in antisocial behaviors such as truancy or the most severe action of self-victimization (suicide). Globally, the teen suicide rate is approximately 7.4 per 100,000.[5] In the United States, there are approximately 8 teen (ages fifteen to nineteen) suicides per 100,000 young people.[6] In Russia, the teen suicide rate is more than 20 per 100,000, and in Lithuania, the teen suicide rate is nearly 24 per 100,000. The worst country, in terms of recognized cases of teen suicides, is Sri Lanka with a rate of more than 46 per 100,000. Overall trends in teen suicide are increasing in both European and non-European countries.[7] Of course, not all of these teen suicides are in direct response to school victimization; however, more and more suicides are attributed to bullying, cyberbullying, and abuse received by individuals within the school environment. Therefore, any act of violence or victimization within the school setting is a concern for students, parents, and societies.

The National Center for Injury Prevention and Control defines school violence as youth violence that occurs on school property, on the way to or from a school-sponsored event, or during a school-sponsored event.[8] For the purpose of this book, incidents of violence that occur on school grounds or incidents that are facilitated through school contacts such as cyberbullying will be the focus. It is acknowledged that thefts and property damage are more common in the school setting than acts of violence or intimidations[9];

however, to better facilitate discussions on school violence, this book will focus only on those violent actions that occur within the school setting.

These traditional actions of violence include physical attacks, psychological abuse, verbal abuse, sexual violence, harassment, bullying, and school shootings. Although not the most common in the school environment, the most recognized form of school violence is a school shooting. These incidents of school shootings are rare and are decreasing, yet they still result in devastating consequences.[10] In addition, in today's world of technology, many incidents of school violence such as intimidation and bullying, which may have historically involved person-to-person contact, are now prevalent in cyberspace.

Between the years of 2000 and 2018, there were approximately 250 school shootings globally with some of the most recent occurring in 2017 and 2018. School violence, although most prevalent in the United States, is not simply a US problem. In 2017, a fifteen-year-old Canadian male student committed suicide after shooting two other students and a teacher on his school campus. During that same year, in Brazil, a private-school student fatally shot two classmates and injured four. Also in 2017, a seventeen-year-old high school student in France, armed with a rifle, two handguns, and two grenades, injured three students and the school's principal. Most recently, in 2018, a thirteen-year-old Russian girl opened fire with a gas pistol and injured seven seventh graders. Hence, school violence is a problem worthy of national and international attention for parents with children of any age.

The purpose of this text is to identify, discuss, and explain many forms of school violence from practical, theoretical, and criminal justice perspectives. For the clarity of this book, the actions of school violence include school shootings, sexual attacks, physical attacks, bullying, cyberbullying, sexting, and sextortion, with each of these actions defined later within this book. These actions may involve one-on-one contact, cliques, gangs, and/or the use of technology.

During the twentieth century, the school massacres in Dunblane, Scotland, in 1996 and at Columbine High School in Colorado in the United States in 1999 gave politicians and the media the events that they had sought to spotlight the evils of the world and the vulnerabilities within the school environment. Reporters, who did little to explore other incidents of child victimization related to child abuse, domestic violence, or youth violence such as gang warfare, quickly focused on the violence of school shootings, which in some cases involved multiple homicide victims.[11] In these discussions of school shootings, the crimes of bullying, peer assaults, and intimidations were also recognized. In fact, in article after article, news report after news report, the vulnerabilities to students while attempting to obtain an education were highlighted for the public. Thus, although research has suggested that young people are safer in school than out of school, the victimization of students while within their learning environments touches every parent's fear.[12]

There are many individuals who consider acts of school violence as new or as ever increasing. These acts are not increasing in rate; however, the severity of the incidents and media coverages often support the existence of such perception to exist.[13] In addition, and something that most people do not consider with an incident of school violence, is the legal considerations of the liability of schools when students are harmed, the liability for wrongful accusations, and the liability for violating students' rights. So, is violence within the school environment really a new problem?

To answer this question, one must first identify the specific acts of violence. As indicated, these reported actions of school violence include school shootings, bullying, intimidation, gang violence, and assaults. In addition, although the majority of these incidents are perpetrated by a student or former student of the school, these acts may also be the criminal actions of an adult. When examining the incidents of school violence in the world, it is suggested that the history of school violence follows the pattern of what one would consider the history of education throughout the world.

Specifically, in 1840, one of the first incidents of a school shooting was recorded when a law professor at the University of Virginia within the United States was shot by a student and later died.[14] In 1913, a former German teacher shot and killed four students and injured more than twenty other students.[15] In 1923, a headmaster killed two students in New Zealand.[16] In 1925, a Lithuanian student killed two students and a teacher.[17] In 1964, in Cologne, a forty-two-year-old male killed eight students and two teachers using a lance and a flame-thrower[18] and, again in the United States, in 1966, the infamous University of Texas Tower Shooting occurred, which resulted in the deaths of thirteen people.

Individuals agree that a child attending school should be concerned with the process of learning, not with avoiding victimization, and that the school environment should be a safe and secure location for both students and teachers. Unfortunately, media portrayals of school violence often leave the public consumers in fear for the safety of children and adult staff members located within the school environment. Most central to the theme of this text, without a safe learning environment, students and teachers may be fearful, assaulted, injured, or killed. In any event, most certainly students will not be learning.

PURPOSE

According to the US Department of Education, during the 2015–2016 school year, approximately 70 percent of all public schools in the United States recorded that one or more violent incidents had taken place.[19] This figure translates to a rate of approximately 18 crimes per 1,000 students enrolled in 2015–2016. During this same time period in Canada, teachers were reporting increases in violent actions within the classroom.[20] Also, during this same period in the European Union (EU) countries, victims of school violence ranged from 7 to 75 percent of the student body, making school violence a problem of global concern.[21]

Current research has shown a decline in the rates of school violence over the past few years, but the few high-profile cases broadcast repeatedly in the media lead the public to other conclusions. This text examines schools as educational settings that range from kindergarten to universities, physical acts of violence, and crimes against students that involve the internet. Acknowledged by this text are the diversity of the locations across the globe, the differences in definitions of crimes, and the differences in perceptions of victimization. However, incidents of school violence, no matter the difference in dynamics, still pose a concern for many individuals and are still a topic worthy of many discussions.

The purpose of this book is to provide accurate and practical information on school violence at a national and international level. This text is designed for students studying crime and criminal justice. Included in this textbook are definitions related to the types and categories of school violence, discussions on victims and offenders, and examples of cases of school violence across the globe. This text assumes a general understanding of the criminal justice system and a general exposure to the school environment. Also included in this textbook is a discussion on pre-incident indicators, the role of mental illness, and information on criminal justice system responses to school violence from both a national and international perspective. In addition, this book will provide information on victimization as it is perpetrated through the internet and focused upon students. Finally, this text discusses adult perpetrators of school violence and the explanations for such attacks.

This book is organized by nine chapters. At the beginning of each chapter are the keywords utilized within the chapter, and case examples are also provided throughout each chapter. In addition, questions on the chapter material and to stimulate classroom discussions or assignments are provided at the end of each chapter. The chapters are as follows. This current chapter, A History of School Violence, provides a general overview of school violence both nationally and internationally in a chronological order. This first chapter provides the reader the necessary background on educational systems throughout the world as well as a general overview of the changes in those systems. In addition, it provides statistical information on the incidents of school violence as well as the rates of teen suicides that may occur as an indirect consequence of victimization by schoolmates.

Chapter 2, Bullying and Cyberbullying, addresses the elements involved in cases of bullying, the characteristics of bullies and victims, and general theories to help explain the action of bullying. In addition, this second chapter discusses the dynamics behind bullying and intimidation within the school setting. It also addresses victimization in cyberspace, which often begins within the school setting. These types of victimizations include cyberbullying, sexting, and sextortion, with information provided on victims, offenders, and the most severe consequence (suicide).

Chapter 3, Cliques and Gangs within the School Environment, addresses the roles of cliques and gangs as related to school violence. Although research suggests that much gang criminal activity in the schools involves property damage and vandalism and that gang presence is declining in schools, gangs should still be considered in discussions of school violence. In schools with a strong presence of gangs, school victimization and the fear of victimization is increased. Lastly, this chapter provides a general overview on theories for understanding gang recruitment, participation, and violence.

Chapter 4, School Shootings and Media Perceptions, addresses the location, the time period, and the victims of these tragic events within the school environment. This chapter also provides information on the offenders of these incidents to include a demographic profile of age and sex. Included within the chapter is an empirical assessment of school shootings with an attempt to identify patterns in the occurrences. Also addressed is the concept of a "copycat," most often discussed in media accounts of tragedies and especially these tragedies that are fueled by multimedia foci.

Chapter 5, Mental Illness and School Violence, addresses the role of mental illness in scenarios of school violence and the research on mental illness in juveniles. Also included in this chapter is a discussion on the mental health implications of internet addiction, which for young people often refers to pathological gaming with youths "addicted" to video games as often cited in explanations of youth violence.

Chapter 6, Warning Factors and Teachers' Perceptions, addresses the roles of teachers in identifying risk factors and potential incidents of violence as well as a discussion on the types of threats and levels of threat risks. Also included in this chapter is a discussion on teachers as victims of school violence.

Chapter 7, Adult Offenders, addresses attempts to explain school shootings as perpetrated by an adult as well as other crimes of violence committed within the school environment by adult perpetrators. School shootings, usually assumed to be in response to a student's frustration, are also perpetrated by adults with little or no connection to the school setting. This chapter discusses these shootings and the location of a school selected as well as a profile of these offenders. Lastly, this chapter discuses other crimes of school violence and the use of technology in some of those crimes.

Chapter 8, Violence in Higher Education, addresses the risk for violence in higher education, the vulnerabilities of open campuses, which are often the environments for a college or university, and the types of violent crimes that occur within higher education. The issues of policy and environmental challenges such as concealed weapons and easy campus access, nontraditional students with life stresses in addition to school pressure, and conflicting cultures that often occur on large international university campuses are also discussed within this chapter. An empirical assessment of school shootings within institutions of higher education is also provided in an attempt to identify trends and patterns of shootings on college campuses.

The final chapter, chapter 9, Controlling the School Environment: Criminal Justice Responses, addresses legislation, zero tolerance, police presence, and the involvement of school staff and communities to address school violence. In addition, this chapter discusses prevention and threat assessments as well as actions that may follow a crisis of school violence. Therefore, this book provides an overview of the multiple issues related to school violence.

WHY STUDY SCHOOL VIOLENCE

During the aftermath of Columbine, many researchers from the disciplines of criminology, psychology, sociology, and public health began focusing on school violence. Their ultimate goal—to reduce the incidents. It was this goal that fueled both reactive and proactive approaches.

Specifically, legislative efforts such as zero tolerance policies and gun control were enacted to reduce the incidents of school violence.[22] In addition, much of the public supported the construction of additional juvenile correctional facilities.[23] Thus, by assuring that the action of violence within a school setting would be met with the strictest of penalties, the rational individual would choose not to commit such as act.

In addition to legislative and policy measures, preventive measures such as counseling for students and expulsions were also utilized.[24] Through these counseling efforts, students are provided the coping skills necessary to address social conflict and problem de-escalation. Through the use of expulsions, students who demonstrate the propensity toward violence are removed from the school environment; thereby, the threat from immediate danger is removed.

Finally, by identifying risk factors for school violence, incidents may be reduced. Specifically, by distinguishing internalized and externalized behaviors, those students at risk for perpetrating acts of violence within the school structure may be identified. Historically, the external behaviors such as aggression and delinquency have been more likely to be utilized to identify at-risk students. By also considering the internalized behaviors such as substance abuse and depression, those students who have historically been overlooked may also be identified as students with a propensity toward an external action such as a school shooting or an internal action such as a suicide.

Incidents of school violence occur across the globe involving victims and offenders of varying ages and backgrounds. As efforts to provide safer environments for students continue, the rates of school violence decline. In fact, for example, more children die from the flu or pneumonia each year in the United States than are killed at school.[25] However, these few high-profile cases of school violence that are broadcast over and over again by the media have led the public to other conclusions. In any event, the exposure of young people to any incident of school violence may lead to a variety of negative consequences to include health problems, depression, drug use, alcohol abuse, self-harm, and suicide. This chapter provides a general overview of the education of children across the globe as well as a brief case history of incidents of severe violence (i.e., school deaths) that have occurred over the centuries. Specifically, included are samples of international and national accounts of school violence over the last two centuries. Therefore, research that identifies the factors that will aid school officials and parents in reducing school violence is essential. Furthermore, the study of school violence and books such as this one will provide the research needed to address these actions of destruction.

HISTORY

The history of school violence follows the pattern of what most would consider the history of education. The following is a brief overview of school violence throughout the centuries of educating children. As revealed in this chronological account, violence within the school environment is not a new phenomenon. In fact, violence has existed since the beginning of formal education, and it is suggested, by these researchers, that school violence will continue long after this book is out of print.

Before 1600

Prior to the 1600s there were no legislatively mandated educational requirements for children anywhere in the world. However, there did exist various institutions of higher education across Europe. In fact, although there is no known date of foundation for Oxford University in England, evidence of teaching ideas exists as early as 1100. Over the next five centuries, many major universities were established, such as the University of Paris (France) around 1150, Cambridge University (England) around 1200, and Charles University in what is now Prague (Czech Republic) around 1350. These universities were for the affluent, and young people without the ability to pay did not attend. Although educational records prior to the nineteenth century are rare, terms such as *schoolmistress, schoolfellow, expulsion,* and *suspension* did exist in the fifteenth century. Therefore, one may assert that the actions of expulsion and suspension were used in language and may have been utilized as related to the inappropriate actions within the school environment even though these school environments were most likely institutions of higher learning.

1600–1800

During the colonial period of American society and throughout the world, few details on the educational system exist. However, what is revealed is the fact that education during that time was unregulated and irregular with the majority of the responsibilities for the education of children resting with the parents.[26] Children were educated throughout various times of the year with learning most often scheduled around their work schedules on the farm and on topics that were of interest to their teachers or their communities at the time. Some of those topics would include animal care and the agriculture of planting. At that time, children were selected for an education based upon the demographic characteristics of gender and socioeconomic status. Males were more likely to be educated than females, and females, if they were educated, were likely educated in secrecy or by listening to the educational lessons provided to the males.[27] In the rare occasion of the education of a female, only young women from very wealthy families would be educated on the subjects of language, arts, and music. One example of such a school for females was the French colony of Acadia, which is still in operation today in Quebec City, Canada.

During this period, there were three basic sources of education across the globe: the family, the church, and the public schools. Each of these three sources had their strengths and weaknesses, with none of these sources of education standardized or available to all children. It is within this period that the education of children younger than college-age became a public concern. In particular, in the United States, in 1642, the Massachusetts Bay Colony passed the first educational law that required all children to be taught to read and write. At that time, the Puritans, who resided within the area, felt that the education of children could strengthen the power of the church and hence create better and more obedient citizens. With this law, each town was required to monitor the parents and the craftsmen who taught children to ensure that these young people learned the basics of reading and writing. If a child was found to be illiterate or unable to understand the principles of the church, the parents or craftsmen could face a fine or lose custody of the child. Although this law did not require the establishment of schools, it did send a clear message to the citizens of the area that the education of children was a community responsibility.[28]

Later, the Massachusetts Act of 1647 mandated that towns in the area provide an education for all children by establishing and supporting public schools; however, it would be nearly two centuries before the education of children in the United States was made truly compulsory. Therefore, Massachusetts was the first state in the United States to pass a comprehensive education law. During this same period in Western Europe, Scotland introduced a tax to pay for the education of teachers to support free education for the children within their communities. In addition, in Central Europe, Russia appointed its first adviser for education, and, in Eastern Europe, Poland established a Commission of National Education to support learning for all children.

For most areas across the globe, children were educated in their homes by their parents or older siblings. These individuals were themselves educated and therefore able to teach the younger children the basics of reading, writing, and sometimes even literature.[29] For those parents who because of their own lack of education in reading and writing or because of financial constraints were unable to teach their children, an apprenticeship program was a viable alternative and readily used to provide skills and training to the young.[30]

In these apprenticeship programs, children were apprenticed out to professionals, taught reading and writing by those professionals, and, in exchange, worked for the professional for a prescribed time period that was normally seven years.[31] These early apprenticeships were a form of what we today refer to as on-the-job training, for boys as young as seven years old trained for skills-based occupations.[32] Unfortunately for many of these boys, these apprenticeships were not only the basis for today's vocational training but also often provided the children who were later the targets for victimization in terms of physical, sexual, and emotional abuse.[33] Children who served as apprentices often became simply slaves to their masters. In fact, these types of "educational programs" sometimes were the locations of what someday would be called acts of school violence. These forms of child labor continue to exist today as children as young as age three still help their parents to make bricks in countries such as Peru.[34] In addition, UNICEF concludes that 90 percent of domestic workers trafficked from West and Central Africa are females under the age of eighteen.[35]

A second source of education during the period was the church. The church both educated and disciplined the child. As the use of religion was a common European practice, many of the early colonist leaders also turned to the church for the education of their children. The church and its officials, with their strict fundamentalist curriculum, focused upon not only teaching children to read and write, but also on developing the moral character of the individual child. This "moral" character was developed by whatever means of discipline necessary. In many cases, an early form of discipline within the school setting was corporal punishment. Common methods of corporal punishment included spanking and paddling. Given that spanking a child as punishment was recommended in the Bible's book of Proverbs, and the fact that many of the early educational systems were regulated by the church, the use of physical punishment as a means of discipline has existed for centuries within the school environment. However, for some of the children assigned to priests and the church in an effort for education, the results were slavery in the form of sexual servitude and labor.[36] Also, despite the use of the church to educate the children of this era, what still resulted was, in most cases, the education of the children from the upper classes of society.

Finally, a third source for educating children during this period was the public school system.[37] In many localities it was mandated that areas with fifty or more households required lessons in reading and writing to the children within the area, and areas with one hundred or more households were required to provide reading, writing, and literature to the children.[38] These town or public schools educated the children for approximately seven years with the aid of teachers called schoolmasters, who were relocated into the area, paid by the citizens of the area to educate their children, and given a free hand in the education and discipline of their students.[39] These schoolmasters were both males and females, which was often associated with conflict between male students and female teachers in a largely patriarchal society. Most children received the education deemed necessary by the community within this public system of education; however, for many, mandatory attendance was not enforced and therefore some children were not educated. In addition, as the schoolmaster was afforded total control over the students, the discipline of the children was at the mercy of the teacher.

In response to these variations in education and incidents of abuse, the public soon began to acknowledge that a more formal approach to education was necessary. In addressing violence in the school setting during this period, efforts were minimal and limited. The education of children was viewed by many as a privilege, and that privilege was most often for the wealthy. In particular, parents, and especially those parents who were not educated, would accept the strict discipline and punishment of their children while they were within the school environment. Students who were disrespectful to their teachers or other adults, who did not memorize their lessons, or who mixed with students of the opposite sex were punished with lashes across their back, legs, hands, and so on.[40] Teachers also used a variety of approaches and weapons for punishment, including blows to the head, strikes to the hand with a ruler, and twisting of ears.[41] In 1793 in Massachusetts, one school reportedly included a whipping post located in the center of the classroom for the convenience of the teacher and to control unruly students.[42] Today, although corporal punishment is forbidden by countries with memberships in the United Nations, there are states within the United States and globally that still utilize corporal punishment as a mode of child discipline.

1800s

During the 1800s the United States, as a new country, began growing and changing. At the same time, the development of modern Europe, through an unprecedented economic transformation of the Industrial Revolution, resulted in population growth in major countries. In many cases this increase in the necessary workforce was met by the use of children. However, there were few changes in the formal educational systems of children. In the majority of the European countries during this period, children attended school from age five to their teens.[43] The Bible remained the major text, teachers continued to control their students with threats and physical punishment, and parents supported the use of corporal punishment by the teachers. However, as a result, in 1853 in the United States, in Louisville, Kentucky, a student shot and killed a schoolmaster in revenge for what the student considered an excessive punishment.

It was during this time period that public officials were concerned about social fragmentation and an undisciplined citizen, and efforts were made to educate individuals who normally would not have received an education.[44] Of course, the majority of the individuals educated were males. However, also during this time period the education of females became an area of interest for the world as the necessity of educated females for participation in society, in the workforce, and with the education of their children was recognized. Specifically, Catholic schools such as the Ursuline Academy in New Orleans (USA) were opened and dedicated to the education of young girls. In addition, at that same time in Russia, Catherine the Great opened free public primary and high schools for girls.

In the early 1800s, missionaries in India opened schools for both girls and boys, and in Eastern Europe, girls were allowed to attend elementary school with boys.[45] Efforts such as these continued across the globe along with corporal punishment in the classroom. Unfortunately, along with these advances were increases in incidents of school violence within the school environment.

For example, in Britain, students who were unsupervised outside of the classroom often participated in irresponsible and destructive behaviors.[46]

Concurrently during this time period, the lines distinguishing public and private schools had begun to fade and most children (at least in the United States) had the opportunity to attend either public or private schools.[47] In most of these cases, the teacher continued to handle the disobedience of students. In 1887 in Tennessee (USA) a student shot and killed a teacher in reaction to a spanking his younger sister had received from the teacher the day before. As socioeconomic status became less of a determining factor for access to education and as children from different ethnic groups were now more likely to attend school, the number of children participating in educational programs increased; thus, the likelihood of conflict within the school environment also increased. For clarity, these conflicts, often referred to as culture conflict theory, suggest that violence is a result of the clash of values that emerges when different groups have varied ideas of acceptable behaviors, hence varied reactions to these behaviors.

During this period, it was first believed (as is often the case today) that disobedient children were the result of a breakdown in the family unit.[48] According to this theory, children who had not been exposed to the norms and social control of a "normal" home life would be less likely to accept the norms of the classroom. This resulted in a child who could not be controlled, who could not be taught. Therefore, power was given to the states to intervene for the "sake of the child."[49] In the United States, as more and more immigrants arrived, conflicts grew and the schools became not only institutions of learning, but also institutions for the transmission of culture and of social control. The public feared that without tight control over the immigrant students that these students would reject the norms of American society. School officials continued to be given free hands in the control and discipline of its children by the states.[50]

As the nation began to change and industrialization became a large part of America's economy, movements of reform within the educational system occurred. The first of these reforms was called the Common School Era. In the Common School Era, the stereotypical "Little House on the Prairie" in a one-room schoolhouse appeared in the United States. At that time it was felt by education officials that one location was needed for all of the students (especially if they were white as the South was still very repressed in terms of nonwhite participants in the educational setting).[51] In this Common School Era, schools were used not only to enforce social control but also to facilitate support for governmental policy. Many of these policies included specific age requirements for attending school and rules and regulations related to attendance and truancy.

During this era, one individual in the United States, Horace Mann, became well known as a school reformer. In Mann's opinion, equity in the schools could be attained through measures such as uniform textbooks or readers.[52] Mann, who became Massachusetts's first superintendent of schools, not only attempted to ensure that each child was educated but was also one of the first individuals to collect information on conflicts within the school setting.[53] Although Mann didn't utilized the phrase "school violence," he did provide evidence of violence within the schools. Specifically, Mann reported in the late 1830s that one school with 250 students had, on average, recorded over 300 floggings for disciplinary problems in a five-day period.[54] In addition, according to Mann, approximately 400 schools were closed on an annual basis because of discipline problems.[55] Thus, the suggestion that is asserted today in reference to juveniles becoming more violent in schools is simply a phrase that was also probably heard in the early 1800s in this country. In another report, in Boston in 1850, the belief was that 65 beatings per day were required to sustain a school of 400 students.[56] This violence in terms of discipline continued to be accepted.

At this same time Europe was also experiencing population and educational growing pains. Along with this growth came the growth of gangs such as the Peaky Blinders in England, which commonly recruited children into their ranks. In the early 1860s the British Parliament had allocated funding for schools; however, not all of the areas in the United Kingdom were treated equally. In the late 1860s, the newly formed National Education League began calling for free, compulsory, and nonreligious education for all children. The result was the British 1870 Education Act, which established a system of school administrators to build and manage schools in the regions most needed throughout England and Wales. In 1880, compulsory school attendance was required for all children between the ages of five and ten; by the end of the century the age was extended to twelve. Eventually, mandatory education for all children became a normal expectation around the world.

1870 EDUCATION ACT

The 1870 Education Act stands as the very first piece of legislation to address education in England. This act established a system of "Boards" to manage schools. Unlike the voluntary/private schools, teaching in the board schools was to be nondenominational. A separate act extended the provisions to the country of Scotland in 1872.

1900s

Back in the United States, the second major reform to the educational system occurred during what was called the Progressive School Era. During this time period, Americanization and patriotism were the foci of society. These foci were reflected in the schools as students were taught the meaning of being a "good citizen," studied past and present war heroes, and recited the Pledge of Allegiance every morning. For most of the baby boomers in the country, and those generations before them, singing "America the Beautiful" and "The Star Spangled Banner" at school and during athletic events were common activities. Across Europe, the 1948 Universal Declaration of Human Rights laid the framework for education in its declaration that everyone had the right to education and that fundamental education should be free.

The Progressive Era that saw the changes of society economically also saw changes in the behaviors of students. Education had become a norm for many children. In the early 1900s it was estimated that 90 percent of all elementary- and secondary-age children were enrolled in school.[57] In the United Kingdom those estimates were similar. Unfortunately, it is also during this time period that the presence of alcohol in schools first surfaced and the "immoral" behaviors of teens began to be recognized. For teens, simple theft, smoking, drinking alcohol, and discipline problems began to flourish. In addition, during this time period, Great Britain furthered its emphasis on education with a revision of the Education Act of 1918 that provided funding for schools and increased the age for mandatory attendance.

1918 EDUCATION ACT (REVISED)

By 1914 Britain had a basic educational system, though for most schoolchildren it did not take them beyond the elementary school age limit of twelve. However, during World War I, there existed the problem of underfunding. As a result, the Education Act of 1918 helped address those needs by providing funding for education through taxes. In addition, the act raised the mandatory school age from twelve to fourteen and made provision for a system of part-time "continuation day" classes for those ages fifteen to eighteen who worked.

In addition, incidents of violence were not limited to only the students, as adults in administrative and teaching positions were also among the perpetrators of school violence. One specific example occurred in Ontario, Canada, when a twenty-eight-year-old headmaster wounded another teacher with three shots from a gun before turning the gun on himself and committing suicide.

As cities across the globe became more and more industrialized, problems related to the increasing number of children moving into the cities were recognized.[58] Culture clashes were documented and teachers began recognizing the need for occasional help in controlling students. Although rural schools in the United States would have had as many as eight hundred students, the cities were the focus of recorded student and staff conflicts.[59] In fact, tardiness and truancy both became issues in the urban schools during the time of the Depression. In addition, reports during that time period indicate that among the problems in schools were the violence and dishonesty of the students, the immorality of the females, the violation of attendance rules, the lack of orderliness by students, and the students not completing their homework.[60]

Outside the United States, in countries also experiencing an economic slump, problems within the school environment were similar. In 1902 in Ontario, Canada, a fourteen-year-old student shot and killed a fifteen-year-old classmate. In 1913 in Bremen, Germany, a twenty-nine-year-old former teacher killed four students and injured more than twenty. In 1923 in New Zealand, the headmaster killed two students and injured nine more. Indeed, as school attendance increased, school violence increased.

To address problems of student behaviors, many schools began the use of disciplinary classrooms that were very much like the "in-school suspension" rooms of today.[61] Within these settings, students attend school while also being disciplined. However, in these cases the discipline involved the separation from their peers while they completed their assignments in a strictly regulated setting. Even today, in-school suspension continues to exist throughout the world with a report from the United Kingdom justifying its use as a means to reduce the number of student absent from school, thereby reducing the pool of recruits to criminal enterprises such as drug dealing.[62]

Also utilized to control those students who failed to conform to the rules of the educational setting during this period were the Central Parental Schools. These Central Parental Schools were very much like the Alternative Schools of today. During the 1930s, it was estimated that 1 out of every 350 school children in the United States was assigned to a Central Parental School.[63] In Europe, Second Chance Schools or Last Chance Schools were provided to those young people who were not allowed to continue their education in a traditional school setting. Common elements of the Second Chance Schools included social supports such as counselors or social workers, reduced lengths of the school day, and a more informal environment.[64]

During the 1950s as the baby boomers in the United States began entering school, the size of enrollments increased dramatically along with the cost of the educational system, and students' involvement in "gangs" began to be noticed as often stunts initiated by students for group membership were recognized as gang activities.[65] Historically, acts that were later identified as acts of school violence were linked to the violence of gangs and the presence of gangs within the school environment.

The third major reform to the educational setting occurred after the 1960s, which called for evaluations and standards of learning. The 1966 International Covenant on Economic, Social, and Cultural Rights recognized the right to free education for everyone. Futhermore, during this era more high schools and college preparatory institutions were established and students were taught in various types of settings with the desire that they become the most academically productive. It is also during this time period that the phrase "school violence" is introduced. During the 1900s the incidents of severe school violence (i.e., shootings) began to be documented across the globe.

In 1983 in Germany a thirty-four-year-old Czech refugee killed three students and injured fifteen others when he opened fire on a sixth-grade classroom. In 1985 in Washington State (USA), a fourteen-year-old student killed herself after killing two fourteen-year-old boys. In 1989 two students in Finland were killed by another fourteen-year-old student. In 1989 in Quebec, Canada, a twenty-five-year-old killed fourteen college students.

It was during the late 1980s that school violence became widely recognized as one of the most critical problems of teen society.[66] Also reported as related to school violence is the fact that from 2000 to 2010, in the United States approximately three million attempted or completed rapes, robberies, assaults, or thefts took place within the school environment on an annual basis.[67] Columbine High School, the most recognized tragedy of a US school shooting at the time, occurred in April of 1999. In this most publicized mass murder, twelve students and one teacher were killed when two students conspired to commit the deadliest shooting in the United States within a school setting.[68] It is during this time period that school violence as it is known today began to be recognized as a global concern.

COLUMBINE HIGH SCHOOL

At approximately 5:00 a.m. on April 20, 1999, students Eric Harris (age eighteen) and Dylan Klebold (age seventeen) began to implement their plan to orchestrate the worst school massacre in US history. Prior to arriving at Columbine High School, they would place backpacks full of explosive devices in a vacated lot just three miles away from the school. They would confirm that the trunks of their cars were filled with explosive devices and the gas tanks were full, and then they would continue to school. In addition, their suicide good-byes (recorded videos) were left at their homes for their parents to find after their mission was accomplished. At approximately 11:10 a.m., Harris and Klebold arrived at Columbine High School. However, instead of parking their vehicles in their assigned adjacent spaces in the senior parking lot, they parked their cars in two different locations in closer proximity to the school. Harris and Klebold then entered their school's cafeteria with two large duffel bags filled with propane bombs. They placed the bags in two strategically located places within the cafeteria. Harris and Klebold returned to their cars to wait for the cafeteria bombs to detonate and to begin dressing in their military "armor" (camouflage pants, T-shirts, trench coats). The bombs in the cafeteria do not go off; however, the one in the vacated lot does. A 9-1-1 call is recorded and alerts the Jefferson County Sheriff's Office (Colorado, USA) of an explosion and fire in the lot. At approximately 11:20 a.m., Harris and Klebold realize that their bombs in the cafeteria are not going to explode, so they enter the school from the sidewalk leading to the cafeteria with shotguns and 9mm firearms. Their first shots, fired toward a couple sitting on the grass outside of the cafeteria eating their lunch, kill the female and injure the male. Their second shots are fired toward three young men as they exit the cafeteria. Their third shots are fired toward a group of students whom, after witnessing the other shooting, began to run. Klebold approaches the three young men who are lying down after exiting the cafeteria and again shoots. Klebold then enters the cafeteria and stands in the doorway. He then goes back outside to report to Harris that the bombs have not detonated. Harris shoots another student, a female, as she attempts to run inside the cafeteria for safety. At 11:22 a.m., the school resource officer (SRO) is notified. A 9-1-1 call comes into the sheriff's office reporting an injured female in the south parking lot of Columbine High School. The deputy dispatched to the scene of the lot explosion a few miles away is advised of a female injured at Columbine. The SRO also hears the dispatcher and heads to the south parking lot. In addition, another police officer on patrol within the area hears the dispatcher and responds to the call at Columbine High School. Teacher Patti Nielson, on hall patrol, observed Harris and Klebold with guns outside of the school. When one of the gunmen fires into the west entrance, Nielson and a male student flee to the library. Once in the library Nielson calls 9-1-1. A teacher directs the students from the cafeteria to the second level of the school and then back down another staircase to safety. The Littleton Fire Department is dispatched to the explosion and grass fire in the vacant lot. The teacher's 9-1-1 call from inside the library reports smoke inside the school. Two additional Jefferson County deputies arrive on the scene. Harris and Klebold, who are now inside the school, exchange gunfire with the deputies and move up and down the hallway outside of the library while randomly shooting. They also toss pipe bombs into the library hallway and one lands in the cafeteria. A second bomb is also recorded as landing in the cafeteria, which causes more smoke. Harris and Klebold leave the hallway and enter the school library. The 9-1-1 recording of Nielson's call, which had remained active, records a male voice yelling "Get up!" Harris and Klebold shoot one student while walking toward the west window of the library. They shoot out the windows and law enforcement return fire. The shooters then shoot the display cabinet near the front door before injuring five and killing three more students. They reload their weapons, and more students are killed or injured before Harris and Klebold leave the library. Multiple law enforcement jurisdictions and emergency workers are now outside of Columbine. Media sources, including CNN's play-by-play accounts of students with their hands above their heads fleeing Columbine through streams of water, broadcast the horror across the nation. At 4:38 p.m., all of the students present at Columbine High School that day were accounted for and the last of the thirteen victims and the two shooters were pronounced dead.

2000+

Since the early 2000s, incidents of school violence (and severe violence such as school shootings) have declined. The US policies such as zero tolerance and the European Union Children and Violence Program and other measures such as video equipment in schools attempt to reduce incidents of school violence.[69] However, they still occur.

In the United States, the 2007 Virginia Tech shooting resulted in 32 college students killed. In addition, the Sandy Hook Elementary School shooting in 2012 resulted in 27 deaths. The 2000 Walisongo School massacre in Indonesia resulted in more than 150 killed. The 2004 Beslan Shooting in Russia resulted in more than 300 killed. The 2014 Peshawar Massacre in Pakistan resulted in nearly 150 killed. The 2015 Garissa University shooting in Kenya resulted in nearly 80 killed. Most recently, in 2018, 17 individuals were killed in Florida's mass shooting, as mentioned previously in this chapter. However, violence also includes violence against one's self.

Specifically, in 2006 Brodie Panlock took her own life at age nineteen. Brodie was spat on and teased daily by her coworkers by being called fat and ugly while working at Melbourne's (California, USA) Café Vamp. Her coworkers were charged and fined for their bullying of Brodie. The owner, Marc Luis Da Cruz, was also fined for failure to provide a safe workplace.[70]

Tyler Long, a seventeen-year-old young man who identified as homosexual and suffered from Asperger's Syndrome, ended his life due to repeatedly being called inappropriate names and students spitting in his food and taking things from him. Tyler's parents reported these incidents to the school and they weren't addressed. Tyler chose to take his own life in 2009. His parents came into his room and found Tyler with a belt around his neck, hanging from his closet rod. But the bullying and remarks did not stop there. Tyler was mocked and made fun of in school for taking his life. Tyler's parents filed a lawsuit against the school, stating school officials ignored the bullying that tormented their son.[71]

In 2010, Phoebe Prince, a fifteen-year young lady from Ireland, moved to South Hadley, Massachusetts, and abruptly ended her life after months of being bullied. Phoebe was threatened on social media, sent abusive threats via text messages, and taunted at school. She feared for her safety according to her friend. The day before Phoebe ended her life, she told her friend that the past few days of her life were close to intolerable. Phoebe's last straw was when one of the bullies yelled across the library calling Phoebe such names as "Irish whore" and "slut." Later that afternoon Phoebe's sister found her hanging from the stairwell of their home.[72]

Lastly, Amanda Todd, a fifteen-year-old Canadian student, ended her life because she was a victim of cyberbullying. Amanda posted a series of postcards on social media stating she was blackmailed into exposing her breasts on a webcam, physically abused, and bullied. Amanda was consistently coerced and threatened. Amanda was beaten at school because she had sex with a guy while his girlfriend was away. When the girlfriend returned, she and fifteen others attacked Amanda. After that incident Amanda attempted suicide by drinking bleach but was ultimately rushed to the hospital, where her stomach was pumped. When she was released from the hospital, she came home to messages mocking her failed attempt at suicide. In 2010, Amanda was found hanging in her home. Her suicide video went viral and gained attention internationally. As of August 2018, the video had more than twelve million views.[73]

Although the rationale for violence within the school setting may vary based upon location, the results remain the same. Young people, attempting to learn within the safe environment of a school, are victims. In some cases, this victimization even results in death.

In summary, the history of school violence follows a history of education across the globe. As more students became engaged in education, more incidents of violence occurred within the school setting. Victims of school violence are most often the students; however, in some cases, staff is also a victim of violence within this setting. The perpetrators of school violence have historically been the students; however, in some incidents of severe violence with multiple victims, the perpetrators are adults and often adults with no formal connection to the educational setting.

Finally, the rationales for the incidents of school violence vary. In most cases of student assailants, the criminal activity is in reaction to a disciplinary action or a peer action or interaction. Adult assailants are often motivated by either religious or political ideologies or they are suffering from mental health issues. Regardless the offenders or the reasons behind their actions, the victimization of children within the school setting is every parent's nightmare. Across the globe, the public continues to be concerned about this issue and reducing these incidents of child victimization within the school setting.

CHAPTER QUESTIONS

1. Who passed the first educational law requiring all children be taught to read and write? What were the consequences if a child was found to be illiterate?
2. What sources were established in an effort to educate children whose parents lacked reading and writing skills?
3. In what year was the age for mandatory school attendance increased and why?
4. Who provided some of the first evidence of violence within the schools, although he did not refer to it as "school violence"? When was the phrase "school violence" introduced?
5. Based upon media perceptions, is there a global increase in school violence? Is this representative of actual statistics?

DISCUSSION QUESTIONS

1. Do you feel as though the acceptable punishment methods throughout history for the misconduct of students in school has aided in the number of incidents of violence we see within schools today? Explain.
2. To what extent do you think bullying or abuse by peers or adults influences the amount of violence within the school environment? Why?
3. Do you feel that violence in video games, television shows, and movies is connected to the number of school violence incidents within today's schools? Explain.

NOTES

1. Michael Nedelman, "9-Year-Old Dies by Suicide after He Was Bullied," accessed on February 1, 2019, at https://www.cnn.com/2018/08/28/health/preteen -suicide-jamel-myles/index/html.

2. Kimberly McCabe and Daniel Murphy, *Child Abuse—Today's Issues* (New York: Taylor and Francis Publishing, 2016), 21–24.

3. National Center for Education Statistics, "Crime, Violence and Discipline 2105–16," accessed on January 5, 2019, at https://nces.ed.gov/pubsearch/pubsinfo .asp?pubid=2017122.

4. Claudia Megele and Peter Buzzi, "School Crime and Violence in European Union," *Encyclopedia of School Crime and Violence*, accessed on January 6, 2019, at https://www.academia.edu/847364/School_Crime_and_Violence_in_European_Union.

5. Danita Wasserman, Qi Cheng, and Guang-Wei Jiang, "Global Suicide Rates among Young People Aged 15–19," *World Psychiatry*, 5(1) (2006): 39–49.

6. Wasserman, Cheng, and Jiang, "Global Suicide Rates among Young People Aged 15–19."

7. Wasserman, Cheng, and Jiang, "Global Suicide Rates among Young People Aged 15–19."

8. National Center for Injury Prevention and Control, *Understanding School Violence—Fact Sheet*. Washington, DC: Center for Disease Control and Prevention, accessed on January 5, 2019, at www.cdc.gov/ViolencePrevention/youthviolence/ schoolviolence/SAVD.html.

9. Kimberly McCabe and Gregory Martin, *School Violence, the Media and Criminal Justice Responses* (New York: Peter Lang Publishing, 2005), 11–20.

10. McCabe and Murphy, *Child Abuse—Today's Issues*.

11. Zach Winn, "The U.S School Shooting Statistics Everyone Should Know," accessed on January 2, 2019, at https://www.campussafetymagazine.com/safety/u-s -school-shooting-statistics-us/.

12. McCabe and Martin, *School Violence, the Media and Criminal Justice Responses*.

13. McCabe and Martin, *School Violence, the Media and Criminal Justice Responses*.

14. Mark Pearl, "The Shocking Campus Shooting in Virginia That You Never Heard of," accessed on January 1, 2019, at https://www.huffingtonpost.com/matthew -pearl/the-professors-assassin_b_1149222.html.

15. David Krajicek, "The Beast of Bremen: Horrific 1913 German School Shooting Proves to Be First of Many," *New York Daily Times*, May 20, 2018, 1–3.

16. Chris Anderson, "Murder in a Small Kiwi School," accessed on January 3, 2019, at http://www.stuff.co.nz/national/8112416/Murder-in-a-small-Kiwi-school.

17. Emil Iracki, "A School Massacre in Vilnius," accessed on January 4, 2019, at http://media.efhr.eu/2013/01/05/school-massacre-vilnius/.

18. Krajicek, "The Beast of Bremen: Horrific 1913 German School Shooting Proves to be First of Many."

19. U.S. Department of Education (March 2018), *Indicators of School Crime and Safety: 2017*, US Department of Education: US Department of Justice Office of Justice Programs.

20. Roman DeAngelis, "This Is a Crisis Right Now: Survey Finds More Violence in Ontario Schools," accessed on January 3, 2019, at https://www.cbc.ca/news/ canada/sudbury/catholic-teachers-survey-violence-schools-1.4180894.

21. European Parliamentarian Research Service [EPRS] (2014), "Back to School," accessed on January 3, 2019, at https://epthinktank.eu/.

22. Russell Skiba, "Zero Tolerance: The Assumptions and the Facts," *Education Policy Brief*, 2(1) (2004). Bloomington, IN: Center for Evaluation and Policy. Indiana University.

23. Gordon Crews, "School Violence Perpetrators Speak: An Examination of Perpetrators' Views on School Violence Offenses, *Journal of the Institute of Justice and International Studies*, 14 (2014): 41–52.

24. Jack Levin and Eric Madfis, "Mass Murder at School and Cumulative Strain: A Sequential Model," *American Behavioral Scientist*, 52 (2009): 1227–45.

25. National Vital Statistics Report, 2017. Final Data for 2016, accessed on January 3, 2019, at https://www.cdc.gov/nchs/data/nvsr/nvsr67/nvsr67_05.pdf.

26. McCabe and Martin, *School Violence, the Media and Criminal Justice Responses*.

27. Elaine Kendall, "Beyond Mother's Knee," *American Heritage*, 24(4) (1973): 73–78.

28. S. Alexander Rippa, *Education in a Free Society: An American History*, eighth edition (New York: Longman Press, 1997).

29. McCabe and Martin, *School Violence, the Media and Criminal Justice Responses*.

30. Gordon Crews and M. Reid Counts, *The Evolution of School Disturbances in America: Colonial Times to Modern Day* (Westport, CT: Praeger, 1997).

31. Joel Spring, *The American School: 1642–1993*, third edition (New York: McGraw-Hill, 1994).

32. Sheldon Cohen, *A History of Colonial Education, 1607–1776* (New York: Wiley, 1974).

33. Kimberly McCabe, *Child Abuse and the Criminal Justice System* (New York: Peter Lang Publishing, 2003).

34. U.S. Department of Labor, "Second Periodic Review of Progress to Address Issues Identified in the U.S. Department of Labor's Public Report of Review of Submission 2015-01 (Peru)," accessed on December 20, 2018, at https://www.dol .gov/sites/default/files/documents/ilab/Peru%20FTA%20Submission%20Second %20Review%20Statement%20Final.pdf.

35. UNICEF, *Child Labor and UNICEF in Actions: Children at the Centre*, accessed on January 5, 2019, at https://www.unicef.org/protection/files/Child_ Labour_and_UNICEF_in_Action.pdf.

36. Kimberly McCabe, *The Trafficking of Persons: National and International Responses* (New York: Peter Lang Publishing, 2008), 4–7.

37. McCabe and Martin, *School Violence, the Media and Criminal Justice Responses*.

38. Joel Spring, *The American School:1642–1993*.

39. Henry Perkinson, *The Imperfect Panacea*, fourth edition (New York: McGraw-Hill, 1995).

40. McCabe and Martin, *School Violence, the Media and Criminal Justice Responses*.

41. Irwin Hyman and James Wise, *Corporal Punishment in American Education* (Philadelphia: Temple University Press, 1979).

42. Hyman and Wise, *Corporal Punishment in American Education.*

43. R. Freeman Butts and Lawrence Cremin, *History of Education in America* (New York: Holt, Rinehart and Winston, 1953).

44. Crews and Counts, *The Evolution of School Disturbances in America: Colonial Times to Modern Day.*

45. McCabe and Martin, *School Violence, the Media and Criminal Justice Responses.*

46. McCabe and Martin, *School Violence, the Media and Criminal Justice Responses.*

47. Crews and Counts, *The Evolution of School Disturbances in America: Colonial Times to Modern Day.*

48. David Rothman, *The Discovery of the Asylum* (Boston: Little & Brown, 1971).

49. Carl Pope, "Juvenile Justice in the Next Millennium." In J. Klosas and S. Stojkovics (eds.), *Crime and Justice in the Year 2120* (New York: Wadsworth, 1995), 100–120.

50. Robert Bohm and Keith Haley, *Introduction to Criminal Justice* (New York: McGraw-Hill, 1997).

51. Spring, *The American School: 1642–1993.*

52. Perkinson, *The Imperfect Panacea.*

53. McCabe and Martin, *School Violence, the Media and Criminal Justice Responses.*

54. Horace Mann and Matthew Smith, *Sequel to the So-Called Correspondence between the Reverend M. H. Smith and Horace Mann* (Boston: W. B. Fowle, 1847).

55. Mann and Smith, *Sequel to the So-Called Correspondence between the Reverend M. H. Smith and Horace Mann.*

56. Walter Hapkiewicz, "Research on Corporal Punishment Effectiveness: Contributions and Limitations," accessed on January 3, 2019, at https://eric.ed .gov/?id=ED102739.

57. Crews and Counts, *The Evolution of School Disturbances in America: Colonial Times to Modern Day.*

58. McCabe and Martin, *School Violence, the Media and Criminal Justice Responses.*

59. Nicholas Butler, *Education in the US: A Series of Monographs* (New York: American Books, 1910).

60. Aubrey Douglass, *The American School System: A Survey of Principles and Practices of Education* (New York: Farrar and Rinehart, 1940).

61. Elwood Cubberley, *Public Education in the United States* (New York: Houghton Mifflin, 1934).

62. Kevin Rawlinson, "County Lines Drug Gangs Recruit Excluded Children," accessed on October 1, 2018, https://www.theguardian.com/global-development/2019/feb/05/county-lines-drug-gangs-blackmailing-tracking-children-social-media.

63. Cubberley, *Public Education in the United States.*

64. Glenda McGregor, Martin Mills, Kitty te Riele, Aspa Baroutsis, and Debra Hayes, *Re-imagining Schooling for Education: Socially Just Alternatives* (London: Palgrave MacMillan, 2017).

65. McCabe and Martin, *School Violence, the Media and Criminal Justice Responses*.

66. Clemens Bartollas, *Juvenile Delinquency*, fifth edition (Needham Heights, MA: Allyn and Bacon, 2000).

67. McCabe and Murphy, *Child Abuse—Today's Issues*.

68. McCabe and Martin, *School Violence, the Media and Criminal Justice Responses*.

69. Megele and Buzzi, "School Crime and Violence in European Union."

70. Alison Caldwell, "Suicide Waitress Driven to the Edge and Pushed," accessed on January 4, 2019, at https://www.abc.net.au/news/2010-02-08/suicide-waitress -driven-to-the-edge-and-pushed/323884.

71. Jim Dubreuil and Eamon McNiff, "Bullied to Death in America's Schools," accessed on November 2, 2018, from https://abcnews.go.com/2020/TheLaw/school -bullying-epidemic-turning-deadly/story?id=11880841.

72. Carlin Miller, "Phoebe Prince's Final Days: Bullied Girl Suffered 'Intolerable' Abuse before Suicide, Say Court Docs," accessed on November 2, 2018, from https://www.cbsnews.com/news/phoebe-princes-final-days-bullied-girl-suffered -intolerable-abuse-before-suicide-say-court-docs/.

73. Michelle Dean, "The Story of Amanda Todd," accessed on November 2, 2018, from https://www.newyorker.com/culture/culture-desk/the-story-of-amanda-todd.

Chapter Two

Bullying and Cyberbullying

KEY WORDS

backbone family	emotional abuse	rejecting
brick-wall family	endomorph	sexting
bullying	hazing	sextortion
corruption	ignoring	social learning theory
cyberbullying	isolation	sociopath
destruction of property/	jellyfish family	terrorizing
vandalism	mesomorph	victim precipitation
ectomorph		

KEY ACRONYMS

(NCES) National Center for Education Statistics
(PACER) Parent Advocacy Coalition for Educational Rights

In 1997, a thirteen-year-old girl in Allenton, England, committed suicide after repeated harassment and taunting about her weight by her classmates. In 2000, a fourteen-year-old Canadian male jumped to his death off a bridge after continued teasing about his appearance and intellect by his classmates. In 2010, a fifteen-year-old American high school student in Massachusetts hanged herself after being victimized through bullying and cyberbullying. Thus, actions of bullying and intimidation within the schools that have historically been perceived as simply "part of going to school" have led to the most severe of consequences for some young people. In August of 2018, a nine-year-old Colorado (USA) boy took his life in reaction to bullying.[1]

Historically, bullying within the school environment has been considered simply a rite of passage, with the first significant article to address bullying published in the late 1800s.[2] In this first scientific paper, bullying was explored through the aspects of the reasons for bullying, the effect of bullying on those bullied, and ways in which bullying may be reduced. Even then the consequences of bullying were publically known when John Flood, a young British soldier and victim of bullying by a fellow soldier, shot and killed his tormentor in 1862.

Over a century later, in 1999, when it was revealed that the shooters at Columbine High School in the United States were also victims of bullying, those involved in education, criminal justice practitioners, and parents throughout the world began to identify bullying as a problem in American schools.

In general, bullying has been viewed by many as a normal part of childhood and attending school.[3] Oftentimes for many students, being a victim of bullying has had a significant impact upon their lives. These victims of bullying often report difficulties such as making friends, maintaining friendships, and even the fear of going to school.[4] Other victims of bullying report the long-term consequences of physical illness and emotional vulnerabilities to include doubts of their own self-worth, feelings of hopelessness, and the inability to have confidence in their abilities to succeed in the world. Unfortunately, although bullying may result in physical violence, it is rarely discussed under the umbrella of school violence. This chapter addresses that limitation. Specifically, this type of violence, which has existed before the beginning of institutionalized education, is the focus of this chapter on school violence.

In the 1970s, the first worldwide systematic approach to studying bullying was conducted.[5] Through this research, it was proposed that legislation should be enacted to prevent these actions within the school environment. In 1983, after three consequential suicides of boys victimized by bullies in Norway, the Norwegian government enacted a nationwide anti-bullying campaign. By the 1990s, both Sweden (the first country) and Norway had enacted anti-bullying laws. The term *bullying* has been used to describe a wide range of behaviors toward an individual to include hazing, teasing, vandalism, robbery, physical attacks, and sexual assaults.[6] For clarity of this chapter, bullying is defined in general terms as the actions that involve the key elements of a physical abuse, verbal abuse, and intimidation, which are intended to cause fear or harm to the victim.[7] Although the majority of the victimizations that occur in today's schools involve minor indignities, bullying is often the foundation for such actions and, when more pronounced, may include incidents of severe violence and physical injury.[8] In addition, and in contrast to the forms of physical bullying in earlier times, bullying in today's modern world often also includes more concentrated outcomes of psychological abuse, which may result when bullying is extended to the cyber community.[9]

In terms of estimates, in the United States, nearly one-third of all students report being a victim of bullying within the last twelve months with 10 percent reporting incidents of bullying at least once a week.[10] In the United Kingdom, approximately 40 percent of students report being bullied within the last year.[11] In China, nearly 50 percent of students report being a victim of bullying.[12] Hence bullying, and especially bullying within the school environment, is a concern across the globe as millions of students are victimized on an annual basis.

Although research suggests that incidents of bullying tend to peak during the middle-school years, there are reports of a growing number of incidents that suggest that bullying is occurring earlier at the levels of preschool and kindergarten[13] and later in the university setting.[14] In particular, although recognized as harassment and not bullying, many university students do not recognize this type of victimization and, for many that do recognize bullying, victims are often blamed for the actions against them.[15] For many, these actions are so common that it is to the point of acceptance; however, in much of the literature on school violence, bullying is labeled a form of the *hidden violence* that exists within the school environment and is often discovered to exist in retrospective reviews of historical cases of school shootings.[16] However, despite the prevalence of bullying, it has not always been given a priority when discussing crimes and violence within the school environment and, as with many crimes, these crimes are addressed in reaction to a tragedy or tragedies. Today, in discussions on schools and the conditions of the school's environment, the subject of bullying is now a common topic and is often included in conversations on child abuse and child emotional abuse[17] with programs and information centers established to focus on anti-bullying efforts. One such program is the 1990 Olweus Bullying Prevention Program, with eleven foci to reduce the incidents of school bullying (see below).

In 2006 in the United States one such center, the Parent Advocacy Coalition for Educational Rights (PACER) Center, founded its National Bullying Prevention Center. Although PACER is an information center for the families of children with disabilities, the National Bullying Prevention Center provides resources designed to benefit *all* students. This center initiated a campaign that led to the decision to make the month of October the National Bullying Prevention month. The campaign's mission is to involve the nation

OLWEUS BULLYING PREVENTION PROGRAM (1990)

- Efforts must consider a whole-school environment.
- One must assess the prevalence of bullying at school.
- A group must be formed to support bullying prevention.
- Staff should be trained on bullying prevention.
- Rules and policies regarding bullying must be established and enforced.
- Students should be involved in regular discussions on bullying.
- Adult supervision should be increased in physical areas with bullying problems.
- Staff must intervene consistently to stop bullying.
- Parental support is a must.
- Support for victims of bullying must be provided on an ongoing basis.
- All efforts to reduce bullying must be continued over time.

to take action at a local level to create safe and supportive schools while also educating students, faculty, and community members on the dangers of bullying and how to prevent it in the future.

EMOTIONAL ABUSE

It has been suggested that emotional abuse is the most common form of child abuse.[18] Unfortunately, as emotional abuse is difficult if not almost impossible to document, it goes unacknowledged, unreported, and unaddressed.[19] Definitions of emotional abuse vary by state, country, and within disciplines, so the number of prosecutions remains at zero and emotional abuse within the school environment continues to flourish. In all cases of bullying, emotional abuse is present.

Emotional abuse is difficult to define; however, it is generally categorized to include six distinct actions: (1) rejecting; (2) isolating; (3) terrorizing; (4) ignoring; (5) corrupting; and (6) destroying personal property. Each of these actions, to some extent, has been documented to exist within the school environment. Although the majority of the research on emotional abuse focuses on parents and caretakers as the perpetrators, more recent work has focused on siblings and peers as related to bullying, intimidation, and the emotional abuse of children.[20] The school setting, because of its physical environment, will contain both the victims and the perpetrators (or bullies) of child-on-child emotional abuse. Thereby, the school setting is the most common environment for peer bullying.

The first category of emotional abuse is rejection. Rejecting within the school environment is related to the refusal of acceptance. Rejection or the rejecting of peers by other peers within the school environment is not a new phenomenon. Discussions on what drives peer rejections has led researchers to identify three general explanations for why young people reject another.

In terms of preferences, in many cases the rejection of one peer by another has simply to do with the rejecter's choice of activities and hobbies. In the case that peers do not engage in those same activities, they may be rejected by those peers that are engaged in the activity.[21] One example of this category of rejection in the school setting is sports. A young man who does not play rugby may not be accepted by those young men who consider themselves rugby players. The preferences for rejecting or not rejecting is not related to the behavior of the rejected child but rather the preferences of those rejecting the child or teen.

Another reason for peer rejection is unfamiliarity. Young people who already have a group of friends may be hesitant to welcome a new person into their group as they do not know the new person and have already established the comfort levels and social boundaries with their current friends. An example in the school setting is the "new kid" in school, who may be from another country or another part of the same country. This new student may speak a different language, may dress differently, or may simply not know anyone. As this new student does not appear similar or known to those students already within the school environment, he or she is unfamiliar to them, therefore, the new student is rejected by the new peers. As with preferences, this rejection is not related to the behaviors of the rejected child but rather related to the perceptions of those rejecting the new student.

Lastly, students are rejected by other peers because of their behaviors. Just as with adults, behaviors or actions that appear unusual or different from the conforming behaviors of society may lead to rejection.[22] The same holds for students within the school environment. An example in the school setting, which may lead to peer rejection, would be the case of students who decide to dress differently from the other students at the school or chooses to spend their free time interacting with teachers. In many cases, these students would be rejected from the general social group of their peers within the school environment.

The second category of emotional abuse is isolation. Isolation within the school environment is related to the absence of social interactions. Isolation or the isolating of students by their peers within the school environment is not uncommon. Historically, research on the isolation of a child, in terms of emotional abuse, usually involved an adult denying the child the opportunity for social interactions with others.[23] This category of emotional abuse is one of the more common categories of abuse in homes with domestic violence, as abusers utilize isolation to maintain control over their victims.[24] In the school setting, isolation is more common in the situation of dating violence. Just as controlling the actions of their partner is critical to adult perpetrators of domestic violence, controlling the actions of a boyfriend or girlfriend is critical for the perpetrator of dating violence. In the university setting, these behaviors will often continue as individuals (particularly males) with a history of bullying in junior and high school view bullying as an acceptable reaction to some individuals.[25]

In these cases, peers who are involved in romantic relationships seek to control the behaviors of their partners by refusing to support their engagement in activities outside of their one-on-one relationship. One example would be the boyfriend who threatens to end the relationship or cause harm to the partner or himself if the partner participates in a school club, sport, or organization. Partners, who do not want the relationship to end or who fear for their safety, will comply with their abuser and allows themselves to be isolated from their peers within the school environment. Another example would be the dating partner who threatens the other with physical violence if they engage in social interactions with any others, who may "take them away" and destroy their relationship.

The third category of emotional abuse is terrorizing. Terrorizing is defined as continuing to fill another with fear either through threats or coercion. Historically, the terrorizing of students is not thought to be as common as some of the other categories of emotional abuse; however, it does occur within the school environment and incidents of terrorizing are increasing with the use of technology.[26] Terrorizing produces widespread fear in victims and is one of the most significant categories of emotional abuse in terms of long-term consequences.[27] One of the newest forms of terrorizing teens is the action of sextortion, a form of sexual exploitation that employs nonphysical forms of coercion to dictate and control the actions of another.[28] To be discussed later in this chapter, sextortion often involves the use of media and often involves the use of sexual images of the victim. In the school setting, and especially with older students who feel embarrassed to report their fear or are humiliated by their actions, the action of terrorizing by a peer ensures control by the perpetrator. In 2015, a seventeen-year-old male from Northern Ireland committed suicide after being a victim of sextortion.[29] In addition, do not discount a teacher as a perpetrator of terrorizing. For students with a fear of public speaking to be intentionally forced to speak in class by a teacher is a nightmare.

Ignoring is one of the more common categories of emotional abuse and is related to a failure of acknowledgment. To ignore someone is to fail to notice the person. Although not as common in the school environment with peer relationships, ignoring may be observed be peers within the school environment. More commonly observed is ignoring in the classroom when a teacher refuses to acknowledge a student's accomplishments, thoughts, or opinions. Just as a parent may intentionally or intentionally ignore their child,[30] a teacher may ignore a student. In instances of unintentional ignoring, the teacher may not continue to ask for input from a particular student if previous requests have been unsuccessful and the student has failed to provide correct answers to questions. Out of habit and in an attempt to engage other students, teachers generally call on students that they feel will know the answers. If a student has not been able to answer questions in the past, the teacher will acknowledge the students that have been able to answer correctly. In some cases of intentional ignoring, teachers who persistently refuse to acknowledge the inputs of some students are perceived to act with impunity.[31] For some reason, beyond the control of the students and without the model of professionalism expected by all educational staff, a teacher may ignore a student. Unfortunately, as teachers provide instruction in a classroom, which is essentially under their control, their actions more often continue without monitoring and without direct supervision; therefore, the behavior continues without punitive consequences for ignoring a student.

Corruption is another category of emotional abuse. Corruption is dishonest or illegal behaviors that often occur by those in power. Corruption within the school environment may apply to the teachers and staff as related to their relationships (to include sexual relationships) with the students as well as to the students themselves. In student cases of corruption, peer pressure to perform certain illegal or delinquent acts is common. Corruption is an action that destroys trust among parties. Children engaged in corruption are also often involved in self-destructive behaviors.[32] Corruption or the corrupting of students within the school environment occurs but often under the umbrella of teen activities. In the school setting, these activities include truancy, skipping classes, smoking, and drinking alcohol. In these cases, the student, often seeking the approval from others, will participate in the behaviors in order to gain acceptance by a peer group. As the teen years are the time for the exploration of self, students within the school environment are at risk for corruption by peers all under the umbrella of acceptance. One example is the young man who engages in the bullying of another to "go along with the group." In these cases, the students are not aware of their corruption by others.

Lastly, the destruction of property or vandalism is a category of emotional abuse, which may occur within the school setting. In this case, these property crimes are an attempt to emotionally abuse the victim. In the school setting, the destruction of property is viewed as a form of juvenile delinquency and, in fact, property crimes far outnumber violent crimes within the school setting.[33] These actions, often in retaliation for some other action, are seen as a means to "right the wrong." One example includes a boyfriend who vandalizes his former partner's car with graffiti after a relationship breakup. Another example includes a student setting fire to a trash bin in a teacher's classroom in reaction to a perceived unfair grade. In this category of emotional abuse, one cannot discount peer influence both in and out of school. The student who has few friends or who is desiring the attention of specific friends is more likely to be corrupted by those peers. While only about 20 percent of the property crimes within the school environment are in an attempt to cause emotional abuse, the majority of these cases are perpetrated by those students between the ages of fourteen and eighteen.[34] Therefore, the elements of a bystander or an unwilling accomplice may be revealed in this category of emotional abuse.

As stated, most cases of child emotional abuse involve a family member as the perpetrator; however, it does occur in the school environment and is often included within the elements of bullying. Given that emotional abuse is a significant part of bullying, the consequences of low self-worth, depression, and powerlessness are a concern for individuals interested in addressing violence within the school environment. When discussing bullying and intimidation within the school setting, emotional abuse is critical to the dynamics of these actions and must be considered in the consequences of bullying and the elements that facilitate bullying.

ELEMENTS OF BULLYING

Nearly two decades ago, three initial elements that exist within all cases of bullying and one outcome element were identified. Those initial elements are: (1) an imbalance of power; (2) an intent to harm; and (3) a threat of further aggression.[35] In addition to these elements, and essential to the process of bullying, is repeated contacts between the bully and victim either in person or in the virtual world. Hence, however hurtful, one event or name calling or taunting is not bullying. The direct outcome element is terror.

The first element of bullying, the imbalance of power, is usually accomplished by physical size. In these events, the bully is usually older or larger. In addition, the bully could be smarter or from a higher socioeconomic strata than his or her victim.[36] This imbalance of power provides the bully the leverage of control over the victim. Since the action of bullying is not one of equally matched rivals, as most bullies do not seek victims of equal abilities, bullying may be thought of as the result of one player initiating the action with some sort of perceived advantage over the other; thus, the victim or the target is vulnerable for attack at the initial stage of confrontation.[37] The victim's fear of pain at the hands of the bully is confirmed and is expected to continue. Within this imbalance of power, bullying occurs and a student is victimized. When there exists a presence of gangs within the school environment (discussed more in the next chapter), there also exists an increased risk for bullying.[38]

In the second element of bullying, the intent to harm, there is no accidental terror or abuses. The significant term in this element is "intent." The bully intends to frighten or inflict pain on the victim and, as a result, receives pleasure from the victim's pain or fear of pain.[39] In these actions of bullying, there exists a form of planning or premeditation.[40] The bully, upon seeing or thinking about his or her victim and the conditions as they exist, decides prior to acting what behavior will be displayed and perhaps even what effect the behavior will have upon the victim. These planned actions of bullying may include name calling, pushing, and such, or the actions may be specific to the victim (e.g., a small child may be forced into a school locker). Without this intent, the bullying would not occur. Therefore, with intent, just as within the criminal justice system, the actions are planned or premeditated.

Once the initial confrontation between the bully and the victim has taken place or has been suggested, the third element of bullying is the threat of further aggression. The victim knows that the bully, perceived as successful in his or her first act toward the victim, will continue to bully the victim. Both the victim and the bully know that the much popularized media story of a victim standing up to and defeating the bully is essentially a myth.[41] As victims know that they are essentially defenseless against the bully, they see the future of more victimizations as inevitable. Consequently, it is unrealistic to expect that a bullying encounter is one single event; therefore, by definition, bullying refers to repeated behaviors. The victim now realizes his or her vulnerabilities and, unfortunately, so does the bully. Therefore, the threats of further aggression continue. The bullying continues until the perpetrator is stopped or until the perpetrator ends the abuse.

The outcome that exists after incidents of bullying is terror.[42] As bullying is a systematic action that is intended to intimidate and maintain dominance over a victim or victims,[43] once this terror from the victim has been established, the bully may continue to act without fear of retaliation. In many cases, bullying will escalate to physical attacks and abuse. In some cases, this escalation of bullying may also be in the form of sexual abuse.[44] The victim, always awaiting another attack, remains in a state of emotional terror.[45] For cases of bullying within the school environment, the outcomes of bullying include fear and anxiety as well as the long-term

consequences of social disruption, decreased learning, and failure to succeed in the classroom.

THEORIES TO EXPLAIN BULLYING

In explaining the action of bullying, multiple perspectives are utilized. This
chapter focuses on three—the biological, the psychological, and the social
perspectives. Specifically, in this chapter, the physical trait perspective is
offered as a biological explanation, sociopathy is offered from the social-
psychological perspective, and the theory of social learning is offered as an
explanation of bullying from the social perspective.

Physical Trait

Historically, publications such as Lombroso's *The Criminal Man*[46] have
attempted to categorize adults by their physical appearance to explain their
behaviors and their asserted propensity to act strangely or violently. Sheldon[47] in his *Varieties of Delinquent Youth* applies that philosophy to young
people as he maintained there existed three categories of body types and
that each type has its own unique associated temperament. Specifically, the
types of body builds were: (1) endomorph; (2) mesomorph; and, (3) ectomorph. The endomorph body type was soft and round with a tendency to
gain weight. Their temperaments were of a relaxed nature that was slow to
react and tolerant of others. The mesomorph body type was one of massive
strength and defined muscular development. Their associated temperament
was assertive with a desire for power and dominance. These individuals
are often ruthless and indifferent to pain (theirs or others). The ectomorph
body type was thin and frail with an associated temperament of inhibition
and social isolation.

   In applying Sheldon's body types to the behavior of bullying, one asserts
that the bully is the mesomorph.[48] The mesomorph is an individual with not
only the physical build and strength to intimidate and provoke fear in others
but also the personality or temperament to desire and command dominance
over others. The target or victim of a bully is most likely the ectomorph. The
victim is perceived to be physically vulnerable and lacks the social integra-
tion or ability to form and sustain the social bond to peers that may reduce
their likelihood of becoming a target.

   If one considers a physical stature as a strong foundation for the bullying-
to-victim relationship, then it stands to reason that in a one-on-one or face-to-
face confrontation, the biological perspective is applicable. However, if the

action of bullying is not face-to-face but rather within a virtual community (i.e., cyberbullying), this perspective is less applicable.

Sociopathy

A social-psychological explanation that is applied to criminal and delinquent behavior is that of sociopathy. The terms psychopathy and antisocial personality are considered synonymous to sociopathy.[49] By definition of behavior, sociopaths are characterized as selfish, impulsive, and emotionally unattached.[50] As these individuals do not feel sympathy or empathy toward others, they often are the perpetrators of many crimes of violence over their life course.[51] For the majority, these abuses begin while the perpetrators are within the school environment.[52]

The cause of sociopathy is uncertain as some researchers look toward the concept of a neurological defect as the cause while some researchers seek explanation from the experience of an emotional trauma during childhood, and some researchers look to the family structure of the abuser.[53] However, it is suggested that, in many cases, youths who begin to bully as a student in the school environment will continue these actions as adults throughout their life.[54] In some cases, these individuals who serve as bullies in the school environment will be classified as sociopaths.

Social Learning

Developed in the 1970s as a revision of Sutherland's *Differential Association*, social learning theory is an attempt to explain behaviors as a result of reinforcement and punishment.[55] Like Sutherland, Akers's *social learning theory*[56] maintains that deviant behavior is learned and that it is a direct outcome of instrumental conditioning and imitation. Instrumental conditioning, which relies upon reinforcement and punishment, allows a behavior to continue once it has been reorganized and imitated from observing the original source. In the school setting, this reinforcement is supported by bystanders' support and administration's failure to punish the abusers.

In discussing the action of bullying, a potential bully observes another bully and then initiates his or her own action of bullying with instrumental conditioning supporting the behavior. Specifically, in Aker's social learning perspective (1985), behavior increases if either a reward is received or a punishment is removed. A bully who obtains power and control over a target and does not receive any sort of punishment will continue bullying. As the target or the bystanders do not intervene to end the abuse, the bullying continues.[57]

CHARACTERISTICS OF BULLIES

Most researchers in both criminal justice and education agree that bullies are not as unique as one might perceive them to be.[58] In particular, all schoolyard bullies tend to have a need for power and control.[59] This need is satisfied at the expense of others through the infliction of injury or through the emotional abuse on their victims. These bullies tend to come from families where physical punishment is the norm and the bonding among parents and children is limited.[60] There are those researchers who suggest that big bullies (parents) create little bullies (their children).[61]

Over a decade ago, Barbara Coloroso identified several of the common traits of bullies. Those common traits include: (1) the desire of domination; (2) the manipulation of others to obtain a goal; (3) the egocentrism of the bully; (4) the view of weakness in the victim; (5) the failure to accept responsibility for their actions; and (6) the need for attention by the bully.[62]

In particular, a bully selects a victim based upon conscientious selection with those individuals smaller in physical frame or inferior in intellectual abilities chosen.[63] Through threats or actions, bullies force their victims to act as they desire. The consequences to the victim are of no concern to the bully as the bully's only interest is his or her satisfaction. From this standpoint, a person perceived weaker by the bully is a possible target. At the same time, bullies will often blame the victimization that they have perpetrated on the weaker status of the victim. Hence, to their self-fulfilling desires, the bully gains notoriety from others through the bullying. Others have attempted to characterize bullies in terms of not their individual traits but rather their family structure.[64]

In examining the family structure, many researchers have suggested that the parenting skills of the bully's parents or major caretakers is a major influence on a child's potential to bully or to commit crimes of violence.[65] Parents, who are most often the models for their children, greatly influence the behaviors of their children.[66] In addition, and more relevant to the adults within the school setting, coaches who shame their players by pronouncing that their male players "hit like a girl" in an attempt to motivate them to play better support the notion that physical violence or threats of violence are warranted.

In general, children who are exposed to violence and intimidation in the home will perceive violence and intimidation as the most appropriate method by which to obtain their desires. Therefore, although parental behaviors are not always directly linked to bullying and other forms of violence in the school setting, they cannot be discounted.[67] Coloroso characterized three kinds of such families and their relationships to bullying.[68] These three types of family structures are the brick wall, the jellyfish, and the backbone. The brick-wall family is concerned with order, control, obedience, and a hierarchy of power. The jellyfish family lacks a core family structure and exists within a laissez-faire atmosphere; and the backbone family provides consistent control with an opportunity for discovery.

The brick-wall family instills in the children that power is obtained through intimidation.[69] To be victorious, one must obtain and maintain power over subordinates. Power results from the actions of physical violence and threats. It is asserted by Coloroso that the bully is most likely a product of a brick-wall family.[70]

In the jellyfish family, two different types of families exist. The first type is one in which the parents, in an attempt to please their children, fail to provide strict rules of conduct or strict supervision.[71] In this family, the children become their own masters. In this type, children, who have never been led to feel they must work for their desires, expects their desires to be fulfilled simply upon their request and may bully a smaller or weaker child into submission. In the other type of jellyfish family, the parents, again in an attempt to please their children, assume all of the responsibilities for their children. A child raised in this environment may be perceived as an easy target to bullies as he is labeled the "Mama's Boy" of the classroom; thus, vulnerable to the intimidations of other students. In one type of jellyfish family, the child becomes the bully. In the other type of jellyfish family, the child becomes the victim.

In the backbone family, the child learns through caring but consistent rules and punishment, which parents utilize in order to empower their children.[72] These children will most often feel respect for themselves and also respect for others. Through these families, communications lines are open, there exists caring for the other family members, and there exists respect for each other. The child from the backbone family is least likely to be involved in bullying as the bully or as the victim.[73]

Family structure has been referenced in many research projects on the aspects of physical bullying.[74] However, with today's reliance on technology and the accessibility of cyberspace for all, the real-world bullying has been extended to the virtual world of cyberbullying.

BULLYING IN COLLEGE

Although not commonly believed to be a problem within the university setting, bullying does occur on college campuses across the world. However, often bullying is not recognized in environments of higher education.[75]

On September 22, 2010, a student studying at Rutgers University posted a Facebook status update via his mobile device reading "jumping off the bridge sorry." and ultimately ended his life by doing just that.[76] This event took place after the student's roommate, as well as another classmate, had supposedly set up a camera in his dorm room and streamed online a video of a sexual encounter that had taken place between the student and another person.

In 2010, the Office of Civil Rights of the Department of Education published the Dear Colleague Letter,[77] which addressed bullying and harassment and included many requirements that were not previously addressed. For example, a major policy that was implemented under this letter was the holding of an offender of cyberbullying accountable for their actions. American college counseling centers have reported that anxiety, depression, and suicidal ideation have been increasing on campuses for the last ten to fifteen years, which may be correlated with the amount of bullying partaking on these campuses. In reference to gender differences, research suggests that within the university setting, male students report being a victim of bullying more than female students, when considering both verbal and physical forms of bullying.[78] In addition, it was reported that, as of 2001, fraternity members were disproportionately represented among offenders of crimes on university campuses.[79]

Hazing

Hazing is defined as a practice of initiating new members into a group, often through harassment and humiliation.[80] In other words, prior to becoming an "official" member of the group, many organizations make their recruits participate in actions that display their loyalty and dedication to the group. In the end, hazing is another form of bullying even though the victims are usually subjecting themselves to the maltreatment in an effort to become part of a desired group. Approximately 73 percent of Greek organization members experienced some form of hazing during their involvement with the organization.[81] Furthermore, although hazing is predominantly discussed in reference to Greek Letter Organizations (further discussed in chapter 3), hazing also occurs between members of athletic teams, honor societies, and clubs on college campuses.

Hazing varies in action severity from group to group. The first recorded death that resulted from hazing was in 1873 at Cornell University.[82] A student, Mortimor Leggett, fell into a gorge after being blindfolded and left alone in the dark by other members of the Kappa Alpha Society and, since

2005, more than sixty college students have died in hazing-related incidents, with five of those students dying in 2013 alone.[83] In 2011, a drum major from Florida A&M University took part in a hazing ritual in which one member of the band would run from one end of a bus to the other end while the rest of the band members kicked and punched them as they ran through.[84] If the student was unable to make it to the other side of the bus without falling down, they were forced to try again. This student did not succeed and left the bus to vomit, but he was pressured by other band members to return to the bus and try again.[85] An hour later the student had collapsed and ended up dying. His cause of death was ruled to be a result of blunt trauma from the hazing ritual. More recently, in 2013, pledges of the Gamma Psi sorority at Young Harris College stated that they were forced to crawl through mud to reach a freezing creek while the older members yelled and spit on them as they completed the challenge.[86] These women also revealed another part of their hazing consisted of them being required to sit on top of washing machines to see if any parts of their body moved while the machines were on. If a sister saw any skin moving, she would circle the body part in a permanent marker and ridicule the pledge for it.[87]

In terms of international legislative efforts, Sweden and Norway led the way in anti-bullying legislation. In addition, in Europe since 1998, the United Kingdom's law requires anti-bullying policies in all state schools. Belgium brought new anti-bullying laws into effect as part of a reform in 2014. In South Africa, laws have been implemented to combat cyberbullying by requiring that Internet Service Providers provide law enforcement the contact details of any individual found to be harassing another. With this law, children under the age of eighteen can also approach the courts without their parent's knowledge. In Australia, each state or territory has formed its own set of anti-bullying policies and applies these policies to public schools. In China, the law requires that people register their real names online, which eliminated the anonymousness of the online community and therefore facilitates investigations into bullying when they are reported to law enforcement officials. Lastly, in Singapore in 2014, cyberbullying was criminalized. Specifically, the cyberbullying of children may result in a fine of up to $5,000 or one year in jail for first-time offenders.

Regarding the United States, as of January 2018, there were only six states that did not have antihazing laws in place (Montana, Wyoming, South Dakota, New Mexico, Alaska, Hawaii); although, in states in which there are legal sanctions for hazing offenders, the sanctions as well as the legal definition of the word itself vary drastically. However, table 2.1 presents examples from five states that have antihazing laws.

Table 2.1. State Legislation Example on Hazing

State	Legal Definition	Criminal Sanctions
California	**West's Ann.Cal.Penal Code §245.6:** "Hazing" means any method of initiation or preinitiation into a student organization or student body, whether or not the organization or body is officially recognized by an educational institution, which is likely to cause serious bodily injury to any former, current, or prospective student of any school, community college, college, university, or other educational institution in this state. The term "hazing" does not include customary athletic events or school-sanctioned events.	**Misdemeanor** (c) A violation of this section that does not result in serious bodily injury is a misdemeanor, punishable by a fine of not less than one hundred dollars ($100), nor more than five thousand dollars ($5,000), or imprisonment in the county jail for not more than one year, or both. (d) Any person who personally engages in hazing that results in death or serious bodily injury as defined in paragraph (4) of subdivision (f) of Section 243 of the Penal Code, is guilty of either a misdemeanor or a felony, and shall be punished by imprisonment in county jail not exceeding one year, or by imprisonment pursuant to subdivision (h) of Section 1170. **Felony** (d) Any person who personally engages in hazing that results in death or serious bodily injury as defined in paragraph (4) of subdivision (f) of Section 243 of the Penal Code, is guilty of either a misdemeanor or a felony, and shall be punished by imprisonment in county jail not exceeding one year, or by imprisonment pursuant to subdivision (h) of Section 1170. **Other Sanctions** (e) The person against whom the hazing is directed may commence a civil action for injury or damages. The action may be brought against any participants in the hazing, or any organization to which the student is seeking membership whose agents, directors, trustees, managers, or officers authorized, requested, commanded, participated in, or ratified the hazing. (f) Prosecution under this section shall not prohibit prosecution under any other provision of law.

State	Legal Definition	Criminal Sanctions
Texas	**§ 37.151-152:** Hazing: Any intentional, knowing, or reckless act, occurring on or off the campus of an educational institution, by one person alone or acting with others, directed against a student, that endangers the mental or physical health or safety of a student for the purpose of pledging, being initiated into, affiliating with, holding office in, or maintaining membership in an organization. (1) "Educational institution" includes a public or private high school. (2) "Pledge" means any person who has been accepted by, is considering an offer of membership from, or is in the process of qualifying for membership in an organization. (3) "Pledging" means any action or activity related to becoming a member of an organization. (4) "Student" means any person who: (A) is registered in or in attendance at an educational institution; (B) has been accepted for admission at the educational institution where the hazing incident occurs; or (C) intends to attend an educational institution during any of its regular sessions after a period of scheduled vacation. (5) "Organization" means a fraternity, sorority, association, corporation, order, society, corps, club, or service, social, or similar group, whose members are primarily students. **§ 37.152 :** (a) A person commits an offense if the person: (1) engages in hazing; (2) solicits, encourages, directs, aids, or attempts to aid another in engaging in hazing; (3) recklessly permits hazing to occur; or (4) has firsthand knowledge of the planning of a specific hazing incident involving a student in	**Misdemeanor** **§ 37.152 (Individual):** (b) The offense of failing to report is a Class B misdemeanor. (c) Any other offense under this section that does not cause serious bodily injury to another is a Class B misdemeanor. (d) Any other offense under this section that causes serious bodily injury to another is a Class A misdemeanor. **§ 37.153 (Institutional):** (b) An offense under this section is a misdemeanor. **Felony** (e) Any other offense under this section that causes the death of another is a state jail felony. **§ 37.152 (Individual):** (f) Except if an offense causes the death of a student, in sentencing a person convicted of an offense under this section, the court may require the person to perform community service, subject to the same conditions imposed on a person placed on community supervision under Chapter 42A, Code of Criminal Procedure, for an appropriate period of time in lieu of confinement in county jail or in lieu of a part of the time the person is sentenced to confinement in county jail. **Other Sanctions** **§ 37.153 (Institutional):** (1) a fine of not less than $5,000 nor more than $10,000; or (2) if the court finds that the offense caused personal injury, property damage, or other loss, a fine of not less than $5,000 nor more than double the amount lost or expenses incurred because of the injury, damage, or loss. **§ 37.155:** In the prosecution of an offense under this subchapter, the court may grant immunity from prosecution for the offense to each person who is subpoenaed to testify

(continued)

Table 2.1 (*continued*)

State	Legal Definition	Criminal Sanctions
Texas	an educational institution, or has firsthand knowledge that a specific hazing incident has occurred, and knowingly fails to report that knowledge in writing to the dean of students or other appropriate official of the institution. (a) An organization commits an offense if the organization condones or encourages hazing or if an officer or any combination of members, pledges, or alumni of the organization commits or assists in the commission of hazing.	for the prosecution and who does testify for the prosecution. Any person reporting a specific hazing incident involving a student in an educational institution to the dean of students or other appropriate official of the institution is immune from civil or criminal liability that might otherwise be incurred or imposed as a result of the report. Immunity extends to participation in any judicial proceeding resulting from the report. A person reporting in bad faith or with malice is not protected by this section. § 37.157: A doctor or other medical practitioner who treats a student who may have been subjected to hazing activities: (1) may report the suspected hazing activities to police or other law enforcement officials; and (2) is immune from civil or other liability that might otherwise be imposed or incurred as a result of the report, unless the report is made in bad faith or with malice.
Virginia	§18.2-56: "Hazing" means to recklessly or intentionally endanger the health or safety of a student or students or to inflict bodily injury on a student or students in connection with or for the purpose of initiation, admission into or affiliation with or as a condition for continued membership in a club, organization, association, fraternity, sorority, or student body regardless of whether the student or students so endangered or injured participated voluntarily in the relevant activity.	**Misdemeanor** Any person found guilty thereof shall be guilty of a Class 1 misdemeanor.

State	Legal Definition	Criminal Sanctions
Colorado	**CO ST §18-9-124:** (a) "Hazing" means any activity by which a person recklessly endangers the health or safety of or causes a risk of bodily injury to an individual for purposes of initiation or admission into or affiliation with any student organization; except that "hazing" does not include customary athletic events or other similar contests or competitions, or authorized training activities conducted by members of the armed forces of the state of Colorado or the United States. (b) "Hazing" includes but is not limited to: (I) Forced and prolonged physical activity; (II) Forced consumption of any food, beverage, medication or controlled substance, whether or not prescribed, in excess of the usual amounts for human consumption or forced consumption of any substance not generally intended for human consumption; (III) Prolonged deprivation of sleep, food, or drink.	**Misdemeanor** (3) It shall be unlawful for any person to engage in hazing. (4) Any person who violates subsection (3) of this section commits a class 3 misdemeanor.
New York	**§ 120.16-17:** Hazing in the first degree. A person is guilty of hazing in the first degree when, in the course of another person's initiation into or affiliation with any organization, he intentionally or recklessly engages in conduct which creates a substantial risk of physical injury to such other person or a third person and thereby causes such injury Hazing in the second degree. A person is guilty of hazing in the second degree when, in the course of another person's initiation or affiliation with any organization, he intentionally or recklessly engages in conduct which creates a substantial risk of physical injury to such other person or a third person.	**Misdemeanor** Hazing in the first degree is a class A misdemeanor. **Other Sanctions** Hazing in the second degree is a violation.

BULLYING TO CYBERBULLYING

Cyberbullying, an extension of bullying, is defined as the use of technology (usually by a teen or preteen) to include a cell phone, a computer, instant messaging, and/or social networking sites to harass, threaten, or intimidate another.[88] For all the negative outcomes of bullying, the most positive consequence is that it is real-world, personal, and immediate.[89] Specifically, in traditional cases of bullying, the victims know the source of the bullying and know, for the most part, why they are a victim of bullying. In these cases, the victims are often being bullied because they are blamed for a failed relationship, they were recognized for an accomplishment while their bully was not, or they have more material possessions than their bully. Thus, in historical cases of bullying the victims know why they are being bullied, the victims know their bully or bullies, and the victims are in the physical proximity of their bully during their victimization.[90] Unfortunately, with cyberbullying this is not always true as the victim may not know who or why or when the bullying may occur.

Cyberbullying exists within the boundless cyberspace.[91] Individuals (adults and children) with the technology skills and the ability to hide behind pseudonymous names are able to disguise their true identities from their victims and from their online community. This secrecy provides bullies the ability to increase their aggression without identifying themselves; thus, the luxury of an attack without the probability of detection. In addition, victims of cyberbullying may be misled about the identity of their bully to the point that (in the victim's mind) their bully is a significant member in their social arena with many supporters when, in actuality, their bully is only a minor character in the reality of their lives and has little or no influence over others.[92]

SEXTING AND SEXTORTION

Sexting is defined as the sending and/or receiving of sexually suggestive images or messages to individuals through a cell phone.[93] The distinction between texting and sexting must be acknowledged. The majority of today's cell phones have the capabilities to send and receive text messages; thus, individuals, through their cell phone may converse without saying a word. Texting is not sexting; however, sexting is a type of texting. As suggested in current research, sexting has increased in rank in terms of parental concerns and school issues throughout the world.[94] The majority of the people who sext with each other are also in relationships with each other. Therefore, in the majority of the cases of sexting, there are multiple contacts (sexts) between parties; in fact, the term sexting assumes the existence of repeated messages and/or images of a sexual nature.[95] For adults (i.e., those age eighteen or older) sexting is not illegal and is common practice among young adults throughout the dating stages of a relationship. However, for those under the age of eighteen, sexting is illegal as it involves the sending of explicit sexual images or messages that are considered forms of child pornography, and it often begins within the school environment.

Sextortion is a severe negative outcome most often as a result of sexting. For clarity, sextortion is defined as a form of sexual abuse where an abuser threatens to reveal sexually explicit images of a victim unless that particular victim meets the specific demands of the perpetrator.[96] These demands include providing more sexually graphic images or videos. Simply stated, sextortion is a form of blackmail in which images are used to force individuals (most likely teens) into performing sexual favors or actions to prevent the release of those images to their friends, family, and the online community.[97] Both of these activities occur in today's virtual cyberspace and both are becoming more common for teen or child sexual exploitation.

Statistics indicate that approximately 95 percent of all teenagers within the United States have their own cell phones and that the majority of those teens send text messages.[98] As parents will attest, in most cases, they are more likely to receive a text from their child than a phone call. In addition, it is not unusual for school administrators and teachers to communicate with students and parents via text messages. However, in some cases, those teen-to-teen text messages become teen-to-teen sext messages. Although sexting is vaguely defined to include the sending or receiving of sexual images or language on a repeated basis, all states and countries address either child pornography or child sexual exploitation. Unfortunately, these images, often circulated to many within the online community, have the propensity to exist forever with emotional and social damage to the victim lasting for years. Accordingly, the victimization of the individual pictured in the images or sexts, often the teen, is considered never ending and never in the past. Therefore, bullying has widened its net to include cyberbullying with incidents increasing the potential targets for violence within the school environment.

CHARACTERISTICS OF VICTIMS AND BYSTANDERS

Although bullies may have a positive perspective on themselves, victims do not.[99] Victims of bullies tend to suffer from low self-esteem, are insecure, and are often unwilling to defend themselves.[100] Whereas the parents of the bullies often allow the child to become independent at early age, often to allow these parents to have more time to focus upon themselves, the victims of bullies may come from homes with very overprotective parents, and are allowed few friends outside of the family.[101]

From a victimology perspective, bullying is explained under the foundation of victim precipitation, which asserts that victims (either passively or actively) provoke their attacks.[102] In cases of bullying, the victim passively precipitates the action merely through their physical appearance or behaviors. In support, many bullies blame their victims for their attacks.[103]

It has been suggested in the area of bullying that there are no innocent bystanders; this is especially true in the school environment. These individuals either support the bullying or they are neutral to the bullying. It has been suggested that there are six different types of bystanders, all with a different dynamic.[104] Those types of bystanders are: (1) the bully/bullies; (2) the follower; (3) the supporters; (4) the disengaged onlookers; (5) the possible defenders; and (6) the defenders.

The bully rules through threats of violence and intimidation, whereas the followers are those that take part in the bullying but are not the initiators of the action. The supporters are those who like the bullying but do not take part, and the disengaged onlookers are those who assert that the bullying of someone else is not their concern. The possible defenders are those that believe the target of the bullying activity should be defended; however, they are not the one to help the person. The defender is that unique individual who actually attempts to help the victim of the bully.[105] Although popular media may contradict the reality, in cases of bullying, there exist few defenders.[106]

Theories of victimization rarely suggest that victims are randomly selected.[107] In fact, most theories suggest either an active or passive role of participation by the victim prior to their victimization. In cases of bullying in the school setting, the role of the victim is often that of passive participation. By identifying the factors that exist in many cases of bullying and cyberbullying within cyberspace, it is determined that in the overwhelming majority of cyberbullying cases those characteristics of victims are either demographic or behavioral.[108]

As with traditional cases of bullying, victims are in many cases smaller in physical stature or perceived as physically weaker than their peers.[109] In other cases, victims of bullying and cyberbullying are overweight, have a strong body odor, or attempt to dress to a role that is not their identity (e.g., dress as a jock when they do not play sports).[110] In other cases of bullying and cyberbullying, victims exhibit antisocial behaviors, act like "little professors," or socialize with very few friends in or out of the school environment. In addition, many victims of bullying have low levels of self-esteem, are insecure, and are often anxious.[111] During the teenage years, these characteristics are more common than unusual. Finally, in traditional cases of bullying, it is not unusual for victims to have been identified as developmentally (intellectually and/or physically) delayed.[112] Whereas many of the characteristics of victims of bullying also apply to cyberbullying, rarely are the victims of cyberbullying physically disabled. However, it is not unusual for victims of cyberbullying to suffer from low self-esteem, academic challenges, and other mental disabilities such as the inability to be flexible on actions and procedures.

In the school environment, it may appear as the victims of bullying and cyberbullying willingly allow the bullying to occur. In cases such as these, perpetrators of bullying and bystanders often observe their victims failing to prohibit the bullying of others. From the perpetrator's perspective, their victim is not likely to report the bullying of others, and thus probably not likely to report the victimization of themselves. From a perpetrator's perspective, if the victim of bullying/cyberbullying is not willing to defend themselves, then they allow the abuse to continue.

Finally, it is not unusual for victims of bullying to attempt to befriend their bully.[113] From the victim's perspective, if they are "friends" with the bully, they are less likely to be the continued victim of the bully. In addition, it is not unusual for victims of bullying to begin to participate in the bullying or cyberbullying of others.

In terms of cyberbullying, one should understand that the number of victims is usually larger than the targets for traditional bullying given that the potential for perpetrators is wider as cyberbullying provides the opportunity to bully an individual without the face-to-face confrontation in traditional cases of bullying.[114]

CONSEQUENCES OF BULLYING WITHIN THE SCHOOL ENVIRONMENT

Bullying may have both short- and long-term consequences for the victim. Short-term consequences can include psychological distress, physical illness, a lack of concentration on schoolwork, and a fear of attending school.[115] Long-term consequences can include low self-esteem, depression, and a reduced capacity for learning.[116] Extreme consequences of bullying within the school environment are demonstrated in cases such as the USA's Columbine school shooting.[117] In response, several anti-bullying organizations (see Table 2.2) now exist.

Often, in many cases of bullying, the victims display behaviors of anxiousness, nervousness, and worry. In other cases, victims themselves become aggressive toward other non-bullying students.[118] Students who are victims of bullying spend much of the time during their school day planning how not to

Table 2.2. Organizations to Address Bullying

Anti-Bullying Organization	About the Organization
STOMP Out Bullying (https://stompoutbullying.org/)	An organization within the United States that works to reduce and prevent bullying, cyberbullying, and other digital abuse, to educate against homophobia, LGBTQ discrimination, racism, and hatred, and to deter violence in schools and communities across the country.
Ditch the Label (https://us.ditchthelabel.org/)	An international organization that works to provide evolving, innovative, and comprehensive emotional and physical support to victims of bullying both in offline and online environments. They are also continuously doing research in an effort to measure, evaluate, and predict changes in the variables related to bullying in an effort to ensure their programs are adequate and beneficial.
No Bully (https://www.nobully.org)/	Although beginning within the United States, this nonprofit organization has become increasingly popular among international communities and was started by a collaborative team of educators, psychologists, and lawyers committed to building a kinder and more compassionate world through ending the bullying crisis.
National Association of People against Bullying (https://www.napab.org/)	A nonprofit foundation that provides anti-bullying services, education, and support to students, families, and school administrators.
PACER's National Bullying Prevention Center (https://www.pacer.org/bullying/)	This organization provides resources to students, parents, and educators on the serious community issue of bullying that impacts the education, health, safety, and overall well-being of students.
The Cybersmile Foundation (https://www.cybersmile.org/)	Founded in 2010, Cybersmile has become the world's leading anti-cyberbullying nonprofit organization. Registered as a nonprofit organization in the United States and as a registered charity in the United Kingdom, this foundation provides expert support, resources, and consultancy to individuals, governments, corporations, and educational institutions around the world.

be a victim. For example, a student who is concerned about being victimized in the bathroom may choose not to eat or drink during the day for fear of having to go to the bathroom or may request permission to go to the bathroom during class time while the other students remain in the classroom. A student worried about victimization on the playground may act out in class to avoid being allowed to go outside and therefore staying inside under the supervision and protection of the teacher. For these students, educational learning is limited, and for the victims who cannot plan for their protection on school grounds, absenteeism becomes an issue.[119]

As suggested, 15 percent of the students in American schools today with persistent absences report bullying as their initial reason for missing school.[120] In the United Kingdom, approximately 20 percent of students report missing school because of bullying.[121] Students who are not attending school are not learning. In addition, schools, which receive funding based upon the number of students in attendance, suffer financially when students are afraid to come to school.[122] In a nutshell, bullying, directly and indirectly, can pose one set of problems for the victim and another set for the educational system.[123]

As glorified in the media over the last decade, bullying can lead to severe consequences such as the school shooting at Columbine High School. Research has suggested that those involved in bullying (perpetrators and victims) within the school environment are likely to choose memberships in gangs, which continue to provide more problems of violence within the school setting. This is especially true for females who are involved in bullying. Reportedly, female gang members were even more likely than males to have been bullied and then bullied someone else while they were in school.[124] Finally, it was suggested over two decades ago that former involvement in school bullying is related to juvenile involvement in violence and weapons;[125] those findings remain true today.[126]

In some rare cases of bullying, students are initially victims of verbalized bullying; however, the verbal abuse escalates into physical abuse. Therefore, the victims are forced to fight to defend themselves and are often injured during these confrontations. Bullying is often the root of other forms of violence.[127] In other rare cases of bullying, the victim decides that the only way to end the victimization is to kill the perpetrator or end their own life.[128]

CHAPTER QUESTIONS

1. In what year was the first significant research article pertaining to bullying published? What were the key components of the article?
2. What are the categories of emotional abuse? Please explain each.
3. Name some common traits most bullies possess.
4. How many states have antihazing laws?
5. Name three short-term and long-term effects of bullying on a victim.

DISCUSSION QUESTIONS

1. As the number of social networking sites increases, do you think the number of suicides will also increase? Explain.
2. Do you feel as though schools are taking bullying and cyberbullying seriously? What steps could be taken in an effort to prevent bullying in the future?
3. Should social networking companies be responsible for all of the content that is posted on their platforms? Why or why not?

NOTES

1. Michael Nedelman, "9-Year-Old Dies by Suicide after He Was Bullied," 2018, accessed on January 3, 2019, at https://www.cnn.com/2018/08/28/health/preteen-suicide-jamel-myles/index.html.

2. Frank Burk, "Teasing and Bullying," *Pedagogical Seminary*, 4 (1897): 336–71.

3. Richard Lawrence, *School Crime and Juvenile Justice* (New York: Oxford University Press, 1998).

4. Nels Ericson, *Addressing the Problems of Juvenile Bullying.* Washington, DC: US Department of Justice. Office of Juvenile Justice and Delinquency Prevention. (2001) (FS-200127).

5. Daniel Olweus, *Aggression in the Schools: Bullies and Whipping Boys* (Washington, DC: Hemisphere Publishing Corp., 1978).

6. Kimberly McCabe, *Child Abuse and the Criminal Justice System* (New York: Peter Lang, 2003).

7. David Farrington, "Understanding and Preventing Bullying." In M. Tonry (ed.), *Crime and Justice: A Review of Research (Volume 17)* (Chicago: University of Chicago Press, 1993), 381–458.

8. Kimberly McCabe and Daniel Murphy, *Child Abuse—Today's Issues* (New York: Taylor and Francis Publishing, 2016).

9. Hyojin Koo, "A Time Line of the Evolution of School Bullying in Differing Social Contexts," *Asia Pacific Education Review*, 8(1) (2007): 107–16.

10. Kimberly McCabe, *Protecting Your Children in Cyberspace: What Parents Need to Know* (Lanham, MD: Rowman and Littlefield Publishers, Inc., 2017).

11. Anti-Bullying Alliance, "The Scale and Impact of Identity-Based Bullying in School, 2017," accessed on December 3, 2018, at https://www.anti-bullyingalliance.org.uk/sites/default/files/field/attachment/The%20scale%20and%20impact%20of%20identity-based%20bullying%20-%20research%20and%20evidence.pdf.

12. Fang Zhao, Jura Hamalainen, and Honglin Chen, "Child Protection in China. Changing Policies and Reactions from the Field of Social Work," *International Journal of Social Welfare*, 26(4) (2017): 329–39.

13. Nicki Crick, Juan Casas, and H.-C. Ku, "Relational and Physical Forms of Peer Victimization in Preschool," *Developmental Psychology*, 35 (1998): 376–85.

14. Kathleen Rospenda, Judith Richman, Jennifer Wolff, and Larisa Burke, "Bullying Victimization among College Students: Negative Consequences for Alcohol Use," *Journal of Addictive Diseases*, 32(4) (2013): 325–42.

15. Meredith McGinley, Kathleen Rospenda, Li Liu, and J. Richman, "Chronic Generalized Harassment during College: Influences on Alcohol and Drug Use," *Journal Youth Adolescence*, 44 (2015): 1898–1913.

16. Kimberly McCabe and Gregory Martin, *School Violence, the Media and Criminal Justice Responses* (New York: Peter Lang, 2015).

17. Ronnie Casella, "What Is Violence about 'School Violence'? The Nature of Violence in a City High School." In J. N. Burstyn, G. Bender, R. Casella, H. W. Gordon, D. P. Guerra, K. V. Luschen, R. Stevens, and K. M. Williams (eds.), *Preventing Violence in Schools. A Challenge to American Democracy* (Mahwah, NJ: Lawrence Erlbaum Associates, 2001).

18. Kimberly McCabe and Daniel Murphy, *Child Abuse—Today's Issues*.

19. Cynthia Crosson-Tower, *Understanding Child Abuse and Neglect*, eighth edition (Boston: Allyn and Bacon, 2010).

20. Kimberly McCabe, *Protecting Your Children in Cyberspace: What Parents Need to Know*.

21. Kimberly McCabe and Daniel Murphy, *Child Abuse—Today's Issues*.

22. Kimberly McCabe and Gregory Martin, *School Violence, the Media and Criminal Justice Responses*.

23. Cynthia Crosson-Tower, *Understanding Child Abuse and Neglect*.

24. Kimberly McCabe and Daniel Murphy, *Child Abuse—Today's Issues*.

25. Tammy Garland, Christina Policastro, Tara Richards, and Karen Miller, "Blaming the Victim: University Student Attitudes toward Bullying," *Journal of Aggression, Maltreatment and Trauma*, 26(1) (2014): 69–87.

26. Kimberly McCabe, *Protecting Your Children in Cyberspace: What Parents Need to Know*.

27. Kimberly McCabe and Daniel Murphy, *Child Abuse—Today's Issues*.

28. Janis Wolak and David Finkelhor, *Sextortion: Findings from a Survey of 1631 Victims* (Durham: University of New Hampshire: Crimes Against Children Research Center, 2016), 5–7.

29. Lizzie Dearden, "Five British Men Have Killed Themselves after Falling Victim to Online Sextortion, Police Reveal," *Independent News*, May 5, 2018, p. 1.

30. Kimberly McCabe, *Child Abuse and the Criminal Justice System*.

31. Rachel McEvoy, Luciana Ballini, Susanne Maltoni, Catherine O'Donnell, Francis Mair, and Anne MacFarland, "A Qualitative Systematic Review of Studies Using the Normalization Process Theory to Research Implementation Processes," *Implementation Science*, 9(2) (2014): 134–40.

32. Kimberly McCabe and Daniel Murphy, *Child Abuse—Today's Issues*.

33. Kimberly McCabe and Gregory Martin, *School Violence, the Media and Criminal Justice Responses*.

34. Kimberly McCabe and Daniel Murphy, *Child Abuse—Today's Issues*.

35. Barbara Coloroso, *The Bully, the Bullied, and the Bystander* (New York: Harper Collins, 2003).

36. Daniel Olweus, *Bullying at School: What We Know and What We Can Do* (Cambridge, MA: Blackwell, 2003).

37. Lee Beaty and Erick Alexeyev, "The Problem of School Bullies: What the Research Tells Us," *Adolescence*, 43(169) (2008): 1–11.

38. National Center for Educational Statistics [NCES], "Gangs and Victimization at School," accessed on January 5, 2019, at http://nces.ed.gov/pubs/web/95740.asp.

39. Barbara Coloroso, *The Bully, the Bullied, and the Bystander*.

40. Kimberly McCabe and Gregory Martin, *School Violence, the Media and Criminal Justice Responses*.

41. Kimberly McCabe, *Child Abuse and the Criminal Justice System*.

42. Barbara Coloroso, *The Bully, the Bullied, and the Bystander*.

43. Daniel Olweus, *Bullying at School: What We Know and What We Can Do*.

44. Kimberly McCabe, *Child Abuse and the Criminal Justice System*.

45. Kimberly McCabe and Daniel Murphy, *Child Abuse—Today's Issues*.

46. Cesare Lombroso, *The Criminal Man* (Milan: Hoepli, 1876).

47. William Sheldon, *Varieties of Delinquent Youth* (New York: Harper and Brothers, 1949).

48. Kimberly McCabe and Gregory Martin, *School Violence, the Media and Criminal Justice Responses*.

49. Daniel Curran and Claire Renzetti, *Theories of Crime*, second edition (Needham Heights, MA: Pearson Education Company, 2001).

50. Robert Hare, "Psychopathy: A Clinical Construct Whose Time Has Come," *Criminal Justice and Behavior*, 23(1) (1996): 25–54.

51. Stephen Hart and Rebecca Dempster, "Impulsivity and Psychopathy." In C. D. Webster and M. A. Jacksons (eds.), *Theory, Assessment, and Treatment* (New York: Guilford, 1997), 212–32.

52. Kimberly McCabe, *Protecting Your Children in Cyberspace: What Parents Need to Know*.

53. Daniel Curran and Claire Renzetti, *Theories of Crime*.

54. Kimberly McCabe and Daniel Murphy, *Child Abuse—Today's Issues*.

55. Ronald Akers, *Deviant Behavior: A Social Learning Approach*, third edition (Belmont, CA: Wadsworth, 1985).

56. Ronald Akers, *Deviant Behavior: A Social Learning Approach*.

57. Kimberly McCabe and Gregory Martin, *School Violence, the Media and Criminal Justice Responses*.

58. Kimberly McCabe and Gregory Martin, *School Violence, the Media and Criminal Justice Responses*.

59. Lee Beaty and Erick Alexeyev, "The Problem of School Bullies: What the Research Tells Us."

60. Daniel Olweus, *Bullying at School: What We Know and What We Can Do*.

61. Kimberly McCabe and Gregory Martin, *School Violence, the Media and Criminal Justice Responses*.

62. Barbara Coloroso, *The Bully, the Bullied, and the Bystander*.

63. Kimberly McCabe and Gregory Martin, *School Violence, the Media and Criminal Justice Responses*.

64. Doug Cooper, and Jennie Snell, "Bullying—Not Just a Kid Thing," *Educational Leadership*, 60(6) (2003): 22–25.

65. David Henry, Patrick Tolan, and Deborah Gorman-Smith, "Longitudinal Family and Peer Group Effects on Violence and Nonviolent Delinquency," *Journal of Child Clinical Psychology*, 30(1) (2001): 172–86.

66. Phillippe Cunningham and Scott Henggler, "Implementation of an Empirically Based Drug and Violence Prevention and Intervention Program in Public School Settings," *Journal of Clinical Child Psychology*, 30(2) (2001): 221–32.

67. Kimberly McCabe and Daniel Murphy, *Child Abuse—Today's Issues*.

68. Barbara Coloroso, *The Bully, the Bullied, and the Bystander*.

69. Kimberly McCabe and Gregory Martin, *School Violence, the Media and Criminal Justice Responses*.

70. Barbara Coloroso, *The Bully, the Bullied, and the Bystander*.

71. Barbara Coloroso, *The Bully, the Bullied, and the Bystander*.

72. Kimberly McCabe and Gregory Martin, *School Violence, the Media and Criminal Justice Responses*.

73. Barbara Coloroso, *The Bully, the Bullied, and the Bystander*.

74. Kimberly McCabe and Gregory Martin, *School Violence, the Media and Criminal Justice Responses*.

75. McGinley, Rospenda, Liu, and Richman, "Chronic Generalized Harassment during College: Influences on Alcohol and Drug Use."

76. Stephanie Chen, "After Student's Death a Weeklong Look into Bullying," 2010, accessed on December 3, 2018, at http://www.cnn.com/2010/LIVING/10/04/bullying.special.explainer/index.html.

77. Dear Colleague Letter, Office of Civil Rights, 2010, accessed on January 3, 2019, at https://www2.ed.gov/about/offices/list/ocr/letters/colleague-201010.html.

78. M. Chapell, S. Hasselman, T. Kitchin, S. Lomon, K. McIvor, and P. Sarullo, "Bullying in Elementary School, High School and College," 2006, accessed on November 3, 2018, at https://ezproxy.lynchburg.edu/login?url=https://search.proquest.com/docview/195943783?accountid=12198.

79. Chapell, Hasselman, Kitchin, Lomon, McIvor, and Sarullo, "Bullying in Elementary School, High School and College."

80. Devon Alvarez, "Death by Hazing: Should There Be a Federal Law against Fraternity and Sorority Hazing?" *Journal of Multidisciplinary Research*, 7(2) (2015): 43–75.

81. Devon Alvarez, "Death by Hazing: Should There Be a Federal Law against Fraternity and Sorority Hazing?"

82. Devon Alvarez, "Death by Hazing: Should There Be a Federal Law against Fraternity and Sorority Hazing?"

83. Devon Alvarez, "Death by Hazing: Should There Be a Federal Law against Fraternity and Sorority Hazing?"

84. *Miami Herald*, "Convictions Upheld in Hazing Death of FAMU Drum Major," 2018, accessed on February 3, 2019, at https://www.miamiherald.com/news/state/florida/article115652918.html.

85. *Miami Herald*, "Convictions Upheld in Hazing Death of FAMU Drum Major."

86. Katie Baker, "Naked Sweethearts and Mud Crawls: A Small College's Big Hazing Problem," April 30, 2013, accessed on January 3, 2019, at https://jezebel .com/naked-sweethearts-and-mud-crawls-small-college-has-big-485060397.

87. Katie Baker, "Naked Sweethearts and Mud Crawls: A Small College's Big Hazing Problem."

88. Frank Schmallenger, *Criminology Today* (Upper Saddle River, NJ: Pearson, 2006), 481.

89. Kimberly McCabe, *Protecting Your Children in Cyberspace: What Parents Need to Know.*

90. Alice Charach, Debra Pepler, and Suzanne Ziegler, "Bullying at School: A Canadian Perspective. A Survey of Problems and Suggestions for Intervention," *Education Canada,* 35(1) (1995): 12–18.

91. Kimberly McCabe, *Child Abuse and the Criminal Justice System.*

92. Kimberly McCabe, *Child Abuse and the Criminal Justice System.*

93. Janis Wolak and David Finkelhor, *Sextortion: Findings from a Survey of 1631 Victims.*

94. Janis Wolak and David Finkelhor, *Sextortion: Findings from a Survey of 1631 Victims.*

95. Benjamin Wittes, Cody Poplin, Quinta Jurecic, and Clara Spera, "Sextortion: Cybersecurity, Teenagers, and Remote Sexual Assault," 2016, accessed on December 13, 2018, at https://www.brookings.edu/wp-content/uploads/2016/05/sextortion1-1.pdf.

96. Benjamin Wittes, Cody Poplin, Quinta Jurecic, and Clara Spera, "Sextortion: Cybersecurity, Teenagers, and Remote Sexual Assault."

97. Janis Wolak and David Finkelhor, *Sextortion: Findings from a Survey of 1631 Victims.*

98. Janis Wolak and David Finkelhor, *Sextortion: Findings from a Survey of 1631 Victims.*

99. Kimberly McCabe and Gregory Martin, *School Violence, the Media and Criminal Justice Responses.*

100. Kimberly McCabe and Gregory Martin, *School Violence, the Media and Criminal Justice Responses.*

101. Daniel Olweus, *Bullying at School: What We Know and What We Can Do.*

102. Stephen Barkan, *Criminology. A Sociological Understanding*, second edition (Upper Saddle River, NJ: Prentice Hall, 2001).

103. Ronald Oliver, John Hoover, and Richard Hazler, "The Perceived Roles of Bullying in Small-Town Midwestern Schools," *Journal of Counseling and Development,* 72(4) (1994): 416–19.

104. Barbara Coloroso, *The Bully, the Bullied, and the Bystander.*

105. Barbara Coloroso, *The Bully, the Bullied, and the Bystander.*

106. Kimberly McCabe and Gregory Martin, *School Violence, the Media and Criminal Justice Responses.*

107. Stephen Barkan, *Criminology. A Sociological Understanding.*

108. Richard Donegan, "Bullying and Cyberbullying: History, Statistics, Law Prevention, and Analysis," *Journal of Undergraduate Research in Communications,* 3(1) (2012): 33-42.

109. Kimberly McCabe and Gregory Martin, *School Violence, the Media and Criminal Justice Responses*.

110. Kimberly McCabe, *Protecting Your Children in Cyberspace: What Parents Need to Know*.

111. Stephen Barkan, *Criminology. A Sociological Understanding*.

112. Kimberly McCabe and Gregory Martin, *School Violence, the Media and Criminal Justice Responses*.

113. Kimberly McCabe, *Protecting Your Children in Cyberspace: What Parents Need to Know*.

114. Kimberly McCabe and Daniel Murphy, *Child Abuse—Today's Issues*.

115. David Farrington, "Understanding and Preventing Bullying."

116. Kimberly McCabe and Gregory Martin, *School Violence, the Media and Criminal Justice Responses*.

117. Kimberly McCabe and Gregory Martin, *School Violence, the Media and Criminal Justice Responses*.

118. Lee Beaty and Erick Alexeyev, "The Problem of School Bullies: What the Research Tells Us."

119. Ronald Stephens, "National Trends in School Violence: Statistics and Prevention Strategies." In A. P. Goldstein and J. C. Conoleys (eds.), *School Violence Intervention: A Practical Handbook* (New York: Guilford Press, 1997), 72–90.

120. David Farrington, "Understanding and Preventing Bullying."

121. Anti-Bullying Alliance, "The Scale and Impact of Identity-Based Bullying in School," 2017, accessed on December 3, 2018, at https://www.anti-bullyingalliance .org.uk/sites/default/files/field/attachment/The%20scale%20and%20impact%20 of%20identity-based%20bullying%20-%20research%20and%20evidence.pdf.

122. Kimberly McCabe and Gregory Martin, *School Violence, the Media and Criminal Justice Responses*.

123. D. Cornell and A. Looper, "Assessment of Violence and Other High-Risk Behaviors with a School Survey," *School Psychological Review*, 27 (1998): 317–30.

124. Shirley Holmes and Susan Brandenburg-Ayers, "Bullying Behavior in Schools: A Predictor of Later Gang Involvement," *Journal of Gang Research*, 5(2) (1998): 1–6.

125. Martin Killias and Juan Rabasa, "Weapons and Athletic Constitutions as Factors Linked to Violence among Male Juveniles: Findings from the Swiss Self-Reported Delinquency Project," *British Journal of Criminology*, 37(3) (1997): 446–57.

126. Kimberly McCabe and Daniel Murphy, *Child Abuse—Today's Issues*.

127. Kimberly McCabe and Daniel Murphy, *Child Abuse—Today's Issues*.

128. Kimberly McCabe, *Protecting Your Children in Cyberspace: What Parents Need to Know*.

Chapter Three

Cliques and Gangs within the School Environment

KEY WORDS

anime
cheerleaders
clique
culture
differential association
drama freaks
franchising
gang
gang territory
Goth
Greek Letter Organizations

hazing
jocks
loners
Lord of the Flies
organization gang
Otaku Killer
party gang
pledging
rushing
Safe School Initiative
   (United States, 2004)

scuttler
serious delinquent gang
sexed in
sluts
social gang
social institutions
socialization
society
strain theory
subculture
youth gangs

KEY ACRONYMS

(GREAT) Gang Resistance Education and Training
(GANG) Get Away N Get Safe
(GLO) Greek Letter Organizations
(SCS) School Crime Supplement Report
(CRIPS) Criminals Running in Packs
(BLOODS) Black Lords of Our Destiny
(MS-13) Mara Salvatrucha

In 2013, gang violence in South Africa resulted in the closure of sixteen schools for two days due to the violence and risk of injuries for attending students.[1] In 2016, four males, assumed to be members of a local gang, waited with firearms outside of a California high school (USA) and injured four students as they were released from school for the day.

In the school environment, there is nothing more important for the teen than to fit in and be accepted by his or her peers. In fact, for many students, efforts to obtain and maintain acceptance by their peers constitutes more of their time during the school day than efforts to advance academically. It is oftentimes more important to be popular than to be smart. Research indicates that when teens compare their peer groups with a group in which they are not members, they consistently favor the group in which they do not belong.[2] The American phrase that "the grass is always greener" appears to ring true in these discussions of teen peer groups and associations. As it is said, you generally want what you do not have; young people and teenagers are no exception.

The importance of not fitting in socially within the school environment cannot be diminished. Students who are perceived as not a member of the favored group are much more likely to be bullied, intimidated, or face the label of a rejected student and to be friendless eight hours a day while in school.[3] In addition, students who do not fit in are often labeled "losers," "weird," or "strange," and no other student in the school environment wants to be associated with someone viewed by their peers as a loser.

Associations and friends within the school environment help teens to discover their own identities. Teens can be classified or categorized by the groups in which they associate, what they do for fun, their interests, or whether they are academically or athletically gifted.

Hence, again and again in discussions on school violence, the subject of peer groups emerges. Oftentimes the peer group of most concern for school administrators is the gang. Schools with an increased presence of gangs also experience increases in drugs and increases in violence in their environments.[4] Efforts in the United States such as Gang Resistance Education and Training (GREAT) are gang violence prevention programs taught in many schools by law enforcement officers for more than twenty-five years. Get Away N Get Safe (GANG)[5] is a similar program started in 2016 in the United Kingdom. However, when one considers the school shooting of Columbine in 1999 and the fact that neither perpetrator was a member of a gang, then it must be acknowledged that even though gang violence is a part of school violence, other groups may also commit acts considered under the definition of school violence. Since Columbine, one particular group—the Gothic culture or Goths—has been a topic of concern within the subject of school violence and is discussed in much of the literature on school violence. In addition, individuals considered the "loners" are a certain subgroup or clique.[6] In addition, anime, "mean girls," and other peer subgroups must be recognized in their contributions to victimization in the school setting. Therefore, this chapter begins with discussions on subgroups, often called cliques, prior to discussions on gangs and their risk to school violence within the educational setting.

CLIQUES

Despite efforts taken over the last three decades by teachers and school administrators not to label or classify students by common characteristics or perceptions of those common characteristics, the grouping by common traits does still occur in schools.[7] As social beings, students, just as adults, will often gravitate toward individuals with similar interests and backgrounds in an effort to establish some sort of familiarity and common connection. This grouping is what is referred to in this section as the formation of a clique. For many, clique memberships are often based upon inequality, racism, and sexism.[8] As long as there are schools, cliques will exist. Cliques exist for the elite, the athletes, the academics, and even the loners. Therefore, despite efforts by school officials not to group students, the school environment is, in fact, an environment in which separatist grouping occurs.[9]

Research suggests that cliques develop more often within the middle school and high school environments than in elementary and primary schools.[10] Until Columbine and the mention of the Trench Coat Mafia, to which perpetrators Harris and Klebold were peripheral members, cliques were perceived as harmless within the school environment. It was acknowledged that cliques may be involved in bullying, hazing, or even physical attacks; however, those attacks targeted specific individuals and never resulted in mass murder. After Columbine, and the mass murders of a variety of students (e.g., females, minorities, football stars, etc.), cliques gained the attention of the media and the public. Although clique members may not be the perpetrators of a school shooting, they may be the targets as it was once suggested by the media that the Columbine shooters chose to target athletes.[11]

The Cambridge Dictionary[12] defines a clique as a small group or subgroup of people who spend time together without welcoming others into their group. *Clique* is a term that is used when describing a group of people with similar interests who feel connected to one another. Members of cliques do not necessarily have to be within the same age cohort; however, in most cases they will be of similar age due to the demographics of the school environment. In general, many cliques consist of people that simply enjoy the same interests and will bond because of their association with the common interests. Some common interest groups that may aid in the formation of a clique are interest in video games, anime, and athletics.

Cliques, often referred to as social circles, are commonly acknowledged in schools. As obtaining a high social status or becoming popular as an individual is important in adolescence, those with memberships in certain affluent cliques may demonstrate power and influence over others as well as receive affection from peers who also wish to be a member of the clique.[13]

Cliques are normative parts of the social development process for individuals regardless of their gender, ethnicity, or popularity. Individuals who are part of a clique are bonded together through shared interests and similar social characteristics such as race, ethnicity, socioeconomic status, and physical appearance. After high school, students may be involved in cliques through fraternities and sororities as they continue their university studies. Cliques have been recognized for the possibility of their involvement in bullying, intimidation, and physical attacks. Cliques in the university settings have been known to participate in hazing—the imposition of often humiliating and sometimes dangerous tasks imposed upon individuals for membership in a group. In addition, cliques may be the structure through which teens taunt and tease other nonclique members.

In general, cliques are the primary vehicles by which adolescents and teens socialize.[14] Therefore, if the actions of a clique are violent, they must be acknowledged in discussions on school violence. In discussions on cliques, historically the more common clique structures exist in every school and include jocks, cheerleaders, drama freaks, sluts, and loners.[15] Those clique members are as described below:

- Jocks—males who participate in sports
- Cheerleaders—females with school spirit
- Drama Freaks—students who are engrossed in acting
- Sluts—females who wear provocative clothing
- Loners—those students without peer groups

Just as in the adult world, the school environment supports a hierarchy among cliques. Often jocks and cheerleaders occupy the top positions, drama freaks and those involved in other club memberships occupy peripheral positions, sluts are placed within the lower social positions, and loners (because of their perceived inability to exist within any clique) occupy the lowest position.[16] It is reasonable to expect that loners (such as Columbine's Harris and Klebold) were often the targets of victimization by other clique members. It was these victimizations at school, media accounts have asserted, that supported their need for mass destruction within their school environment.[17]

Cliques can have a significant impact on the lives of young people, especially those individuals who become victims of abuse by those cliques.[18] Children can be subjected to violence and ridicule by members of a clique with this humiliation happening in front of their peers. For males, the experience often includes physical attacks or threats of a physical attack while the same holds true for females; however, females are more likely the targets of verbal abuse and cyberbullying.[19] One popular work of literature that portrays cliques in their most negative form—William Golding's[20] *Lord of the Flies*— is an excellent example, as it focuses on a group of British boys stranded on an island and their attempt to establish a hierarchy of leadership.

As with any organization, and as illustrated in *Lord of the Flies*, within most cliques there exists a hierarchy or a pecking order with the role of the leaders to exercise control over the other members. In many instances, as rivals compete for the leadership position, undermining other members of the clique becomes a vital component of the power play. Once the leadership position is attained, maintaining that position and the status within the clique requires measures that, in their extremes, are often violent.[21] This same sort of leadership through violence is also present in criminal gangs; for this reason, juvenile gangs (discussed later in this chapter) are also significant in discussions on school violence. In cliques and gangs, the way in which males and females attain the leadership position is often achieved differently. Males will often gain status as a result of athletic prowess,[22] while females will often gain status as a result of social success.[23] Unfortunately, as females tend to rely on public opinion to maintain their hierarchy, in the long run, the self-esteem of those females tends to be lower than the self-esteem of those females not involved in the cliques, while an end to a relationship with a popular boyfriend may also end their leadership position. For males, as long as their physical strength is maintained, and another male does not challenge that strength, the leadership position is secure.

By the media accounts of Columbine, it soon became those individuals who were bullied into becoming loners who became the concern of officials wishing to identify the risk factors of cliques as related to school violence.[24] However, it should be acknowledged that the overwhelming number of cliques such as Goths and those interested in anime throughout schools are often nonviolent and not a threat to school safety.[25]

Gothic Subculture

The Gothic subculture, or Goths, is a clique that originated in England in the 1980s with its roots in the punk-rock music genre. With the 1999 mass

shooting at Columbine and the labeling of the two perpetrators as "Goth" kids
and the shootings of two more boys (killing one) in Canada a week later by
a fourteen-year-old wearing a trench coat and carrying a rifle,[26] the Gothic
culture has been brought to the forefront of global conversations of school
violence, but little empirical evidence exists that directly links the Goth subculture to school shootings. However, students who identify themselves as
Goth are at an increased risk for hate shootings both inside and outside of the
school system[27] and for suicide.[28]

At one time, the Gothic culture or the term Goth was a label used to refer to
mainly the uncivilized and uneducated individuals during the Middle Ages of
northwestern Europe.[29] Today we use the term Goth to refer to nonconform-
ing youths who may or may not celebrate pagan religions, with the sexual
empowerment of women significant in the subculture. The Goths often wear
heavy white facial makeup with black eyeliner and lipstick. The members
dress in black, dye their hair either black, blue, or pink, and wear silver jewelry and chains or restraints around their neck, waist, arms, and legs. Some
smoke clove cigarettes, use vapes, engage in body piercing and tattoos, and
relax in coffee shops.

With books such as *Frankenstein*, magazines such as *Ghostly*, and movies
such as *The Matrix* and *Blade Runner*, Goths have helped to support the culture for over three decades. Although the Goth subculture is essentially nonviolent, the media quickly turns its attention to stories involving the Gothic
subculture, especially stories of violence.

There are also those who suggest Goth members have at one time in their
academic histories been labeled by teachers and fellow students as different
in the school environment.[30] Thus, the look of Goth, as a membership in this
school clique, allows students to take control of their actions and their feelings of being excluded from other cliques. The use of Goth is simply a means
for a student to identify himself or herself as different and, for the majority of
Goths, their tendencies are toward nonviolent, pacifistic, passive, and tolerant
lifestyles within the school environment.

Anime

Another popular trend in today's schools across the globe is the use of anime.
This version of Asian culture takes its original form from a type of Japanese
art that dates back as far as 900 AD. Originally, it was viewed as Buddhist
art that depicted scenes of life after death. In the sixteenth century, silk-bound
books were popular entertainment among the rich as these books depicted situations from daily life.[31] The first commercialized version of Japanese anime

was in the early twentieth century, where it remained essentially unchanged until the late 1960s and its spread to the international community.[32]

Anime is short for the technique of creating animated cartoons using pencils and a springboard. In the 1990s anime was further popularized by television shows such as Pokémon. As many of the settings for anime are high schools and middle schools, students across the globe are attracted to the art and the stories portrayed through anime. Contrary to Western comics that target young teens and children, anime acquires many audiences as their topics target young children and also adults. Unfortunately, anime has also acquired an extremely negative perception through the Otaku Killer, a Japanese serial killer and anime fanatic who killed four young girls in the late 1980s,[33] and researchers who suggest that anime contributes to aggressive and violent behaviors in young people.[34] The subjects of anime include comical daily life, perversions involving sex, images of violence, fantasy world, paranormal phenomena, and death.[35] Most recently, China has issued restrictions on violent anime and online cartoons and especially those anime that depict subjects such as extreme fighting, terrorists attacks, the use of nuclear weapons, hardcore pornography, and the supernatural.[36]

Imagine the attention these graphic novels receive when introduced to young people through peers within a school setting. These students, who are members of a clique that enjoy anime, may be of concern to parents who discover that the thirteen-year-old male sitting beside their daughter in math class is also reading stories based around the theme of violent sexual encounters. Just as with other cliques, students who are testing boundaries and seeking the outrageous and unconventional will seek others interested in anime for a sense of belonging.

As discussed, in regard to groups within the school environment, there are numerous cliques that exist today that revolve specifically around the original themes of Goth and anime. One needs only to search the internet to find thousands in existence. Cliques that are quirky or unusual are often naturally appealing to young people and especially appealing to those young people who may not be members of a large popular group at school. A quiet and unassertive character, which has been the target of victimization by their peers, many find solace in the membership of such a clique. However, a student who has been a victim of repeated incidents of school violence may finally retaliate with violence, assumed to be supported by his or her clique.

Cliques in the middle and high schools pose unique threats to the school environment. In these years of development, students are establishing their own identities, and their interactions with peers both positively and negatively affect who these students will become as adults.

Table 3.1.   General Stages of Psychosocial Development

Age	Virtue	Significant Relationship	Questions
9–12	Competence	Neighbors, School	Can I make it in the world? Am I doing it right?
13–19	Fidelity	Peers, Role Model	Who am I? Who can I be?
20–29	Love	Friends, Partners	Can I love? Will I fit in?

There are eight stages of psychosocial development from infancy to adult-hood. Specifically, as illustrated in table 3.1, between the ages of nine and nineteen, social development with specific virtues develops.[37]

As suggested, personal development continues throughout one's life.[38] Consequently, cliques and their membership continue for many within environments of higher education. Specifically, within universities and colleges, cliques are often perceived in the form of Greek life or fraternity or sororities and are often popularized by American culture.

Greek Life

Greek Letter Organizations (GLO), more commonly known as Greek life, is a common option many college campuses have for their students to participate in. Although predominantly seen within the United States, such groups have also been established in countries such as Canada and France. Throughout history membership was based upon academic honors and professional interest, but in recent years there has been a shift to membership being socially oriented. With that being said, this system is composed of many organizations ranging in purposes, although the majority share some common characteristics. GLOs will often participate in philanthropic activities, educate members on different ideals surrounding their philanthropy, host parties, and aid in the creation of networks once graduated from a university.

A main component shared by these organizations is secrecy. The purpose of this is to ensure members feel as though they are different from the everyday student, so, although the organizations themselves are not a secret, they will be given information from other members that they are not supposed to share with anyone outside of the organization. Another shared component by many GLOs is the membership of only one sex. For example, GLOs made up of only female members are referred to as sororities, whereas a GLO with only male members is called a fraternity.

These organizations will also have a set of symbols that represent them, as well as the possibility of certain colors indicating their membership, secret handshakes, or code words. Another common element among the majority of GLOs is their selection process. This process has two steps, rushing and pledging. Rushing is the time in which potential new members are sought out and exhibit their personal traits and qualifications that would make them a valuable member to the organization. Pledging refers to the second part of the recruitment process in which those who have been chosen by the GLO to be new members of the organization are placed on a probation for their first few months so they are able to prove themselves to the other members.

Therefore, even while attending university, students may be victims of cliques. In 2017 at Florida State University (USA) a twenty-year-old fraternity pledge died of alcohol poisoning after consuming alcohol at a house party the night before.[39] In 2018 at the University of the Philippines, two fraternities were engaged in violent acts with each other, including a school shooting.[40] Therefore, cliques and their influences are a subject of concern when discussing school violence, and this includes discussion of school violence at the university level.

CLIQUES AND SCHOOL VIOLENCE

Over the last few years, the majority of schools within the United Kingdom report few or no gangs;[41] however, violence attributed to groups of students (i.e., cliques) does still exist within the school environment. The British House of Commons[42] does not recognize a unified definition for the term *gang*, so gang activities are attributed to cliques in the United Kingdom.

The division of school students into different cliques can cause major tension, as many refer to this division into cliques "social apartheid."[43] It is reported that school violence perpetrators, such as the Columbine shooters, sought a makeshift clique after their rejection from the stereotypical, "normal" groups.[44]

An examination of fifteen US school shootings from 1995–2001 found that the majority of the cases involved bullying by individuals and groups.[45] Although rejection played a part in these shootings, it was noted that the perpetrators also displayed other risk factors unique to those victims. This helps to explain why not all students who experience bullying or rejection become violent within the school setting. In the United States, the 2004 *Safe School Initiative* suggested that oftentimes perpetrators of a school shooting felt bullied or persecuted by their peers.[46]

In addition, the US Campus Violence Prevention Center found that in 2001, fraternity members were disproportionately represented among offenders of crimes on university campuses.[47] Concern to uphold masculinity or femininity, a set group of inclusion and group protection, high consumption of alcohol, and an importance paced on superiority may be reasons that members of Greek life are overrepresented among offenders in this setting. Researchers have suggested that students' drinking styles correlate more closely with behaviors of their immediate social network than with drinking practices of students in general at their colleges.[48] This is especially the case in cliques such as fraternities.

As a result of GLOs being composed of students extending from freshman to seniors from all over the world, upperclass members may purchase alcohol for an organizational social event, and although some members are not of age, the likelihood of alcohol consumption by all increases. Even further, research suggests that members of these cliques are more likely to excessively consume alcohol due to their preconceived notions stating that it is an essential part of Greek culture.[49] As a result, students involved may believe that the more they drink the more highly they will be seen by peers. Aside from the physical damages excessive alcohol consumption may cause, it is also likely to decrease one's ability to make rational decisions. For example, under the influence of alcohol one may be at an increased risk of getting behind the wheel while not sober or getting into a fight, which may cause harm to not only the individual who drank excessively, but also others within the campus environment.

In 2006 a woman reported that she was held against her will and raped at a fraternity at the University of Arkansas; in that same year, a college freshman from Penn State University said that she was raped at a fraternity party on her campus as well.[50] Research has also suggested that, compared to nonfraternity men, fraternity men have been found to have more traditional attitudes toward women and are a more sexually permissive peer group. As a result of the traditional attitudes these men hold toward women, it is implied that members of fraternities see themselves as being superior to women, with women's main purpose being sexual pleasure for them. This, in combination with holding a more accepting viewpoint on rape myths, reassures their idea that mistreating and sexually harassing women is an acceptable practice. Women on university campuses across the world are at an increased risk of sexual victimization, especially at parties where drinking occurs, as a result of this traditional attitude as well.[51]

Large Greek life systems may also be a risk factor when referencing bullying on college campuses. In most Greek organizations while pledging and becoming an official member, those who are in this position are instructed to partake in actions to show they are loyal and dedicated to the group; this is considered hazing. Hazing is generally referred to as a practice of initiating new members into a group through harassment and humiliation.[52] Approximately three-fourths of GLO members experience some form of hazing during their involvement with the organization.[53] Examples of these practices range anywhere from something as innocent as having pledges (those attempting to gain membership in the group) memorize the Greek alphabet, to horrific incidents in which new members are made to preform sexual acts on animals or other members of the group. The first recorded death that resulted from hazing was at Cornell University in 1873 when a student fell into a gorge after being blindfolded and left alone in the dark by other members of his fraternity.[54] Hence, cliques are significant when discussing school violence at the university level.

GANGS

More recently, in 2018, a Newcastle University student (UK) died the day after participating in a traditional British pub crawl the night before. As research suggests, schools with gangs are likely to have an increase in school violence.[55] In addition, high levels of victimization within a school environment are not always reflective of the overall outside community.[56] The US 2007 School Crime Supplement Report (hereafter SCS) documented that approximately 15 percent of America's students report the presence of street gangs at school. In countries within the European Union, research suggests that there currently exist more than five thousand gangs with some of their younger members still attending school.[57] Although the presence of gangs in the United States and United Kingdom schools has declined,[58] the presence of street gangs at school is still a concern for parents, teachers, and the students themselves. If gangs are present at school, then a climate of fear and intimidation is certainly possible;[59] students in fear cannot be expected to concentrate on their studies. For clarity of definition, a gang is defined as a group of persons (three or more) assembled and acting or working together.[60] For the purpose of this book, gangs are discussed in terms of their formation, theoretical foundations, and their associations to violence as it is applied to the school environment.

Gangs pose a threat to the safety of our children both inside and outside the school environment.[61] In 2018, a two-year-old in Chicago (USA) was killed when gang violence was extended to his backyard.[62] In the same year in London, a fifteen-year-old was stabbed in a gang conflict after school.[63] Gang members endanger our children through violent activities, drug dealing, theft, and member recruitment. Furthermore, it should be acknowledged that most violent gang activity occurs not on school property, but near the property.[64] In addition, most of the gang activities within the school setting are not only nonviolent, but also noncriminal.

Unfortunately, as the media will report, this is not always the case. In Maryland (USA) in 2018, a member of the gang MS-13 attacked a student and threatened a teacher.[65] Earlier, in Honduras, a teacher and four students were injured when a clatter of bullets pierced the roof of their school.[66]

Findings from the 2017 SCS report suggest that student characteristics are associated with not only membership in gangs, but also the reporting of gang activities. In the United Kingdom youths between the ages of twelve and thirteen are now joining gangs, with approximately 8 percent of those individuals being females.[67] In particular, students' awareness of gangs and gang activities increase with age and race or ethnicity.[68] Specifically, older students and nonwhite (black and Hispanic) students were more likely to report gang presence in their schools. In addition, in research on gangs and the effect of gangs on student recruitment, it is suggested that gang activity is also related to the student characteristic of family income. The 2017 SCS report supports the notion of an increase in gang activity among lower-income students in that schools in urban areas with lower socioeconomic students report the most gang-related incidents. However, it should be noted that gangs may be present in all areas. Some researchers have suggested that gang membership is more appealing to lower socioeconomic youths, and others have suggested that law enforcement efforts are more concentrated in the lower socioeconomic areas; thus, more gang activity is recorded.[69] Regardless of the reasons behind gang activity, there are more gangs identified within the lower socioeconomic schools than in rural and upper socioeconomic area's schools.

Gangs can be defined in various ways; however, the US Department of Justice defines a gang as an association of three or more individuals, who collectively identify themselves by adopting a group identity, which is used to create an atmosphere of fear and intimidation, frequently by employing one or more of the following: a common name, slogan, identifying sign, symbol, tattoo, or other physical marking, style or color of clothing, hairstyle, hand sign, or graffiti. However, in order to understand the culture of a gang we must first understand the concepts of society and culture. A society is a group of people who share an exclusive territory and a common culture, while a culture can be recognized as a totality of learned socially transmitted customs, knowledge, material objects, and behavior.[70] Among customs are norms of behavior, which are supported by the reactions of the society's members. Many members of a society share common language, beliefs, values, and symbols. A major characteristic of societies is their tendency to form social institutions. The most common institutions are family, faith organizations, schools, government, commerce, and military justice systems. Social institutions house internal organizations where members hold ranks, which is what their role contains within the social institutions. Within a gang community each individual is given a role to fulfill. A society's culture, norms, language, beliefs, values, and symbols are all examples of a generation process called socialization. The understanding of the nature of human society and culture are important in order to understand gangs and their behavior as gangs are a part of the society, which is often referred to as a subculture. A subculture is defined as a small portion of the larger part of the society we live in. Some gangs or subcultures are identified as motorcycle gangs, prison gangs, hate groups, adult organized crime groups, terrorist's organizations, and street gangs.[71]

Historically, even before gangs were recognized as a formal organization, gang members existed. Specifically, in the 1800s the English term *scuttler* was used to describe males between the ages of fourteen and eighteen who would fight in one of two bands of youth.[72]

The role of a gang varies for each person; however, the most desired reason one joins a gang is to belong or to experience companionship. All gangs have in common a need to claim a turf or territory.[73] Gang territory can range from a block, to a street, a neighborhood, or even a city. These territories may also be extended to the school environment. Members of gangs are often recognized by what they wear, the colors they display, or the tattoos they have. These visible characteristics indicate not only a luxury or power but may also be a matter of survival for some.[74] Globally, the majority of gangs solicit members that are between the ages of twelve and twenty-four. As gang members will engage in criminal activity or acts of juvenile delinquency that if committed by an adult would be crimes, it is essential that these gangs attract young people as members.

Youth gangs are described as a group of youths or young adults that are willing to identify as a gang. Youth behavior is often unstable; sometimes changing from week to week; and for many youths, their tenure in a gang is only about one year. Although there exist many reasons for youth gang members to be temporary, it has been suggested that youth gangs are more like "near groups," which are characterized by shifting membership, loosely defined roles, and limited cohesion.[75] As one of the key components to a youth gang is criminality, many would assume that the presence of leadership would be among the top correlations, but it is not. Additionally, some of the other key identifiers to youth gangs are having three or more members, member ages between twelve and twenty-four, a shared name or symbol, members viewing themselves as a gang or being recognized by others as a gang, the group having a degree of organization and permanence, or group members involved in an elevated level of criminal activity.[76]

Although most youth gangs cause little concern in the school environment, drug gangs within schools are organized and extremely dangerous.[77] These members are responsible for distributing, selling, and carrying illicit drugs such as cocaine, heroin, methamphetamine, and opioids. These members are possessing large amounts of drugs and cash in order to protect dealers and other members from the police and rival gangs. Some of the lower-end drug dealers are not able to drive fancy cars, flaunt gold jewelry, or get rich, but they are expected to work around the clock for low wages, which is enforced through fear or threats made by superior members.[78]

Gangs have their own standards and characteristics that vary based on national, regional, and local levels. The US National Gang Intelligence Center and National Drug Intelligence Center collaborated to produce reports on various gangs. In 2011 the UK Home Office provided funding for three levels of gang intervention: primary, secondary, and tertiary. In addition to the macro-level explanations of gang membership, micro- or individual-based theories also have been used to explain a youth joining a gang. This struggle with the various definitions of gangs and the failure to recognize gang activities makes it especially challenging for practitioners and researchers to accurately measure a gang's impact. In addition, schools that fail to define certain behaviors as gang related may not be able to provide an effective solution. However, schools that inaccurately diagnose a problem as gang related might be prescribing gang interventions that are inappropriate for the solution.[79]

In regard to school structure and gang activities, one cannot discount the association between guns and gangs. Specifically, in the United States, students who knew or saw other students carrying a gun at school were more likely to report gang activity at school. This link between guns at school and the presence of gangs supports the previous works of violence and gangs.[80] In particular, where there are gangs, there is the potential for guns. Where there are guns, there is the potential for violence. From those countries with strict gun laws, weapons such as knives in schools are often indicators of gangs and violence.

THEORETICAL EXPLANATIONS
FOR GANG MEMBERSHIP

Students join gangs for a variety of reasons. Historically, some researchers suggest that gang membership is a way in which students who cannot achieve success in the legitimate world obtain success in the illegitimate world.[81] In addition, other historical researchers have suggested that peer pressure[82] or the search for a male role model influences gang membership and fuels the desire for gang membership.[83] Lastly, some researchers suggest that gang membership is simply an extension of a youth's already established delinquency.[84] However, the most commonly applied theories to gang membership are Robert Merton's strain theory and Edwin Sutherland's differential association.

Strain Theory

In Merton's examination of the societal structure of America, he suggested that material success was everyone's major goal and that by not obtaining that goal of material success a strain was placed upon the individual.[85] Consequently, and simply stated, strain theory asserts that individuals who are unable to obtain their material goals by legitimate means will seek illegitimate means and avoid the strain of failure.[86]

In the school environment, where socioeconomic status is often critical to obtaining the finest clothes, jewelry, and cars, those students within the lower socioeconomic strata fail to have the "accessories" necessary for "successful" school years. For those students, the possible gain of material goods through gang membership is an appealing option. As illegal gang activities may produce revenue for its members, young people who join gangs may earn the money necessary to purchase their desired items or they may simply steal those items as part of their gang activities.[87]

Differential Association

One of the most popular interpersonal theories is Sutherland's differential association.[88] In the theory of differential association, a person becomes delinquent when social conditions are more favorable to delinquency than to non-delinquency. Specifically, Sutherland's differential association is based upon nine propositions: (1) criminal behavior is learned; (2) criminal behavior is learned in interaction with other persons in a process of communication; (3) the principal part of the learning of criminal behavior occurs within intimate personal groups; (4) when criminal behavior is learned, it includes techniques of committing the crime; (5) the specific direction of motives and drives is learned from definitions of legal codes that are favorable and unfavorable; (6) a person becomes delinquent because of an excess of definitions favorable to violations of the law; (7) differential association may vary in frequency, duration, priority, and intensity; (8) the process of learning criminal behavior by association with criminal and anticriminal patterns incorporates all the mechanisms that are involved in any other learning;

and (9) although criminal behavior is an expression of needs and values, it is not explained by those general needs and values.[89]

In the school environment, and especially in the gang environment, where there exist multiple opportunities for social interactions and social learning among students, criminal behavior and violence is easily learned. Students who associate with groups or gangs that are engaging in delinquent activities are more likely to participate in those delinquent activities.[90]

In addition to macro-level explanations of gang membership, micro- or individual-based theories also have been used to explain youth gangs. Research has suggested that gang membership satisfies the five basic needs of physiology (hunger, thirst, shelter), safety, social, esteem, and self-actualization.[91] Specifically, for many young people, gang membership provides them food, a place to stay, security, protection, an acceptance that they may not have received from their family, and the perceived ability to participate in something and do a good job.

In a nutshell, gang membership may provide its members a feeling of power, control, and importance—something that they may have never experienced before. In addition, as gangs tend to strike fear in people, membership may enhance feelings of self-respect and importance. As we all desire the feeling of importance, gang membership, which produces that feeling, is appealing. Those feelings of importance or power may be manifested through different types of power. In addition to the political power and control that comes from gang membership, there is also an element of economic power that most gang members find appealing. As discussed, gang members are able to acquire material possessions and even monetary rewards through gang membership that otherwise they might not have available to them or others in their social strata.[92]

Historically, there were two gangs that popularized the phrase street gangs. Those two groups were the CRIPS and the BLOODS. The CRIPS, or Criminals Running in Packs, originated in Los Angeles, California, in the late 1960s but are now documented in a variety of locations across the globe.[93] The members of the CRIPS wore blue and their motto was *beat a person down before they beat you.* They are still an active street gang today and are found across the nation.

The BLOODS, or Black Lords of Our Destiny, also originated in Los Angeles, California, in the late 1960s.[94] The members of the BLOODS wore red and believed in teaching their young recruits through the experience of battle.[95] The BLOODS are still an active street gang and are also found across the globe. Today, one of the most prolific youth gangs is MS-13, or Mara Salvatrucha, an international youth gang that originated in the United States and now occupies positions of power in Canada, Mexico, and countries throughout Central America and Europe.

The allure of gang membership and gang opportunities for young people at the bottom of the social ladder is the economic prospect for an instant increase in social status. It is the youth's attempt to climb out of the lower class and upward to the middle or upper class in American society. Unfortunately, in many cases the harm outweighs the benefits, as often in their attempts at economic prosperity, young people who are engaged in illegal activities become the clients of the criminal justice system or the local mortuary.[96]

In addition, youths tend to gravitate toward gangs as a result of a perceived lack of avenues for success in the world. Since gang members tend to be unsuccessful in the educational setting, employment options are limited. Delinquency and violence may provide the avenue for materialism.[97] As motivation to join a gang may result from nothing other than a desire for peer acceptance, it is unfortunate that some of those desires for friendship lead to such comradeships that include illegal behaviors and violence.[98] However, as discussed with cliques, belonging and acceptance in the lives of young people is highly valued, and for most young people, therefore, no price is too high to pay.

Another reason for joining a gang is hate.[99] According to the Bureau of Justice Statistics, 31 percent of the violent offenders of hate crimes are under the age of eighteen,[100] with some of those incidents occurring in the school environment. Thus, nearly one-third of individuals targeting others because of a hatred toward a certain group or lifestyle spend most of their day within the school setting. Many individuals will participate in hate-related victimization within a group rather than alone; therefore, gang memberships facilitate these victimizations. As over one-half of hate crimes are motivated by racial bias, and approximately 25 percent by sexual-orientation bias, the school environment, which is filled with a variety of different types of students and a diversity of ideas, is a natural setting for a hate crime.[101]

PROFILE

Historically, gang members were white and were the children of recently arrived and poor immigrants. In discussing the characteristics or the profile of gang members today, it is acknowledged that gang members still tend to be poor and live in the lower-income, urban communities.[102] However, while today gang members are predominantly male, young, and members of a minority group, most are temporary members. In addition, today females, although not stereotypically considered gang members, also join gangs with approximately 10 percent of all gang members in the United States being female and 8 percent of gang members in the United Kingdom being female.[103] Although female gang members are less common, they are still a concern.

Many female gang members engage in a range of delinquent acts, including theft and violence, which also includes unprotected sexual intercourse (sometimes with HIV positive partners) as part of their gang initiation.[104]

Female gang membership is a phenomenon that appears to be escalating globally.[105] Although female gang members commit crimes of violence less often than their male counterparts, they do engage in acts of violence more often than nongang males or females.[106] Females join gangs for many of the same reasons that males join gangs; however, some researchers have suggested that female gang membership may also be influenced by the female's desire to escape abuse within the home.[107] Through gang membership, the female, who has often suffered the victimization and forced submission within the home, gains the role of abuser instead of the abused.

For a female to become a gang member, there is often an initiating process just as is the case for males.[108] In participating in this process of tests or rituals, females obtain membership just as is the case for males. Some of those tests include carrying a weapon, committing property crimes, shooting other people, and physically assaulting other people. Another initiation may be what is phrased as being "sexed in" the gang.[109] A newer trend in being "sexed in" a gang is that female gang members must have unprotected intercourse with a partner that is known to be HIV positive.[110] The dangerousness of this activity and the completion of these activities support the female's worthiness to gang membership.

Another area of concern regarding the proliferation of gang activities across the globe involves the subject of franchising.[111] Franchising involves the purposive spread of gangs from large urban areas of the country to the smaller and even rural areas of the country. In many cases this process involves the exportation of drug-trafficking gang members to areas outside of the large urban areas to establish a foothold on the local drug market.[112] Specifically, although the BLOODS, the CRIPS, and MS-13 were gangs established in the US state of California, nearly every state in America and multiple countries report the presence of those gang members. Consider the fact that just as the fast-food restaurant McDonald's franchises to obtain a larger part of the market, so do gangs, as franchising provides new venues for potential profit for various criminal enterprises. Current gang members relocate to the new areas and attempt to recruit new members in that locality. As often the new gang members are young teens, they, of course, are present in the school setting.[113] Some franchising is not planned but results through the simple migration of gang members from one area to another. A young teen, who may have been in trouble within the city, may be relocated to a grandmother's or some other family member's home (outside of the teen's current proximity) in another region of the country. The migrating teen then becomes a resource in the new locality for gang membership. This teen or seasoned gang member, placed within a new location, recruits others within the new area for gang membership.[114] As the new school students, teachers, and administrators begin recognizing the colors and graffiti often associated with gang presence, they begin to become concerned about their perceived gang problem as gangs are perceived as violent. Therefore, gang franchising is another explanation to the perceived increases in incidents of gang violence within the school environment.

GANGS AND SCHOOL CRIME

The actual impact of gangs on school and school violence is extremely difficult to measure. This is due in part because the incidents of school crime are often not tracked by perpetrator, but rather by the offense itself, as well as the lack of a clearly recognized definition of the term *gang*. Globally, law enforcement records the incident of a crime often without information on the motive or perpetrator of the crime, so the record of the incident will not be identified as a gang-related robbery. In addition, without gang members claiming responsibility for the incident, law enforcement officials are left with determining if the crime was a crime involving a student or a crime perpetrated by a gang member who is also a student. Hence, their activities are different and they vary among the types of gangs.

Research describes four different types of gangs: (1) social; (2) party; (3) serious delinquent; and (4) organization.[115] An example of a social gang is one whose members engage in high rates of drug use and drug sales but little else. An example of a party gang member is one who engages in high rates of drug use, but not drug sales. An example of the serious delinquent gang is one who engages in a wide range of serious and minor acts of delinquency, but rarely drugs. Lastly, the organization gang members are heavily involved in delinquency and drug sale. Therefore, the most common types of gangs found in the setting of the school are the social gangs, the party gangs, and the serious delinquent gangs.[116]

Students should be able to consider their schools as a safe haven and a place to learn that is free of violence and crime. As suggested by researchers, when there is the perception of crime or violence, the educational process is disrupted and students' ability to learn is lessened. This impacts students, teachers, and even the administrative staff. Victimizations in a school can have a lasting impact causing depression and anxiety, which can cause truancy and lead to poor academic performance, quitting school, and violent behavior.[117]

Gangs in schools have a major impact on the learning environment as both staff members and students may feel intimidated or unsafe.[118] These gangs are created as an offset of the cultural customs and patterns from each geographical location.[119] Gangs can affect any school regardless of size, location, or ethnicity of students.

In August 2018, despite the heavy police presence, shots rang out at a football game in Jacksonville, Florida. One person died and two were injured. This incident was identified as being gang related. This school shooting was the second shooting in a week that was identified as being related to gang violence.[120] Some researchers suggest that these gangs within schools are the new bullies.[121] The 2017 School Crime Supplement to the National Crime Victimization Survey reported that one-fourth of students who reported a gang presence in their school also reported criminal victimization. In addition, research suggests that schools with gang-related crimes have a higher rate for violent crimes such as rape or robbery.[122] Schools that have reported gang-related crimes also have a higher rate for threats involving the use of a weapon. Overall, gang-related crimes in schools exhibit a positive correlation to attacks with weapons and gun possession by students.[123] Of all gang membership, over one-third consists of youth under the age of eighteen.[124] Youth members in gangs have a higher rate of violent victimization than their nongang-affiliated counterparts. However, victimization rates within schools are equivalent for gang-affiliated and nongang-affiliated students.[125]

In 2015, 11 percent of students ages twelve to eighteen reported a gang presence in their academic institution, with the greatest percentages of gangs reported in schools occurring in urban areas.[126] Globally, gangs are more prevalent in public schools than private schools; however, the number of gang-related incidents of school violence is decreasing.[127]

Nongang-affiliated students tend to normalize the actions of gang-affiliated students.[128] It is reported that the most common actions of gangs in schools is to fight, assemble in certain areas, and cause classroom disruptions. As students have begun to normalize these actions, their reactions typically do not involve tremendous fear.[129] Lastly, theft occurrences are positively correlated to gang presence at schools.[130] Also, the presence of gangs at a school increases the risk of violent crime by 37 percent.[131]

Consequently, gangs and the perpetrators of gang violence within the school environment create an issue of concern for many across the world. Programs that train teachers and parents to identify risk factors are one way to address this concern. Teachers, as discussed later in this book, who are trained to notice changes in the personalities and behaviors of students are better able to identify risk factors for gang involvement and gang violence.

In the school environment, students group themselves by individual characteristics such as athletic abilities, academic performance, and socioeconomic status. However, this grouping may not be beneficial to the school setting. It is acknowledged that the majority of the groups that exist within the school setting are nonviolent; however, that is not always the case. As groups (gangs, cliques, subgroups, etc.) may be the perpetrators of violence or the targets of violence, the identification of these groups is a necessary component to reducing the incidents of school violence.

CHAPTER QUESTIONS

1. What peer group is of most concern for the majority of school administrations?
2. How are clique members usually described?
3. What is considered to be the "most desired" reason one would join a gang?
4. What are the nine propositions of differential association?
5. What are the four types of gangs?

DISCUSSION QUESTIONS

1. Do you feel as though rural areas around the globe experience problems with gangs, or do you believe gang presence is unique to metropolitan areas? Explain.
2. In your opinion, do you think membership in a gang or clique prevents one from being bullied? Why?
3. Throughout your years in school, would you consider the prevalence of gangs within the school environment to have increased, decreased, or remained the same? Explain.

NOTES

1. BBC News, *South African Gang Violence Shuts Down Cape Town Schools*, August 15, 2013.
2. Mark Tarrant, "Adolescent Peer Groups and Social Identity," *Social Development*, 11(1) (2002):110–23.
3. Michael Lease and Jennifer Axelrod, "Position in the Peer Groups' Perceived Organizational Structure: Relation to Social Status and Friendship," *Journal of Early Adolescence*, 21(4) (2001): 377–404.

4. James Howell, "Youth Gangs: An Overview," *Juvenile Justice Bulletin* (Washington, DC: US Department of Justice. Office of Juvenile Justice and Delinquency Prevention, 1998).

5. HM Government, *Ending Gang and Youth Violence: A Cross Government Report* (London: The Stationery Office, 2011).

6. Kimberly McCabe and Gregory Martin, *School Violence, the Media and Criminal Justice Responses* (New York: Peter Lang, 2005).

7. Kimberly McCabe and Gregory Martin, *School Violence, the Media and Criminal Justice Responses.*

8. Kimberly McCabe and Gregory Martin, *School Violence, the Media and Criminal Justice Responses.*

9. Gordon Crews and M. Reid Counts, *The Evolution of School Disturbances in America* (Westport, CT: Praeger, 1997).

10. Michael Lease and Jennifer Axelrod, "Position in the Peer Groups' Perceived Organizational Structure: Relation to Social Status and Friendship."

11. Kimberly McCabe and Gregory Martin, *School Violence, the Media and Criminal Justice Responses.*

12. *Cambridge Academic Content Dictionary* (Cambridge, UK: Cambridge University Press, 2017).

13. Jan Dijkstra, Siegwart Lindenberg, Frank Verhulst, John Ormel, and Rene Veenstra, "The Relation between Popularity and Aggressive, Destructive, and Norm-Breaking Behaviors: Moderating Effects of Athletic Abilities, Physical Attractiveness, and Prosociality," *Journal of Research on Adolescence*, 19(3) (2009): 401–13.

14. Kimberly McCabe, *Child Abuse and the Criminal Justice System* (New York: Peter Lang, 2003).

15. Wayne Wooten, *Renegade Kids, Suburban Outlaws* (New York: Wadsworth, 1995).

16. Wayne Wooten, *Renegade Kids, Suburban Outlaws.*

17. Kimberly McCabe and Gregory Martin, *School Violence, the Media and Criminal Justice Responses.*

18. Kimberly McCabe and Gregory Martin, *School Violence, the Media and Criminal Justice Responses.*

19. Kimberly McCabe, *Protecting Your Children in Cyberspace: What Parents Need to Know* (Lanham, MD: Rowman and Littlefield Publishers, Inc., 2017).

20. William Golding, *Lord of the Flies* (London: Faber and Faber Publishers, 1954).

21. Patricia Adler and Peter Adler, *Peer Power: Preadolescent Culture and Identity* (New Brunswick, NJ: Rutgers University Press, 1998).

22. David Eder, "The Cycle of Popularity: Interpersonal Relations among Female Adolescents," *Sociology of Education*, 58 (1985): 154–65.

23. David Eder, "The Cycle of Popularity: Interpersonal Relations among Female Adolescents."

24. Kimberly McCabe and Gregory Martin, *School Violence, the Media and Criminal Justice Responses.*

25. Douglas Thompkins, "School Violence: Gangs and a Culture of Fear," *Annals of the American Academy of Political and Social Science*, 567 (2000): 54–71.

26. Anne McIlroy, "Schoolboy Killing Stuns Canada," *The Guardian*, April 29, 1999.

27. Catherine Smyth, "Call for Hate Crime Law Change," *Manchester Evening News*, 2008, March 18, 2012. http://www.manchestereveningnews.co.uk/news/greater-manchester-news/call-for-hate-crimes-law-change-949182.

28. Polly Curtis and John Carvel, "Teen Goths More Prone to Suicide Study Shows," *The Guardian*, April 14, 2006.

29. Kimberly McCabe and Gregory Martin, *School Violence, the Media and Criminal Justice Responses*.

30. G. Trasler, "School, Delinquency, and the Youth Culture in Britain and North America," *Theoretical Perspectives on School Crime* (Hackensack, NJ: National Council on Crime and Delinquency, 1978), 1440–91.

31. Nicole Gaouette, "Get Your Mange Here," *Christian Science Monitor*, February 8, 1999.

32. Susan Napier, *Anime from Akira to Howl's Movie Castle: Experiencing Contemporary Japanese Animation* (New York: St. Martin's Press, 2016), 10.

33. Charles Bolton, Istvan Csiesery-Ronay, and Takayuki Tatsume, *Robot Ghosts and Weird Dreams: Japanese Science Fiction from Origins to Anime* (Minnesota: University of Minnesota Press, 2008).

34. Kimberly McCabe and Gregory Martin, *School Violence, the Media and Criminal Justice Responses*.

35. Toshihisa Izawa, "What Are Mange and Anime?" 2001, accessed on January 7, 2019, at http://www.mit.edu/people/rei/expl.html.

36. L. Kehon, "China Cracks Down on Violent Anime Online Cartoons," BBC News, April 1, 2015, accessed on January 5, 2019, at https://www.bbc.com/news/technology-32149754.

37. Erik Erikson, *Childhood and Society* (New York: W. W. Norton and Company, 1950).

38. Erik Erikson, *Childhood and Society*.

39. Karl Etters, "Coffee Family Enters Settlement in Hazing Death Lawsuit," *Tallahassee Democrat*, June 13, 2018.

40. Sofia Tomacruz, *UP Says Warring Fraternities Involved in Two Incidents on Campus*, November 15, 2018, accessed February 1, 2019, at https://www.rappler.com/nation/216767-up-diliman-alpha-phi-beta-upsilon-sigma-phi-fraternity-wars-november-2018.

41. Hannah Smithson and Rob Ralphs, "Youth in the UK: 99 Problems but the Gang Ain't One," *Safer Communities Brighton*, 15(1) (2016): 11–23.

42. House of Commons Home Affairs Committee Report, *Gangs and Youth Crime. Report of Session 2014015* (London: The Stationery Office, 2015).

43. Jessie Klein, "Cultural Capital and High School Bullies: How Social Inequality Impacts School Violence," *Men and Masculinity*, 9(1) (2006): 53–75.

44. Jessie Klein, "Cultural Capital and High School Bullies: How Social Inequality Impacts School Violence."

45. Mark Leary, Robin Kowalski, Laura Smith, and Stephen Phillips, 2003, *Teasing, Rejection, and Violence*, accessed on February 1, 2019, at https://psycnet .apa.org/record/2003-03966-003.

46. Kimberly McCabe and Daniel Murphy, *Child Abuse—Today's Issues* (New York: Taylor and Francis Publishing, 2016).

47. Kimberly McCabe and Daniel Murphy, *Child Abuse—Today's Issues*.

48. Barry Caudill, "High-Risk Drinking among College Fraternity Members: A National Perspective," *Journal of American College Health*, 55(3) (2006): 141–55.

49. Rose Marie Ward, Marina Galante, Rudra Trivedi, and Juliana Kahrs, "An Examination of Drunkorexia, Greek Affiliation, and Alcohol Consumption," *Journal of Alcohol & Drug Education*, 59(3) (2015): 48–66.

50. Sarah Murnen, "Athletic Participation, Fraternity Membership, and Sexual Aggression among College Men: A Meta-Analytic Review," *Sex Roles*, 57(1/2) (2007): 145–57.

51. Sarah Murnen, "Athletic Participation, Fraternity Membership, and Sexual Aggression among College Men: A Meta-Analytic Review."

52. Devon Alvarez, "Death by Hazing: Should There Be a Federal Law against Fraternity and Sorority Hazing?" *Journal of Multidisciplinary Research* (1947-2900) 7(2) (2015): 43–75.

53. Devon Alvarez, "Death by Hazing: Should There Be a Federal Law against Fraternity and Sorority Hazing?"

54. Devon Alvarez, "Death by Hazing: Should There Be a Federal Law against Fraternity and Sorority Hazing?"

55. James Howell, "Youth Gangs: An Overview."

56. Dena Carson and Finn Esbensen, "Gangs in School: Exploring the Experiences of Gang Involved Youth," *Youth Violence and Juvenile Justice*, 17(1) (2017): 3–23.

57. Katherine Mansfield, "EU Home to More Than 5000 Criminal Gangs Who Make Billions from Migrant Crisis," *Express*, March 13, 2017.

58. Hannah Smithson, Rob Ralphs, and Patrick Williams, "Used and Abused: The Problematic Usages of the Term Gang and Its Implications for Ethnic Minorities," *British Journal of Criminology*, 53(1) (2013):113–28.

59. Hannah Smithson, Rob Ralphs, and Patrick Williams, "Used and Abused: The Problematic Usages of the Term Gang and Its Implications for Ethnic Minorities."

60. Robert Agnew, "Foundation for a General Strain Theory of Crime and Delinquency," *Criminology*, 30(1) (1992): 47–88.

61. Ronald Stephens, "National Trends in School Violence: Statistics and Prevention Strategies." In A. P. Goldstein and J. C. Conoleys (eds.), *School Violence Intervention: A Practical Handbook* (New York: Guilford Press, 1997), 72–90.

62. Megan Crepeau, Anna Spoerre, and Jeremy Gorner, "Prosecutor: 2 Year Old Boy Killed after Gang Leader Gives Order to Shoot," *Chicago Tribune*, October 23, 2018, accessed on January 9, 2019, at http://www.chicagotribune.com/news/local/ breaking/ct-met-arrest-boy-killed-20181022-story.html.

63. Zahid Mahmood, "Knives and Gangs: What's Driving Britain's Broken Boys to Crime?" CNN World, December 15, 2018, accessed on February 1, 2019, at https:// www.cnn.com/2018/12/15/uk/london-knife-crime-boys-intl-gbr/index.html.

64. Kimberly McCabe and Gregory Martin, *School Violence, the Media and Criminal Justice Responses*.

65. Michael Miller, "A Ticking Time Bomb: MS-13 Threatens a Middle School, Warn Teachers, Parents, Students," *Washington Post*, June 11, 2018.

66. Noe Leiva, "Gang Wars Mean School Can Be a Battleground in Honduras," *Their World*, March 28, 2017, accessed on February 1, 2019, at https://theirworld.org/news/gang-wars-hit-honduras-schools.

67. Hannah Smithson and Rob Ralphs, "Youth in the UK: 99 Problems but the Gang Ain't One."

68. Thomas Regulus, "The Effects of Gangs on Student Performance and Delinquency in Public Schools," *Journal of Gang Research*, 2(1) (1994): 1–13.

69. Kimberly McCabe and Gregory Martin, *School Violence, the Media and Criminal Justice Responses*.

70. Thomas Regulus, "The Effects of Gangs on Student Performance and Delinquency in Public Schools."

71. Kimberly McCabe and Gregory Martin, *School Violence, the Media and Criminal Justice Responses*.

72. A Devive, "Scuttlers and Scuttling," *Manchester Guardian*, 1890.

73. Kimberly McCabe and Gregory Martin, *School Violence, the Media and Criminal Justice Responses*.

74. Joan Moore and John Hagedorn, "Female Gangs. A Focus on Research," *Juvenile Justice Bulletin* (Washington, DC: Bureau of Justice Statistics. Office of Juvenile Justice and Delinquency Prevention 2001).

75. Lewis Yablonsky, "The Delinquent Gang as a Near-Group," *Social Problems*, 7(2) (1959): 1–15.

76. Kimberly McCabe and Gregory Martin, *School Violence, the Media and Criminal Justice Responses*.

77. Kimberly McCabe and Gregory Martin, *School Violence, the Media and Criminal Justice Responses*.

78. Jan Moore and John Earl, "Why Do Kids Join Criminal Street Gangs," 1997, accessed on December 12, 2018, at https://people.missouristate.edu/michaelcarlie/what_i_learned_about/gangs/why_do_kids_join_criminal_street.htm.

79. Kimberly McCabe and Gregory Martin, *School Violence, the Media and Criminal Justice Responses*.

80. David Cornell and A. Looper, "Assessment of Violence and Other High-Risk Behaviors with a School Survey," *School Psychological Review*, 27 (1998): 317–30.

81. Richard Cloward and Lloyd Ohlin, *Delinquency and Opportunity* (New York: Free Press, 1960).

82. Edwin Sutherland, *Principles of Criminology*, second edition (Philadelphia: J. B. Lippincott, 1934).

83. Walter Miller, "Lower Class Culture as a Generating Milieu of Gang Delinquency," *Journal of Social Issues*, 14 (1958): 12.

84. Finn-Aage Esbensen, "Preventing Adolescent Gang Involvement," US Department of Justice, September 2000, accessed on January 3, 2019, at https://www.ncjrs.gov/pdffiles1/ojjdp/182210.pdf.

85. Robert Merton, *Social Theory and Social Structure* (New York: Free Press, 1975).

86. Robert Merton, *Social Theory and Social Structure*.

87. Kimberly McCabe and Gregory Martin, *School Violence, the Media and Criminal Justice Responses*.

88. Edwin Sutherland, *Principles of Criminology*.

89. Edwin Sutherland, *Principles of Criminology*.

90. Kimberly McCabe and Gregory Martin, *School Violence, the Media and Criminal Justice Responses*.

91. Abraham Maslow, *Motivation and Personality*, third edition (New York: Harper and Row, 1987).

92. Leon Bing, *Do or Die* (New York: Harper Collins, 1991).

93. Mary Jackson and Paul Knepper, *Delinquency and Justice: A Cultural Perspective* (Boston: Allyn and Bacon, 2003).

94. Mary Jackson and Paul Knepper, *Delinquency and Justice: A Cultural Perspective*.

95. Mary Jackson and Paul Knepper, *Delinquency and Justice: A Cultural Perspective*.

96. Kimberly McCabe and Gregory Martin, *School Violence, the Media and Criminal Justice Responses*.

97. Lewis Yablonsky and Martin Haskell, *Juvenile Delinquency*, fourth edition (New York: Harper and Row, 1988).

98. Lewis Yablonsky and Martin Haskell, *Juvenile Delinquency*.

99. Kimberly McCabe, *Protecting Your Children in Cyberspace: What Parents Need to Know*.

100. Kevin Strom, *Hate Crimes Reported in NIBRS, 1997–99* (Washington, DC: Bureau of Justice Statistics. US Department of Justice. Office of Justice Programs, 2001).

101. Kimberly McCabe, *Protecting Your Children in Cyberspace: What Parents Need to Know*.

102. Robert Agnew, "Foundation for a General Strain Theory of Crime and Delinquency."

103. Kimberly McCabe and Daniel Murphy, *Child Abuse—Today's Issues*.

104. Kimberly McCabe and Gregory Martin, *School Violence, the Media and Criminal Justice Responses*

105. Joan Moore and John Hagedorn, "Female Gangs. A Focus on Research."

106. Joan Moore and John Hagedorn, "Female Gangs. A Focus on Research."

107. Kimberly McCabe and Gregory Martin, *School Violence, the Media and Criminal Justice Responses*.

108. Kimberly McCabe and Gregory Martin, *School Violence, the Media and Criminal Justice Responses*.

109. Robert Walker, "Gangs or Us: Gangsta Girls, 2003," accessed on January 31, 2019, at http://ww.gangorus.com/gangstagirls.html.

110. Robert Walker, "Gangs or Us: Gangsta Girls, 2003."

111. Jeffrey Fagan, "The Second Organization of Drug Use and Drug Dealing among Urban Gangs," *Criminology*, 27 (1989): 633–69.

112. James Howell, "Youth Gangs: An Overview."

113. Hannah Smithson, Rob Ralphs, and Patrick Williams, "Used and Abused: The Problematic Usages of the Term Gang and Its Implications for Ethnic Minorities."

114. Patricia Adler and Peter Adler, *Peer Power: Preadolescent Culture and Identity.*

115. Jeffrey Fagan, "The Second Organization of Drug Use and Drug Dealing among Urban Gangs."

116. Jeffrey Fagan, "The Second Organization of Drug Use and Drug Dealing among Urban Gangs."

117. Kathryn Brookmeyer, Kostas Fanti, and Christopher Henrich, "Schools, Parents, and Youth Violence: A Multilevel, Ecological Analysis," *Journal of Clinical Child and Adolescent Psychology,* 35(4) (2006): 504–14.

118. Simon Robers, Jana Kemp, Amy Rathbun, Rachel Morgan, and Thomas Snyder, "Indicators of School Crime: 2013," 2014, accessed on January 23, 2019, at https://www.bjs.gov/content/pub/pdf/iscs13.pdf.

119. Douglas Thompkins, "School Violence: Gangs and a Culture of Fear," *Annals of the American Academy of Political and Social Science*, 567 (2000): 54–71.

120. Amy Rock, "1 Dead, 2 Injured in Gang-Related Shooting at Raines High School," August 28, 2018, accessed January 8, 2019, at https://www.campussafety magazine.com/safety/raines-high-school-shooting.

121. Douglas Thompkins, "School Violence: Gangs and a Culture of Fear."

122. Charles Crawford and Ronald Burns, "Reducing School Violence," *Policing*, 39(3) (2016): 455–77.

123. Charles Crawford and Ronald Burns, "Reducing School Violence."

124. Joanna Kubik, Megan Docherty, P. Boxer, Bonita Veysey, and Michael Ostermann, "Examining the Moderating Role of Gang Involvement on the Context and Impact of Victimization," *Journal of Criminological Research, Policy, and Practice*, 2(2) (2016): 107–21.

125. Joanna Kubik, Megan Docherty, P. Boxer, Bonita Veysey, and Michael Ostermann, "Examining the Moderating Role of Gang Involvement on the Context and Impact of Victimization."

126. Lauren Musu-Gillette, Anlan Zhang, Ke Wang, Jizhi Zhang, Jana Kemp, Melissa Diliberti, and B. Oudekerk, *Indicators of School Crime and Safety: 2017* (NCES 2018-036/NCJ 251413) (National Center for Education Statistics, U.S. Department of Education, and Bureau of Justice Statistics, Office of Justice Programs, U.S. Department of Justice. Washington, DC, 2018).

127. Hannah Smithson and Rob Ralphs, "Youth in the UK: 99 Problems but the Gang Ain't One."

128. Dena Carson and Finn Esbensen, "Gangs in School: Exploring the Experiences of Gang Involved Youth."

129. Dena Carson and Finn Esbensen, "Gangs in School: Exploring the Experiences of Gang Involved Youth."

130. Martin Bouchard, Wei Wang, and Eric Beauregard, "Social Capital, Opportunity, and School-Based Violence," *Violence and Victims*, 27(5) (2012): 656–73.

131. Martin Bouchard, Wei Wang, and Eric Beauregard, "Social Capital, Opportunity, and School-Based Violence."

Chapter Four

School Shootings and Media Perceptions

KEY WORDS

copycat offender	general strain theory	rational hate
criminal category	investigative journalism	rejected category
cycle of violence	irrational hate	social bond theory
disturbed category	psychological projection	

KEY ACRONYMS

(K–12) Schools including grades kindergarten through twelfth grade
(SRO) School Resource Officer

In today's society, the majority of a person's news on violence and victimization in the world is obtained through the media. Individuals gain information on the weather, social conflicts, and even their horoscopes through the radio, newspapers, television, the internet, and online news outlets. Information on the subject of school shootings and victimization within the schools is no different.

In the late 1940s a functional analysis was conducted to explore how social artifacts (such as the media) could lead to the development of theories to explain their need and responsibilities.[1] Within this research, it was determined that the function of the media was to survey the environment, correlate the past of society in responding to the environment, and transmit that social heritage from one generation to the next.[2]

A decade later it was suggested that the media served four purposes. The first was a surveillance of world events. The second was the interpretation of facts and figures. The third was a resource for socialization, and the fourth was the manipulation of public perceptions and sentiment.[3] In today's world of fake news accounts, one must consider the impact of media manipulation on accounts of school violence and school shootings. As is commonly known, the media largely determines what they report and the extent of their coverage.[4] If the media interprets the meaning behind such covered events as school shootings and then places these events in context for their audiences with their speculations provided on the causes and consequences of such recorded actions, the media is, in effect, an agent of socialization on the issue of school violence. Therefore, it is essential that books such as this one provide the most accurate of information on this subject that touches everyone across the globe. As early as the 1970s, researchers suggested that individuals receive their political socialization or political identities through the media.[5] As this remains the case, one must consider the consequences for the inaccurate reporting of incidents of school violence.[6]

Within the media, social and political manipulation will often take place through what is called investigative journalism.[7] This type of journalism— sometimes referred to as "mudraking" is an attempt to present sensationalized coverage on some event that attracts a large media audience.[8] The coverage of Columbine on April 20, 1999, and the Virginia Tech shooting in 2006 are examples of this extensive media coverage.

Up until the last few years, the media's influence on American behaviors has been largely discounted due to the stringent criterion of statistical significance and the relative impossibility of quantifying the complexities of social stimuli and action with the majority of individuals feeling overwhelmed by the media's coverage of events.[9]

There has been no direct link supported (empirically) that suggests that viewing violence will cause an individual to behave violently. In fact, recent research suggests that young adults are now better at separating fact from fiction than their older counterparts.[10] As discussed in the previous chapter, this also applies to the calls for restrictions on online games for teens and of anime with violent subjects. However, recent research has suggested that the media may, in fact, play a part in affecting the perceptions and behaviors of individuals.[11] In fact, some researchers point to a direct link between media and politics and suggest that the media is anything but objective in covering highly politically related events.[12] In particular, researchers have suggested that the media has a great impact on people's perceptions of unfamiliar issues[13] as well as sensationalized events such as a school shooting.[14]

On the subject of school violence, which for many individuals is equated to Columbine, the effect of media coverage to this one particular event cannot be ignored. The school shooting at Columbine and Virginia Tech gave US politicians and the world media the events that they had sought to spotlight the cruel and evil world of teens.[15] Reporters, who did little to explore other incidents within the country related to child abuse, domestic violence, or gang warfare, quickly covered these school shootings to discuss the problems of youth culture and the consequences of bullying and violent video games. The common results were the public's anxiety about and sometimes fearfulness of teens and their propensity toward violence.[16] So it is reasonable to assume that when incidents occur such as the shooting at Columbine, adults desire information on the topic to show support for their perceptions.[17] When considering the public trust in the media within the international arena, approximately 60 percent of those individuals living within the countries of the European Union trust the media, with the lowest levels of trust reported within the United Kingdom.[18] The media, with its goal to gain the attention of the public, supports that desire. However, in the overwhelming majority of the cases, the perception of the violent teen with the intent of mass destruction in the school environment is not the case. Unfortunately, as a result of media influences, the majority of teens fear a school shooting could happen at their school.[19]

Prior to the twentieth century, the fear of gun crime was associated with urban neighborhoods, especially within those of inner cities or with gang problems. In a nation that experiences a persistent fear of crime, school shooting incidents significantly deepen that fear. The US Center for Disease Control reported in 2003 that approximately 125 incidents of students using guns in school-related homicides or suicides occurred between July of 1992 and June of 1999, with approximately 95 percent of those cases involving male shooters and approximately 30 percent committing suicide. Although the ownership of handguns was prohibited in the United Kingdom after the school shooting at Dunblane Primary School in Scotland, more than a thousand weapons have been confiscated in schools within the United Kingdom between 2011 and 2013, with forty children having been found with handguns.[20] In February of 2019, a university student in the United Kingdom was arrested for manufacturing guns with a 3-D printer.[21] Specifically, 93.5 percent of the shooters were male, 26.8 percent of the shooters committed suicide, 69.1 percent of the shooters committed homicide, and 15.6 percent of the shooters had killed more than one person.[22] Although more common in the United States, school shootings occur across the globe. In Canada four individuals were killed in a 2016 high school shooting. In 2017 in France, three students and a teacher were killed in a school shooting. Lastly, in April of 2015, 147 individuals were killed at a school shooting at a university in Kenya. School shootings may occur at any school level and tend to not only affect those who are local to the incident but also those across the nation who hear about the shootings through different types of media.

Once the late 1990s came to an end and the US Columbine High School shooting had occurred, those of the middle and upper classes throughout the world began to pay more attention to the uprise in violence, the victimization of children, and specifically to school shootings in grades K–12. The Virginia Tech shooting of 2007, identified as the most tragic of all school shootings in the United States, brought the subject of school violence and student safety to the university level.

As a result of such incidents and a special attention being paid to the topic, institutions of learning around the world have increased their security, and politicians have also started to implement policies on how to handle and prevent such situations. Unfortunately, for the last decade parents have feared for their children's safety while attending school. However, most recently, as a result of government efforts, it is reported that the majority of young people feel as though their government is interested in addressing school violence.[23]

Table 4.1 provides information on the number of school (K–12) shootings in the United States from 1997–2017. Identified in this table are the year, the month, the number of perpetrators, the age of the perpetrator(s), the number of fatalities, and the number injured. In addition, the end result of the shooting (arrest or suicide) is provided.

Of the 113 school shootings evaluated, there were fifty-six cases that resulted in a fatality. In most cases, there was one person killed; however, in several cases, the school shooting resulted in more than ten individuals killed, with the 2007 Virginia Tech shooting identified as the most severe as it resulted in thirty-three fatalities. In addition, the majority of the school shootings that occurred during the time period resulted in two individuals injured with one shooting, the Thurston High School (Ohio), resulting in approximately twenty students and staff experiencing injuries

When considering the common characteristics of these school shootings in the United States, the majority occurred in the months of January (n = 16), October (n = 16), and September (n = 15). In terms of offender demographics, more than 95 percent were male and approximately 90 percent were under the age of eighteen. Mental illness, to be discussed later in this text, was noted to exist in approximately 20 percent of the cases; however, as this information has only been recently considered in these cases, the proportion of perpetrators of school shootings with mental illness is assumed to be greater than officially reported. In reference to the school shooting dynamic, the majority occurred on an open campus (another topic to be discussed later in this book)

Table 4.1. Frequency Table of Variables of Interest for US, K–12 School Shootings (1997–2017) (N=113)

Variable	N	Percent*	Variable	N	Percent*
Number of School			Intent:		
Shootings per State:			Yes	69	83.1
0	12	24.0	No	14	16.9
1–3	28	56.0	Missing	30	
4–6	8	16.0			
7–9	1	2.0			
10+	1	2.0	Offender Has Mental		
Year:			Illness:		
1997–2002	27	23.8	Mental Illness Present	23	12.39
2003–2007	17	15.2	Missing	90	87.61
2008–2012	26	23.0			
2013–2017	43	38.0	Campus Type:		
Month:			Open Campus	78	86.7
January–March	38	33.6	Closed Campus	12	13.3
April–June	20	17.8	Missing	23	
July–September	21	18.6			
October–December	34	30.1	Fatalities:		
Sex of Offender:			0	56	50.0
Female	5	5.9	1–10	54	48.2
Male	80	94.1	11–20	1	0.9
Missing	28		21–30	1	0.9
			Missing	1	
Number of Offenders:			Injuries:		
One Offender	92	87.6	0	38	33.9
More than One	13	12.4	1–10	70	62.5
Missing	8		11–20	2	1.8
			21–30	2	1.8
			Missing	1	
Age of Offender:					
Under 18	77	88.5			
Over 18	10	11.5			
Missing	26				

*Percent rounded

Table 4.2. Descriptive Statistics of Number of Fatalities and Number of Persons Injured for US, K–12 School Shootings (1997–2017) (N=113)

Variable	n	Min.	Max.	Mean (Std.)
Fatalities	113	00.00	27.00	1.28 (3.11)
Injuries	113	00.00	23.00	2.14 (3.75)

and were carried out by a single offender. As previously discussed in terms of copycat killings and media influence, many of the school shootings in the United States occurred after Columbine. Lastly, approximately 20 percent of the school shootings in the United States resulted in the shooter's suicide or an attempted suicide.

RISK FACTORS FOR SCHOOL SHOOTINGS

Research has been conducted in an effort to differentiate characteristics of school shooters.[24] These analyses led to the conclusion that school shooting offenders can often be categorized into three groups: disturbed, rejected, and criminal.[25] The disturbed category of offender can be described as having emotional and/or mental health problems and include risk factors such as intense emotions surrounding relationship breakups, past suicide attempts, abuse at home, or suspension/expulsion from school. An example of a disturbed shooter is demonstrated in the case of Thomas Witt Hamilton from Glasgow, Scotland (age forty-three), who in March of 1996 killed seventeen and injured fifteen at Dunblane Primary School. This perpetrator's history included complaints regarding his behaviors toward young boys, being blackballed by the Scouts' Association, and a failed business. The rejected category offender uses this event "to send a message" with risk factors related to this category including medication, mental illness, violent media, being a victim of bullying, suicidal thoughts, violent writings, loner behavior, and keeping a journal. An example of a rejected school shooter is Eric Harris (age eighteen), senior at Columbine High School (1999), who was rejected by the military, a victim of being ridiculed and bullied at school, with a history of mental health counseling, who also recorded a video suicide message prior to his shooting. Lastly, the criminal category includes those who use the incident as part of a criminal activity. Risk factors for the criminal category of school shooters include weapon fascination, past convictions, past violent behavior, violence against the family, and multiple past offenses.[26] An example of a criminal shooter is Matti Juhani Saari (age twenty), who was responsible for the Kauhajoki, Finland, shooting in 2008. This perpetrator had been dismissed from the Finnish army with charges and a court appearance pending, had a fascination with massacres and firearms, and possessed previous videos of himself with threats of violence toward others.

Although determining categories of offenders may aid in the identification of risk factors related to these incidents, these categories do not encompass the complex spectrum of risk factors and other variables that influence a student to bring a gun into the school environment. When examining these events it is important to recognize that each of these incidents is different and, depending on the gender, social status, mental health status, cognitive development, and especially age of the perpetrator, the reasoning and responses to these events vary.

Research examining 160 incidents of school shootings within the United States concluded that 53 percent of these incidents occur within a K–12 school.[27] The Department of Education and the Secret Service (2002) also conducted research on incidents of school gun violence and concluded that 81 percent of the incidents were carried out by an individual offender, 59 percent of the attacks happened during the school day, and 71percent of the offenders felt bullied or threatened by others within the school environment prior to their attack.[28]

RISK FACTORS FOR K–12 SCHOOLS

A *Washington Post* article published in April of 2018 stated that seven out of ten school shooting offenders are under the age of eighteen. Over the last few years the students that attend grades K–12 are the most common victims of a school shooting. In response, there has been much research on the dynamics of school shootings within this age group, which allows for conclusions to be made as to why these events take place and also how to prevent them in the future.[29]

Relationships within the School

When examining school shootings within this age group, one must take into account the relationships these child perpetrators have with the teachers within this environment.[30] Failure to recognize symptoms of a troubled adolescent by school support systems such as teachers, guidance counselors, and school resource officers (SROs) increases the likelihood that a troubled teen will partake in an extreme form of violence.[31] Research on perpetrators of school shootings concluded that there existed three main themes between student and teacher relationships.[32] Those themes were: teachers labeling students or targeting the wrong students, teachers stereotyping students or trying to put students into clearly defined categories, and teachers feeling the need to understand the commonalities within their problem students.[33] Furthermore, one study concluded that 53 percent of students describe their schools and school officials as quick to put people into categories.[34] As asserted by labeling theory, children will act as they feel those supervising them expect.[35] If students believe they are being put into categories and judged by the people that are supposed to protect them, their actions toward school violence—if they are labeled as violent—seems expected. In addition, if a child feels that their victimization is expected and therefore the teachers and administrators are seen as simply observers of the abuse, then the child often believing that bringing a gun to school is their only way to maintain their safety also seems to be a reasonable consequence.

Aside from teachers and school officials, another portion of the school environment that research suggests may be correlated with an increased probability of a child committing a shooting is the relationships among the students. Students who are perceived by peers to be socially withdrawn tend to measure lower in moral reasoning, which may increase their likelihood of partaking in a school shooting.[36] Students who are withdrawn or rejected by peers also have more opportunities for cognitive imbalances and as a result they develop moral reasoning more slowly than others.[37] As a result of this, they may also be labeled as an outsider or loner. According to students, the three factors that most influence group boundaries at school are style (60 percent), athletic achievement (53 percent), and appearance (52 percent).[38] This is no different from the research that suggests that attractive and well-dressed adults, across the globe, are more likely to be successful.[39] As discussed in the previous chapter, within the adolescent community identity is very closely tied with peer relations and if a student is socially isolated, bullied, or socially excluded by peers, one may take extreme forms of violence as a result. In addition, although all schools have different student cliques form, the establishment of gangs or groups within an institution may significantly increase the overall social isolation of students as they may feel as though they do not fit in with anyone if they are "not worthy" of being a part of the school's "cool" gang.

Bullying

When these incidents occur within the grades K–12, a major theme that appears over and over again, especially within the media, is that of bullying.[40] Research has suggested that male students are more likely to be victims of bullying both verbally and physically within all age groups; however, females are more likely to be victims of cyberbullying.[41] In reference to weapons, more than one-third of boys and nearly one-fifth of girls who had been bullied in school reported bringing a weapon to school.[42]

School Resource Officers

As the number of school shooting incidents arise within grades K–12, the conversation of how to limit these occurrences has become popular among both law enforcement and school officials. For years many schools have placed law enforcement officers, known as school resource officers, within their schools in an effort to discourage students from partaking in such actions.[43]

SROs are not going to completely eliminate school shootings, as was demonstrated by the fact that there was a SRO on the school grounds of Columbine High School in 1999;[44] however, research does suggest that the presence of a SRO does deter crime and reduce the severity of crimes.[45]

Research states that both law enforcement executives and school principals agree that SROs should be placed within their jurisdictions, and the usage of SROs is also more supported than that of arming teachers or school administrators.[46] Furthermore, law enforcement executives believe that arming a school employee is not the best response to a school shooting, and both law enforcement executives and school employees agree that the most effective school safety method overall, and the best response to a school shooting, is the use of SROs. Although both school and law enforcement executives prefer that SROs be in schools rather than arming teachers, it is also speculated that none of these measures is actually effective in preventing school shootings and that there is a need for law enforcement, school administrators, and policy makers to work together in an effort to develop a better strategy to prevent events like these in the future from proceeding.[47]

Mental Illness

When a school shooting occurs, many people speculate that it is a result of a preexisting mental illness that the individual possesses. When asking perpetrators of these crimes about why they had been involved in the incidents, many gave responses indicating different symptoms related to different mental illnesses.[48] Examples of such responses that indicated this were thoughts of suicide, feeling sorry for themselves, expecting to have been killed, not caring about their future, feelings of helplessness, feeling as though they do not belong to a group, or finding themselves in a dark place, especially one in which they have felt to have been in for a while and could not get out.

School attachment is not only an example of a social bond within the school setting, it is also related to crime and delinquency among adolescents and the mental health of adolescents.[49] If efforts are implemented to reinforce juvenile investment in school as well as emphasizing positive associations with school, it could be beneficial in the future when dealing with issues associated with both negative mental health within K–12 students as well as deviance and violence within the school, such as a school shooting.[50]

Family and Relationships

Parent-child relationships may also play a role in the potential for a child to become the perpetrator of a school shooting. Parents may also play a role in a child becoming a perpetrator of an incident of school violence in teaching children about appropriate behaviors, being an example of these behaviors, encouraging their child to act in that way, punishing a child if they do not act in an appropriate way, and also to aid in the development of the child's empathy.[51]

Also, relationships between siblings are important. For example, Harris and Klebow (Columbine shooters) expressed negative sentiments toward their college-aged brothers in their suicide videos created prior to the school massacre.[52] Research supports that the first peer relationships are often established within the family between siblings and those relationships are, in many ways, the building blocks or foundations for future peer relationships.[53] In addition, abuse at the hands of a sibling often is overlooked in the literature on child abuse, within the family, and by the criminal justice system. However, this abuse often creates long-term consequences, with the most negative outcomes to include outward displays of violence and suicide.[54]

Social Factors

Oftentimes, when young perpetrators of school violence are asked why they chose to hurt other students, the response of revenge is heard.[55] As the environment of bullying, intimidation, and victimization within the school was a part of their everyday lives, many students may state that the severity of their violence was not planned but rather they were simply trying to prove to themselves that they were no longer allowing the abuse. In addition, a few student perpetrators of a school shooting may assert that they were acting under the orders of their clique or gang.[56] Some students suggest that they are simply a product of their upbringing and surroundings, the influence of unemployment and poverty within their home neighborhoods, and broken relationships[57] that are present within their lives.

In addition, the theme of revenge was indicated by responses such as the victim being to blame, revenge as the only option, believing they had been wronged by someone within the school, believing they had been wronged by a parent, or responding to threats.[58] This defense mechanism, called *psychological projection*, occurs when an individual justifies an impulse or action by denying themselves the responsibility while attributing the responsibility to others.[59] Psychological projection, often utilized in explaining acts of family violence to include child abuse, is also applicable in cases of teens attempting to defer the responsibility of a school shooting by blaming other areas and individuals within their lives or environment.

Gun Availability

It is obvious that it would be impossible for a school shooting to occur if a child did not have access to a gun. In the United States, gun violence is listed as one of the major causes of death and has been listed as one of the supporting reasons for the rates of school shootings occurring at more than fifty times the rates of the remaining world.[60]

A significant factor to examine while investigating such incidents is the overall availability of guns within the community or, more specifically, how easy it is for a youth to attain such a weapon within their community. After Scotland's 1996 school shooting, laws were enacted that prohibited the ownership of specific handguns throughout the country. The result has been no more school shootings in Scotland.

RISK FACTORS FOR COLLEGES AND UNIVERSITIES

Shootings are among the deadliest types of emergencies a university may face. Recent research suggests that school shootings within the university setting are increasing throughout the world.[61] In particular, in the United States, research on university shootings for the years of 2001–2002 and 2005–2006 concluded that there were a total of forty recorded shooting incidents on or near college campuses and that this number had increased 23 percent for the 2006–2007 to 2010–2011 compared academic years and more than 100 percent by 2014–2015.[62]

Bullying, Harassment, and Mental Illness

When a school shooting takes place within a school of grades K–12, the first rationale usually asserted by the media for the motive is bullying. However, when a shooting occurs on a university campus, bullying is rarely mentioned, instead the rationale oftentimes mentioned is mental illness.[63] Although much research has correlated bullying with school shootings,[64] in universities, male students report being a victim of bullying (both verbally and physically) more than female students. In one extreme example that took place at Swarthmore College (USA), a student was bullied from age four until he was in college, which influenced his decision to shoot a student at his college who he considered to be his tormenter. This indicates that, although not as common as in the

K–12 environment, these incidents do happen on college campuses as a result
of bullying and harassment. American college counselors have asserted that
anxiety, depression, and suicidal ideation have been increasing on campuses
for the last ten to fifteen years, which may be correlated with the amount of
bullying happening on these campuses.[65]

In universities outside of the United States, the cases of school shootings
are less prevalent; however, in France in 2012, the shooting of a rabbi and
three children at Jensen School was explained as a revenge killing. The 2009
Azerbaijan State Oil Academy shooting in Baku resulted in the murder of
twelve individuals, with the perpetrator having a history of mental illness.
Finally, in the 2008 Finland college shooting, ten people were killed. This
perpetrator also had a history of mental illness. In each of these university
mass shootings, the perpetrators committed suicide at the scene, which is also
an indication of severe mental illness and hopelessness.[66] Therefore, it may be
time for colleges across the globe and college counseling centers to take bullying, harassment, and mental illness into account when attempting to reduce
their incidents of school shootings.

One must also consider the social factors of a society when examining their
incidents of a school shooting at the university level. Concealed weapons is
one of these social factors in the United States. When a school shooting occurs on a college campus, the first conversation that is brought up is that of
gun carrying on these campuses. Male students exhibit a higher level of approval for the legalization of concealed weapons on campuses than females
do, and "pro-firearm" perspectives are more representative of those associated with the Republican Party in most cases. Further research concluded
that female students and African-American students showed less support for
the right to carry guns on campus.[67] Students whose parents own firearms or
students who have friends who carry a concealed weapon have significantly
higher levels of approval of legalizing concealed firearms on college campuses as well as those who live off campus, which could be a result of their
familiarity with the weapons. However, the majority of university students
disapproved of the legalization of concealed weapons on campuses.[68] Therefore, these results indicated that the student's perceptions of the legalization
of concealed carry weapons on their campuses depended much on their political and weapon socialization.

Another social factor related to school violence on university campuses
may be the issue of hate.[69] Just as the France shooter of 2012 proclaimed hate
for the Jews, the perpetrator of the 2015 church shooting in South Carolina
(USA) expressed his hatred for African Americans.[70] Hence, hate is becoming another social element that fuels mass murders and mass shootings.

The outcomes of hate in history are legendary with the obvious results of mass murder. However, when adults attempt to explain why someone hates something or someone, the rational becomes less apparent;[71] this lack of justification also applies to teens. So, as attempts to combat hate are limited and, in many cases, ignored, how does one objectively end an action with subjective, socially based dynamics?

Hate is divided into two categories: rational and irrational.[72] Rational hate results from acts perceived as unjust while irrational hate is demonstrated as a hatred of a demographic or behavioral characteristic of a person or groups of people and is often without the experience of personalized victimization. In explaining rational hate, the focus by the perpetrator (in this case the school shooter) is usually the unjust action performed against them or another within their inner circle and their inability to effect change or their own perceived helplessness to prevent the victimization. Irrational hate, the category of hate involving most actions of mass destruction such as a school shooting, is much more difficult to understand. Some suggest, just as the notion of the cycle of violence in family violence,[73] that this behavior or philosophy is passed down from generation to generation as a learned behavior. It is also this category of hate that rarely results from a personal account of abuse or victimization by the target of hate.[74] In the school environment, irrational hate is often displayed in jokes about certain races, gender, or religions or in actions of discrimination toward an individual based upon their appearance. Irrational hate allows the hater, most often a very insecure individual, to elevate themselves above their hated subject. From this vantage point, the hated individual is perceived as less worthy and, therefore, deserving of the bias, discrimination, and, eventually, hate. It is this category of irrational hate that fuels the memberships and actions of those involved in hate groups or groups that facilitate hate and destruction against others, and it is these groups that may be of interest to young people who feel victimized by their peers within the school environment.

THEORIES TO EXPLAIN SCHOOL SHOOTINGS

Much of the concern raised in reference to school shootings is derived from our inability to understand and predict such tragic incidents. As a result of these shootings occurring in seemingly safe schools where the community is essentially crime free, researchers search for causes of these heinous events. Some theoretical explanations include social bond and general strain theory.

Social Bond Theory

Travis Hirschi's social bond theory[75] states that individuals do not commit crimes because of the social reinforcements that exist within the state of a social bond. A social bond is something within a person's environment that connects them to society's ethical restrictions. Furthermore, researchers suggest that delinquency is a consequence of a person's bonds to society being weak or broken.[76] Social bond theory asserts that delinquency results in the reduction of one's personal stakes in conformity. The bonds, which one creates with society, include involvement, attachment, commitment, and belief. Those with a lack of these bonds to society are at an increased likelihood for acting in a violent manner with significant outcomes for society.

Those who are most likely to engage in deviant behavior also most likely display behavioral signs at a young age such as a lack of a close bond with their parents. In addition, they may not be supervised effectively, and may not be disciplined in a consistent manner at home. This could translate over into the school environment if not addressed. Also, if a child reports having a great number of close friends, or involvement within their age category, their moral reasoning is reported to be increased, which also translates into children who are withdrawn or rejected by peers having a slower development of their moral reasoning, which may increase their likelihood of partaking in a deviant action.[77]

Research conducted examining social bonds and delinquency within schools has had significant success. Some research concludes that overall levels of school attachment within a school decrease alcohol use among adolescents.[78] Further research also suggested that school attachment has a strong correlation with mental health among adolescents, with lower levels of school attachment serving as a risk factor for negative mental health states.[79] These mental health issues may include illnesses such as depression and anxiety, which have also been proven to be risk factors for school violence, or more specifically school shootings.

Social Bonds and School Shootings

When talking about the specific bonds of involvement, attachment, commitment, and belief, in relation to school shootings, one may be able to look back on specific incidents throughout history and determine which social bonds were broken for certain offenders. For example, the shooters in the Columbine shooting did not have a belief in the predictable norms of society. These students were noted as praising Hitler or the devil and also being racists, which exhibits their lack of belief in the regular norms of the society in which they lived. These shooters also lacked involvement and attachment within their schools, as they did not fit in with any of the social cliques on campus, so they began their own. The students also lacked the proper attachment and involvement within their families as the boys admitted to having weak relationships with their parents. A characteristic found to be prevalent in many male school shooters is the feeling of anger for someone, or society overall, which is another example of how irregular social bonds can influence one to commit a school shooting.

General Strain Theory

Robert Agnew's general strain theory[80] focuses on different types of strain, coping with strain, and how the exposure to different sources of strain react to different stressors within people's lives through unhealthy coping mechanisms, such as through criminal activity. With general strain theory, a person may commit a crime in an effort to divert or terminate a stressor within their life such as the end of a relationship or death of a loved one, which in turn may cause the individual to experience different emotions such as depression or anxiety. This theory suggests that as a result of these types of triggers, an individual may seek some sort of revenge or attempt to lessen the emotions they are feeling by turning to criminal or deviant activities.

According to general strain theory, three types of strain based upon negative relationships with others include: (1) an individual preventing the person from achieving goals; (2) an individual removing, or threatening to remove, a stimuli that the person believes is positive to their life; and (3) an individual who presents or threatens to present the person with a stimuli that is seen as negative by the person.[81] In the theory, there exists two major types of coping strategies. The first is for those who seek to minimize or eliminate the source of strain. The second approach applies to those who seek to satisfy their need for revenge. Furthermore, general strain theory emphasizes the fact that when one blames these stressors on others, it is likely that a desire for revenge will emerge in an effort to eliminate the stressor. This desire for revenge was utilized as a rational for the 2012 France school shooting.

In reference to adolescents, the relationships within the school as well as their home lives may increase the amount of strain a child faces, and the fact that they are unable to separate themselves from the causes of their stressors may increase their likelihood of turning to delinquency. For example, if the strain in a child's life is a result of their poor home life, it is likely they are unable to escape this stressor since that is where they have to live, where their parents are, and they most likely are unable to attain alternate sources of living without facing punishment for their actions of trying to get away.

Strain Theory and School Shootings

While a moral panic has broken out within the world regarding school shootings, the search continues for answers in reference to the causes of these events. After a school shooting occurs, the media emphasizes different stressors within the shooter's life as well as turning attention to the overall strain that caused the specific incident.[82] For the specific instances of school shootings, the presentation of negative stimuli or the removal of positive stimuli from the student's life are most likely to provoke an incident as a result of their inability to recognize how to healthily handle such stressors. For example, in the 2007 shooting at Virginia Tech, potential stressors were noted as having been possibly correlated to why the student committed the incident. When looking back at the shooter's life, mental illness was noted, which may be seen as a negative stimuli that stressed him, or the social isolation he had faced throughout his life as a result of the mental illness may have also been a negative stimuli that increased his likelihood to commit such an act.[83] As the case was investigated further, strain may have resulted from the fact that he performed poorer academically than his sister did, which may have resulted in his not being valued as highly by his family or community.

SCHOOL SHOOTINGS AND THE MEDIA

The mass media plays an enormous role in the construction of society today more than ever.[84] In a place where newspapers, radios, and televisions were once the main media sources, modern technology has increased the role the media plays throughout all aspects of our lives. The increased use of cellular devices with internet streaming capabilities, social networking sites, and many other devices have made it significantly easier for individuals to access information of interest as well as publicize information of their own ideals or

On February 14, 2008, twenty-seven-year-old student Steven Kazmierczak killed five students and injured seventeen when he opened fire into a crowd of students on the campus of Northern Illinois University. Kazmierczak was prescribed medications for anxiety, for depression, and as a sleep aid, although he had stopped taking the prescriptions about three weeks prior to the shooting. According to a report published by the US Fire Administration, he is also believed to have studied the actions of Seung-Hui Cho, the perpetrator of the 2007 Virginia Tech shooting.

beliefs. As a result, there are those who suggest that the media often serves as an accomplice in school shootings.[85] The media's purpose is to provide news—the choice of that news coverage is theirs.[86] There are also those who suggest that mass shootings in schools were extremely rare until the media's coverage of Columbine.[87] Today, in addition to the media, the use of cell phones with internet capability allows news sources to reach an active audience whereas in the past they were only able to reach listless audiences.[88]

The role of the media is to report events such as these that take place within our society in a way that is easily understandable by the public, while filling in the gaps in their information if the facts do not explain the entirety. Although the majority of people are never directly affected by crime, their beliefs and perceptions of becoming victimized are highly influenced as a result of the media. In particular, fear of these incidents is heightened when society believes the victims demographically resemble themselves or loved ones.

Despite the fact that school shootings usually occur in less than ten minutes, the media coverage of such events extends for days, weeks, months, and sometimes years after the actual shooting incident hypothesizing motives or discussing the shooter's life, and with this overrepresentation of the extreme incidents within the media a moral panic erupts. Although contradictory to what the media portrays, the levels of crime in schools are low, but as a result of the media they are exposed to, students believe their chances of becoming victimized at school are high and they fear this regularly. In other words, since students see media and news sources constantly reporting incidents in which they resemble the victims, they perceive the same sort of incident as a real risk to themselves as well. Media coverage also attempts to fill in gaps of information between the public and societal officials. While attempting to discover motives for school shootings, news outlets will point fingers at movies, videogames, availability of guns, parenting, mental illness, bullying, and many more factors as motivations. Lastly, preceding these advancements, the media was not often utilized as a way for a potential school shooter to send threats or showcase their intentions, which has now been seen in many cases of school shootings over the past decade. As illustrated in table 4.3 in the media's coverage of Virginia Tech (USA), millions of viewers and potential copycats had received the details of the mass shooting.

Table 4.3. Media Coverage of School Violence

Media Coverage	Number of Viewers
Fox News	1.8 million viewers
CNN	1.4 million viewers
MSNBC	108.8 million website viewers

The Copycat Effect

A major concern with the overemphasis of school shooting incidents within the media is the idea that it will spark a contagion or "copycat" offender. A copycat offender may be defined as a violence-prone individual, or individuals, who imitate forms of violence attractive to them based upon examples that are usually popularized by the mass media. For years, research has suggested that the media inspires copycats in crimes of severe violence such as murder.[89] In many news accounts on school shootings, details are provided on the perpetrators, their modes of attack, and the outcomes of the murder sprees.[90]

Although the media does not deliberately encourage the imitation of such incidents, it has been identified as an accomplice in the correlation with the consequence of one of these events occurring. For example, recent shooting offenders have admitted to idolizing and studying the actions of shooters, such as those who partook in the Columbine High School shooting.[91] More specifically, within the four weeks after this incident, there were up to 350 students across the United States arrested on charges of having raised a threat against their school.[92]

Teenagers are the most vulnerable to fall into this fascination as a result of peer pressure, parental arguments, interactions with peers, and also the overall anxiety that is associated with being a teen. It is hypothesized that these events are usually the outcome of the shooter wanting to get revenge at someone, or something. These individuals take such a drastic step in order to obtain this revenge to gain social reaction in an effort to show others the anger or sadness they have been caused. Once these incidents occur the media covers the story and the offender is granted the social reaction they had planned for. With the increase of different forms of media, there has also been an increase in the occurrence of school shooters using the media to disburse messages as to why they were going to partake in the action or to emphasize the idea of revenge. Shooters who utilize the media in this way may be doing so in an effort to help create their story and ensure the public knows their motivations behind the event.[93]

The media business is an industry that attempts to make daily events exciting and relevant while also keeping the attention of the audience.[94] For example, continually broadcasting disastrous situations holds the attention of individuals within our society since they are eye-catching and people want to understand why they are happening. In a society where the public's favorite stories are graphic or violent in nature, and as a result of limitations in space or time, the media typically focuses on broadcasting incidents that are the most extreme in an effort to capture the audience's attention.

The rarity of these types of school shootings events are almost impossible to determine, despite what is portrayed in the media, yet policymakers have been increasing the security within schools and implementing programs in an effort to reduce school violence, although these approaches have not yet proven to be effective. Specific examples of these prevention tactics that have been taken are the utilization of metal detectors, zero-tolerance policies, increased SRO and police presence on campus, and strict disciplinary enforcement, to name a few. Although these protocols may aid in the lessening of such events by acting as a deterrent for this behavior, it is suggested that school administrators can control school crime by focusing on the social control within these institutions.[95] Administrators can do this by monitoring student movement, locking entrances, installing security cameras, installing bulletproof glass, and creating crisis management teams and plans for when these situations do arise.

CHAPTER QUESTIONS

1. What are the four main purposes the media serves?
2. What are the three categories of school shooters?
3. Approximately what percent of school shootings within the United States (1840–2017) were carried out by an individual offender?
4. Hate is divided into two categories; what are the categories?
5. What are the two major coping strategies discussed?

DISCUSSION QUESTIONS

1. In your opinion, would stricter gun laws reduce the number of school shootings within the United States? Explain.
2. What are your thoughts on the increase in the number of SROs in schools in an effort to reduce school violence, specifically gun violence on school campuses? Explain.
3. Do you feel as though the cycle of violence influences one's likelihood to become an offender of school violence? If so, in what ways?

NOTES

1. Robert Merton, *Social Theory and Social Structure* (New York: Free Press, 1975).

2. Charles Wright, *Mass Communications: A Sociological Perspective* (New York: Random House, 1959).

3. Harold Lasswell, *Political Communications: Public Language of Political Elites in India and the United States* (Chicago: University of Chicago Press, 1969).

4. Doris Graber, *Mass Media and American Politics* (Washington, DC: CQ Press, 1997).

5. Sidney Kraus and Dennis Davis, *The Effects of Mass Communication and Political Behavior* (UK: Cambridge University Press, 1976).

6. Kimberly McCabe and Gregory Martin, *School Violence, the Media and Criminal Justice Responses* (New York: Peter Lang, 2005).

7. Doris Graber, *Mass Media and American Politics*.

8. David Protess and D. Leff, *The Journalism of Outrage: Investigative Reporting and Agenda Building in American Society* (New York: Guilford Publications, 1991).

9. Kimberly McCabe and Gregory Martin, *School Violence, the Media and Criminal Justice Responses*.

10. Tim Cook, "Disclaiming the Media: The American Public's Changing Attitude toward the Media," *Political Communication*, 24(3) (2017): 259–81.

11. Kimberly McCabe, *Protecting Your Children in Cyberspace: What Parents Need to Know* (Lanham, MD: Rowman and Littlefield Publishers, Inc., 2017).

12. Tim Cook, "Disclaiming the Media: The American Public's Changing Attitude toward the Media."

13. Steven Livingston and Todd Eaches, "Humanitarian Crisis and US Foreign Policy: Somalia and the CNN Effect Reconsidered," *Political Communication*, 12(4) (1995): 413–29.

14. Stanley Feldman and Lee Sigelman, "The Political Impact of Prime-Time Television: The Day After," *Journal of Politics*, 47(2) (1985): 556–78.

15. Kimberly McCabe and Daniel Murphy, *Child Abuse—Today's Issues* (New York: Taylor and Francis Publishing, 2016).

16. Kimberly McCabe and Sharon Gregory, "Recognizing Illegal Activities of Computer Users," *Social Science Computer Review*, 16(4) (1998): 419–22.

17. Kimberly McCabe and Gregory Martin, *School Violence, the Media and Criminal Justice Responses*.

18. Louis Ryan, "Differential Embedding: Polish Immigrants in London Negotiating Belonging over Time," *Journal of Ethnic and Migration Studies*, 44(2) (2017): 233–51.

19. Kimberly McCabe and Gregory Martin, *School Violence, the Media and Criminal Justice Responses*.

20. Clare Scott, "Australian Cosplayer Faces Prison for 3D Printed Replica Guns," August 6, 2018, accessed on January 3, 2019, at https://3dprint.com/221568/cosplay-3d-printed-replica-guns/.

21. Clare Scott, "Australian Cosplayer Faces Prison for 3D Printed Replica Guns."

22. Zach Winn, "The U.S. School Shooting Statistics Everyone Should Know," 2017, accessed on November 12, 2018, at https://www.campussafetymagazine.com/safety/u-s-school-shooting-statistics-us/.

23. Kimberly McCabe, *Protecting Your Children in Cyberspace: What Parents Need to Know*.

24. Stephen Thompson and Ken Kyle, "Understanding Mass School Shootings: Links between Personhood and Power in the Competitive School Environment," *Journal of Primary Prevention*, 26(5) (2005): 419–38.

25. Maria Ioannou, Laura Hammond, and Olivia Simpson, "A Model for Differentiating School Shooters Characteristics," *Journal of Criminal Psychology*, 5(3) (2015): 188–200.

26. Maria Ioannou, Laura Hammond, and Olivia Simpson, "A Model for Differentiating School Shooters Characteristics."

27. Zach Winn, "The U.S. School Shooting Statistics Everyone Should Know."

28. Brian Vossekuil, Robert Fein, Marissa Reddy, Randy Borum, and William Modzeleski, *The Final Report and Findings of the Safe School Initiative: Implications for the Prevention of School Attacks in the United States* (U.S. Department of Education, Office of Elementary and Secondary Education, Safe and Drug-Free Schools Program and U.S. Secret Service, National Threat Assessment Center, Washington, DC, 2002).

29. Stephen Watts, Karl Province, and Kayla Toohy, "The Kids Aren't Alright: School Attachment, Depressive Symptoms, and Gun Carrying at School," *American Journal of Criminal Justice* (2018): 1–20.

30. Kimberly McCabe and Gregory Martin, *School Violence, the Media and Criminal Justice Responses*.

31. Martin Bouchard, Wei Wang, and Eric Beauregard, "Social Capital, Opportunity, and School-Based Violence," *Violence and Victims*, 27(5) (2012): 656–73.

32. Gordon Crews, "School Violence Perpetrators Speak: An Examination of Perpetrators' Views on School Violence," *Journal of the Institute of Justice and International Studies*, 14 (2014): 41–52.

33. Gordon Crews, "School Violence Perpetrators Speak: An Examination of Perpetrators' Views on School Violence."

34. Stephen Thompson and Ken Kyle, "Understanding Mass School Shootings: Links between Personhood and Power in the Competitive School Environment."

35. Frank Tannenbaum, *Crime and Community* (London and Columbia: London and New York: Columbia University Press, 1938).

36. Kimberly McCabe and Gregory Martin, *School Violence, the Media and Criminal Justice Responses*.

37. Stephen Watts, Karl Province, and Kayla Toohy, "The Kids Aren't Alright: School Attachment, Depressive Symptoms, and Gun Carrying at School."

38. Stephen Thompson and Ken Kyle, "Understanding Mass School Shootings: Links between Personhood and Power in the Competitive School Environment."

39. Melissa Stanger, "Attractive People Are Simply More Successful," *Business Insider*, October 9, 2012, accessed on November 4, 2019, at https://www.business insider.com/attractive-people-are-more-successful-2012-9.

40. Kimberly McCabe and Daniel Murphy, *Child Abuse—Today's Issues*.

41. Kimberly McCabe, *Protecting Your Children in Cyberspace: What Parents Need to Know*.

42. Mark Chapell, Stephanie Hasselman, Theresa Kitchin, Satiya Lomon, K. McIvor, and P. Sarullo, "Bullying in Elementary School, High School and College," 2006, accessed on November 3, 2018, at https://ezproxy.lynchburg.edu/login?url=https://search.proquest.com/docview/195943783?accountid=12198.

43. Kimberly McCabe, *Protecting Your Children in Cyberspace: What Parents Need to Know.*

44. Kimberly McCabe and Gregory Martin, *School Violence, the Media and Criminal Justice Responses.*

45. Kimberly McCabe and Daniel Murphy, *Child Abuse—Today's Issues.*

46. Margaret Chrusciel, Scott Wolfe, J. Andrew Hansen, J. Rojek, and Robert Kaminski, "Law Enforcement Executive and Principal Perspectives on School Safety Measures," *Policing*, 38(1) (2015): 24–39, accessed on November 7, 2018, at https://ezproxy.lynchburg.edu/login?url=https://search-proquest-com.ezproxy.lynchburg.edu/docview/1660587976?accountid=12198.

47. Margaret Chrusciel, Scott Wolfe, J. Andrew Hansen, J. Rojek, and Robert Kaminski, "Law Enforcement Executive and Principal Perspectives on School Safety Measures."

48. Gordon Crews, "School Violence Perpetrators Speak: An Examination of Perpetrators' Views on School Violence."

49. Stephen Watts, Karl Province, and Kayla Toohy, "The Kids Aren't Alright: School Attachment, Depressive Symptoms, and Gun Carrying at School."

50. Martin Bouchard, Wei Wang, and Eric Beauregard, "Social Capital, Opportunity, and School-Based Violence."

51. Beth Rosenthal, "Exposure to Community Violence in Adolescence: Trauma Symptoms," *Adolescence*, 35(138) (2000): 261–84.

52. Kimberly McCabe and Gregory Martin, *School Violence, the Media and Criminal Justice Responses.*

53. Kimberly McCabe, *Child Abuse and the Criminal Justice System.*

54. Kimberly McCabe and Daniel Murphy, *Child Abuse—Today's Issues.*

55. Kimberly McCabe and Daniel Murphy, *Child Abuse—Today's Issues.*

56. Kimberly McCabe and Gregory Martin, *School Violence, the Media and Criminal Justice Responses.*

57. Beth Rosenthal, "Exposure to Community Violence in Adolescence: Trauma Symptoms."

58. Gordon Crews, "School Violence Perpetrators Speak: An Examination of Perpetrators' Views on School Violence."

59. Rin Nohara, "Psychological Projection Effects on Family Violence," *British Psychological Society Magazine*, 7(6) (2010): 1–4.

60. Chip Grabow and Lisa Rose, "The US Has Had 57 Times as Many School Shootings as Other Major Industrialized Nations Combined," CNN, 2018, accessed on January 3, 2019, at https://www.cnn.com/2018/05/21/us/school-shooting-us-versus-world-trnd/index.html.

61. Zach Winn, "The U.S School Shooting Statistics Everyone Should Know."

62. *Campus Safety Magazine*, "Study Finds Increase in School Shootings at Colleges in U.S.," April 27, 2018, accessed on November 7, 2018, at https://www.campus

safetymagazine.com/news/study_finds_increase_in_school_shootings_at_colleges_in_u-s/.

63. Kimberly McCabe and Daniel Murphy, *Child Abuse—Today's Issues.*

64. Mark Chapell, Stephanie Hasselman, Theresa Kitchin, Satiya Lomon, K. McIvor, and P. Sarullo, "Bullying in Elementary School, High School and College."

65. Mark Chapell, Stephanie Hasselman, Theresa Kitchin, Satiya Lomon, K. McIvor, and P. Sarullo, "Bullying in Elementary School, High School and College."

66. Kimberly McCabe, *Protecting Your Children in Cyberspace: What Parents Need to Know.*

67. H. Jaymi Elsass, Jaclyn Schildkraut, and Mark Stafford, "Studying School Shootings: Challenges and Considerations for Research," *American Journal of Criminal Justice,* 41(3) (2016): 444–64.

68. Hyunseok Jang, Ricki Dierenfeldt, and Chang Lee, "Who Wants to Allow Concealed Weapons on the College Campus?" *Security Journal,* 27(3) (2014): 304–19.

69. Kimberly McCabe, *Protecting Your Children in Cyberspace: What Parents Need to Know.*

70. Sarah Mervosh, "Here's a Look at Some of the Worse Mass Shootings in Houses of Worship in Recent Years," *New York Times,* October 28, 2018, accessed on January 2, 2019, at https://www.post-gazette.com/news/crime-courts/2018/10/28/houses-of-worship-synagogue-Pittsburgh-mass-shootings-religious/stories/201810280203.

71. Kimberly McCabe, *Protecting Your Children in Cyberspace: What Parents Need to Know.*

72. John Schafer and Joe Navarro, "The Seven Stage Hate Model," *Law Enforcement Bulletin,* 72(3) (2003): 1–9.

73. Larry Siegel, *Criminology: The Core,* fifth edition (New York: Wadsworth, 2014).

74. Kimberly McCabe, *Protecting Your Children in Cyberspace: What Parents Need to Know.*

75. Travis Hirschi, *Causes of Delinquency* (Berkeley: University of California Press, 1969).

76. Frank Schmalleger, *Criminology Today,* fourth edition (Upper Saddle River, NJ: Pearson, 2006).

77. Stephen Thompson and Ken Kyle, "Understanding Mass School Shootings: Links between Personhood and Power in the Competitive School Environment."

78. Kimberly Henry and Michael Slater, "The Contextual Effect of School Attachment on Young Adolescents' Alcohol Use," *Journal of School Health,* 77(2) (2007): 67–74.

79. Stephen Watts, Karl Province, and Kayla Toohy, "The Kids Aren't Alright: School Attachment, Depressive Symptoms, and Gun Carrying at School."

80. Robert Agnew, "Foundation for a General Strain Theory of Crime and Delinquency," *Criminology,* 30(1) (1992): 47–88.

81. Robert Agnew, "Foundation for a General Strain Theory of Crime and Delinquency."

82. Kimberly McCabe and Gregory Martin, *School Violence, the Media and Criminal Justice Responses*.

83. CNN Library, *Virginia Tech Shooting Fast Facts*, May 2, 2018, accessed on January 3, 2019, at https://www.cnn.com/2013/10/31/us/virginia-tech-shootings-fast-facts/index.html.

84. Kimberly McCabe and Gregory Martin, *School Violence, the Media and Criminal Justice Responses*.

85. Zeynep Tufekci, "The Media Needs to Stop Inspiring Copycat Murders. Here's How," *The Atlantic*, December 19, 2012, accessed on November 3, 2018, at https://www.theatlantic.com/national/archive/2012/12/the-media-needs-to-stop-inspiring-copycat-murders-heres-how/266439/.

86. Kimberly McCabe and Gregory Martin, *School Violence, the Media and Criminal Justice Responses*.

87. Kimberly McCabe and Gregory Martin, *School Violence, the Media and Criminal Justice Responses*.

88. Kimberly McCabe, *Protecting Your Children in Cyberspace: What Parents Need to Know*.

89. Zeynep Tufekci, "The Media Needs to Stop Inspiring Copycat Murders. Here's How."

90. Kimberly McCabe and Gregory Martin, *School Violence, the Media and Criminal Justice Responses*.

91. Stephen Diamond, "Sex, Madness and Mass Murder in Santa Barbara," 2014, *Psychology Today*, accessed on November 3, 2018, at https://www.psychologytoday.com/us/blog/evil-deeds/201405/sex-madness-and-mass-murder-in-santa-barbara.

92. Antonio Preti, "School Shootings as a Culturally Forced Way of Expressing Suicidal Hostile Intentions," *JAAPL*, 36(4) (2008): 544–50.

93. Zeynep Tufekci, "The Media Needs to Stop Inspiring Copycat Murders. Here's How."

94. Kimberly McCabe and Gregory Martin, *School Violence, the Media and Criminal Justice Responses*.

95. Thomas Capozzi and R. Steve McVey, *Kids Killing Kids: Managing Violence and Gangs in Schools* (New York: Routledge, 2000).

Chapter Five

Mental Illness and School Violence

KEY WORDS

anorexia nervosa
antisocial personality
  disorder
attention-deficit/hyper-
  activity disorder
behavior therapy
binge eating disorder
bipolar disorder
bulimia nervosa
chronic
clinical depression
cognitive-behavioral
  therapy
combined type
comorbid

conduct disorder
co-occurring condition
Diagnostic and Statisti-
  cal Manual of Mental
  Disorders
dialectical behavior
  therapy
family therapy
generalized anxiety
  disorder
internet addiction dis-
  order
mental health
mental illness

oppositional defiant
  disorder
peer group therapy
persistent depressive
  disorder
predominantly com-
  bined type
predominantly hyper-
  active-impulsive type
protective factor
risk factor
seasonal affective dis-
  order
suicide
suicide attempt

The conversation surrounding mental illness in relation to school violence was brought to the attention of the public after post-event examinations of the perpetrators of the April 1999 massacre at Columbine High School in Colorado (USA). Prior to this incident many social scientists believed school violence to be an extreme reaction to bullying, childhood trauma, and media coverage,[1] as it was asserted that children choose violence in order to gain control,[2] in retaliation for abuse,[3] or because violence was seen as an appropriate response.[4]

KEY ACRONYMS

(ADHD) Attention-deficit/hyperactivity disorder
(ASPD) Antisocial personality disorder
(BED) Binge eating disorder
(BJS) Bureau of Justice statistics
(DSM or DSM-5) *Diagnostic and Statistical Manal of Mental Disorders*
(GAD) Generalized anxiety disorder
(IAD) Internet addiction disorder
(NIH) National Institutes of Health
(ODD) Oppositional defiant disorder

Once this tragic event occurred, researchers from many disciplines began dissecting the case and examining the differing variables within these teens' lives that may have influenced their likelihood of such violent behaviors. Upon the analysis of the lives of Eric Harris and Dylan Klebold (Columbine High School), it was discovered that Klebold has suffered from both depression and suicidal thoughts, while Harris was a homicidal psychopath, who was also prescribed an antidepressant. Prior to the examination of Columbine's young killers, most often the attacks on schools were attributed to mentally ill adults such as Charles Whitman, the twenty-five-year-old perpetrator of the 1966 University of Texas (USA) Tower Shooting, who killed fifteen people, and Thomas Hamilton, the forty-three-year-old perpetrator in the 1996 Dunblane Primary School (Scotland) mass shooting.

In many cases, perpetrators of school violence have not been officially diagnosed with any sort of mental illness, which is especially true of the many young shooters of recent times. Unfortunately, many attackers exhibit a history of suicidal thoughts or reports of extreme sadness.[5] In addition, significant life changes such as the death of a loved one, public humiliation, or the end to a romantic relationship may ignite an emotional response from someone suffering from a mental illness, which may in turn lead to their involvement in violence within the school.

On April 16, 2007, thirty-two people were killed and seventeen were injured by student Seung-Hui Cho on the campus of Virginia Tech. Cho was a senior studying English, and he ultimately committed suicide. To date, this massacre is known as the deadliest school shooting in the history of the United States. Cho had a history of mental illness.

One example of this scenario was the Virginia Tech (USA) shooting. On April 16, 2007, Seung-Hui Cho, a senior at Virginia Polytechnic Institute and State University (Virginia Tech—USA), killed thirty-two people before taking his own life. Once the investigation into Cho's life began, it was clear to many that he had suffered from a mental illness. In fact, this mental illness had been recognized formally by university officials.[6] Specifically, a professor of Cho's recalled being informed by a colleague about the disturbing piece of writing that Cho had written, as well as his unusual conduct with other students within the classroom. After spending more time with Cho, the professor had observed the unusual behaviors firsthand and had reported her suspicions to both the campus police and the campus counseling center. As Cho had not threatened anyone, and it was concluded that he did not pose a threat to himself or others, he chose not to receive counseling. Not long after his professor had reported his worrisome behaviors, Cho threatened to commit suicide and was treated at an off-campus counseling center. He was released once it was considered, in his mental health assessment, that he no longer was a risk to himself or others. After his release, Cho did receive counseling from the university's counseling center; however, he was never provided a specific diagnosis. After the mass shooting, the investigation into his life discovered that Cho had been court-ordered to seek outpatient care in 2015 two years prior to the tragedy after making suicidal remarks to his roommates. Hence, there are those who suggest that the Virginia Tech shooting, identified as the deadliest school shooting in history, could have been avoided if the perpetrator had received the treatment he required.

MENTAL HEALTH AND MENTAL ILLNESSES

Before discussing the ways in which mental health clinicians are able to diagnose a mental illness, one must understand the definition of mental health. Mental health references our emotional, psychological, and social well-being meaning it impacts the ways in which individuals think, feel, and act. Mental health, in many ways, influences how individuals handle stressful situations, how they interest and relate to others, and how they determine their daily choices.[7] Mental health problems may be influenced by biological factors, life experiences, and family histories of mental health problems, which can affect our overall thinking, mood, and behavior.[8] It is suggested that having positive mental health allows for people to appreciate and strive to reach their full potential, cope with the stresses of life in a healthy way, work more efficiently, and make significant contributions to their communities overall.[9] Negative mental health or mental illness, as is commonly the phrase, without treatment restricts individuals from fulfilling their needs and/or desires.

Essentially, the early warning signs that individuals may be struggling with their mental health may present as eating or sleeping excessively, or not enough, having low energy, experiencing extreme mood swings, or the increased use of alcohol or drugs. Research on the relationships between drugs and violence suggests that over one-third of the incidences of workplace violence occurred when the offender was consuming alcohol or drugs.[10] On university campuses, more than 40 percent of the crimes committed against students involved a perpetrator using drugs or alcohol.[11] In an effort to maintain positive mental health, it is proposed that one must maintain a good mind-set, obtain sufficient sleep, connect with others socially, be physically active, and develop coping skills for everyday activities to increase the positivity in not only one's overall health, but more specifically one's mental health.[12]

A mental illness, or mental disorder, is a condition that affects one's thinking, feelings, mood, and behavior.[13] Mental illnesses may be occasional, or they may be chronic, meaning they have continued for long periods of time.

There are many different types of mental illnesses, and these illnesses can all impact one's capabilities to relate to others and to function normally in everyday life. Common mental disorders include anxiety disorders, depression, eating disorders, personality disorders, and psychotic disorders.[14] In order to officially be diagnosed with a mental illness, one must complete a physical exam and possibly undergo lab tests from a doctor and an additional psychological examination. The psychological examination will contain questions referencing the individual's thoughts, feelings, and behaviors.[15] It should be noted that not all mass shooters have a history of criminal behavior or mental illness. One example is the 2013 Washington, D.C. (USA) Navy Yard shooter, who never committed a crime and had never been involuntarily committed to a psychiatric hospital.[16]

Mental illness is a global problem. The World Health Organization, hereafter WHO, reports that one in four individuals across the globe will be affected by mental or neurological disorders at some point in their lifetime.[17] Unfortu-

The University of California (Los Angeles) shooting occurred on June 1, 2016. This incident involved a thirty-eight-year-old former PhD student who shot and killed an associate professor in a murder then suicide. There was a history of online hostile comments about the professor by the shooter for several months prior to the event. The shooter struggled with mental health problems such as depression.

Table 5.1. Common Mental Illnesses across the Globe

Mental Illness	Global Population (%)	Males vs. Females
Depression	4%	3%, 4.5%
Anxiety Disorders	4%	3%, 4.7%
Bipolar Disorder	0.6%	0.55%, 0.65%
Schizophrenia	0.3%	0.29%, 0.28%

nately, nearly two-thirds never seek the help of a professional.[18] In addition, many governments do not fund mental health initiatives and programs. In terms of the more common mental illnesses across the globe, they include depression, anxiety disorders, bipolar disorder, and schizophrenia. Information on these illnesses is provided in table 5.1.

Researchers agree that the best way to treat mental disorders and mental illness is first through the proper identification or diagnosis of the condition.[19] With approximately 50 percent of all mental illnesses beginning by the age of fourteen,[20] early diagnoses are critical.

Diagnostic and Statistical Manual of Mental Disorders (DSM or DSM-5)

The *Diagnostic and Statistical Manual of Mental Disorders* (DSM or DSM-5) is the handbook most commonly utilized throughout the majority of the world as it serves as the most influential guide in the diagnosis of mental illnesses or disorders.[21] This handbook was originally produced in 1952 and has been periodically reviewed and revised to maintain the most accurate and reliable information. These reviews ensure that all of the advancements in research and knowledge surrounding the topic of mental illness throughout the years are utilized in this most significant phase of seeking mental health treatment—the phase of diagnosis of the illness.

The DSM-5 comprises descriptions, indicators, and other standards for diagnosing mental disorders while also providing a common language for mental health practitioners to communicate about their patients.[22] A common language within the DSM-5 for practitioners enables them to form consistent, reliable, valid diagnoses that may be used in the research of mental disorders in the future. In addition, these commonalities also aid in the development of alternative medications and/or treatment options for those who suffer from a variety of mental disorders.

The original 1952 DSM is now referred to as the DSM-5, which in 2013 was revised to identify the newer forms of mental illness. The DSM-5 Task Force, Work Groups, and Study Groups are composed of experts from many disciplines, including neuroscience, genetics, social and behavioral sciences, public health, statistics, epidemiology, and nosology, and they utilize their expertise to review and revise the publication.[23] As a result of the advances in the science behind mental health throughout recent history, it was important that the DSM was reviewed. The DSM-5 changes include better character-izations of the symptoms and behaviors for those individuals who desire clinical assistance but whose symptoms are not clearly defined in the DSM. The DSM-5 does not contain information on how to treat those with a mental disorder; however, as mentioned, determining the correct diagnoses is the first step in the direction of being able to properly treat any medical issue.

RISK AND PROTECTIVE FACTORS

As with other health problems, mental health issues may arise in certain in-dividuals as a result of differing risk factors. The World Health Organization defines a risk factor as any attribute, characteristic, or exposure of an indi-vidual that would increase their likelihood of developing a disease or injury. Risk factors vary and may relate to the individual, their family, community, or life events. In particular, the most commonly genetically associated mental disorders are autism, attention-deficit hyperactivity disorder, bipolar disorder, depression, and schizophrenia.[24] A protective factor is described as character-istics, conditions, or behaviors that reduce the effects of stressful life events.[25] Early interventions, exercise, and social support are all protective factors for mental illness.[26] Table 5.2 lists risk factors and protective factors as applied to children, families, schools, and the community as provided by the US Center for Disease Control.

COMMON MENTAL ILLNESSES
IN TEENS AND ADOLESCENCE

Children with mental health problems are often the victims of violence by peers.[27] In addition, there are those researchers who suggest that zero toler-ance policies within the school leave little room for flexibility of discre-tion within attempting to correct behaviors of a student with mental health problems; therefore, in some case, these policies actually increase violent behaviors in certain children.[28] The more common mental illnesses in ado-lescence and teens include oppositional defiant disorder, attention-deficit/hyperactivity disorder, conduct disorder, depression, generalized anxiety disorder, antisocial personality disorder, and, the most recently identified, internet addiction disorder.[29]

Table 5.2. Risk and Protective Factors for Suicide

Actor	Risk Factor	Protective Factor
Child	• Genetics • Low IQ • Learning disabilities • Developmental delays • Difficulty in communication • Physical illness • Difficult temperament	• Secure attachment experience • Good sociability • Having a belief in control • Positive attitude • Capacity to reflect • Outgoing temperament as an infant
Family	• Presence of domestic violence • Inconsistent discipline • Hostile relationships • Abuse • Neglect • History of parental mental illness • History of criminality or alcohol/substance abuse within the home • Death • Rejection of relationships	• At least one supportive adult • Affection • Consistent discipline • Supportive long-term relationships • Support for education
School	• Bullying • Cyberbullying • Lack of positive interaction between peers • Deviant peer influences • Peer pressure • Poor relationships between school staff and students	• Clear policies in reference to bullying/cyberbullying • Code of conduct for staff • School promotion of positive mental health • Healthy relationships between school staff and students • Positive classroom management • Effective safeguarding and child protection policies
Community	• Low socioeconomic status • Homelessness • War • Discrimination • Gangs • Organized crime networks	• Good housing • Range of leisure activities • Opportunities for valued social roles • High importance of school • High standards of living

Oppositional Defiant Disorder (ODD)

Oppositional defiant disorder (hereafter ODD) is a type of behavior disorder that may interfere with a child's ability to create and maintain relationships with parents, peers, and teachers. ODD is demonstrated in children as a constant pattern of uncooperative and defiant behaviors that interfere with their daily activities. ODD explains a hostile attitude and the exhibition of hostile

When we put him into preschool at age four, he would act out and tear up other children's toys. There was an underlying anger or annoyance with him that we couldn't quite put our finger on.

behaviors toward authority figures. Although often researchers do not know exactly what causes this disorder, two theories that are offered as explanations are developmental theory and learning theory.

When examining ODD through developmental theory, researchers suggest that this behavior disorder begins when the child is young. Those suffering from ODD may have difficulties learning to be independent from a parent or guardian. As a result of these struggles to become detached from this person, developmental issues may arise that last beyond their beginning years.[30]

Learning theory proposes the idea that the negative indicators of this disorder are learned attitudes.[31] It is suggested that children with ODD will copy the effects of negative reinforcement methods used by parents, or those in an authority figure. When exposed to negative reinforcement that is often the result of a peer relationship, a clique, or gang membership, the child's ODD behaviors will increase as a result of gaining the response they had hoped for from the authority figure or just their attention.[32]

The symptoms of this behavior disorder may be presented at home or in school or both, with about 1 to 16 percent of all school-age children having ODD.[33] Symptoms vary, although common signs of ODD are deliberate attempts to irritate others, frequent angry episodes, use of hateful words while upset, and spiteful attitudes. Unfortunately, these are also often the characteristics of the teen years.

Within the school environment, children or teens who suffer from ODD may be uncooperative, defiant, or hostile when dealing with their peers or teachers. Although all children may exhibit similar traits, those who suffer from this behavior disorder will present these symptoms more often than others, especially when tired, upset, or hungry.[34] In addition, children with ODD may exhibit frequent temper tantrums within the school environment and be easily irritated by their peers, as well as intentionally partaking in actions that annoy others, blaming others for their misbehaviors, being touchy with classmates, and speaking harshly to both peers and authority figures.[35] These children may also argue with teachers or other authority figures regularly while also questioning rules and refusing to do what is asked of them.[36]

Early treatment of ODD can help prevent future behavior problems, but success may depend on the child's symptoms, age, and health status. One type of treatment for those with this disability is cognitive-behavioral therapy. Through this therapy children learn how to better communicate with others while also learning how to manage their anger and control their impulses.[37] Family therapy is another treatment for those with ODD, which helps the family improve their communication skills as a whole and aids those within the family who do not suffer from ODD to better understand the disorder and how to support their loved one who does. Peer group therapy is another form of treatment for those with ODD. This form of therapy helps children better develop their social and interpersonal skills with others within their age group.[38]

Although this behavior disorder is common, those who suffer from mood or anxiety disorders, conduct disorder, or attention-deficit/hyperactivity disorder (to be discussed next) may be more likely to be diagnosed with ODD.[39] In fact, ODD is very likely to be comorbid with attention deficit disorder (ADD) or ADHD. Comorbid is defined as: "existing simultaneously with and usually independently of another medical condition."[40]

Attention-Deficit/Hyperactivity Disorder (ADHD)

"I was having trouble getting my work done, I would also get in trouble in class for doing impulsive things—for being crazy."

As of 1994, the American Psychiatric Association divided attention-deficit/ hyperactivity disorder (ADHD), formally known as attention deficit disorder (ADD), into subtypes based upon three main features or symptoms of the disorder: inattentiveness, impulsivity, and hyperactivity.

The subtypes of ADHD are: (1) predominantly combined type, (2) predominantly inattentive type, and (3) predominantly hyperactive-impulsive type. The combined type has multiple symptoms of inattention, impulsivity, and hyperactivity. The predominantly combined type exhibits multiple symptoms of inattention, with few or no symptoms of hyperactivity-impulsivity, while the predominantly hyperactive-impulsive type has multiple symptoms of hyperactivity-impulsivity, with few or no symptoms of inattention.

ADHD is a neurobiologically based developmental disability that affects many school-age children.[41] Research suggests that ADHD is transferred by genetics and results from a chemical imbalance or deficiency in certain neurotransmitters that are utilized by the brain to regulate behavior. At one time ADD/ADHD was one of the most commonly treated mental illnesses in the American schools.[42]

As previously mentioned, the main symptoms of ADHD are inattention, hyperactivity, and impulsivity. Signs of inattention in a child are not seeming to listen when directly spoken to, losing things that are necessary for tasks, and forgetfulness in daily activities. Hyperactivity may present itself as a child seeming to always be moving, as excessive running around when inappropriate, or as a child having difficulties when attempting to partake in leisure activities or quiet time. Signs of impulsivity in children are most often exhibited through a child's inability to wait their turn or their lack of ability to hold back comments while someone else is speaking.

Within the school environment, children or teens who suffer from ADHD and present symptoms of inattention may make careless mistakes on their classwork, have difficulty following through with instructions in reference to completing assignments, exhibit difficulty organizing tasks, and also often avoid tasks that require continuous mental effort such as homework. Hyperactivity may be presented by children within a school as fidgeting while seated, increased occurrences of asking to leave their seat, and excessive talking. Symptoms of impulsivity in reference to ADHD and the school environment are a child who is unable to wait for a question to be finished being asked before stating an answer aloud, interruption of peers within classroom discussions, and the inability for a student to wait their turn.

Behavior therapy has been used as a way for children to learn or strengthen positive behaviors they wish to practice while also eliminating the problem behaviors that have been occurring. This type of therapy is beneficial not only for the child who suffers from ADHD, but also their parents as it equips them with new skills and knowledge about the disorder that aids in their understanding of how to interact with the individual. Aside from therapy, medications may also be prescribed to those suffering from ADHD as well.

Conduct Disorder

"He stole things from his brother, he broke his father's tools, he didn't do his homework. In eighth grade, he refused to wear clean clothes for weeks, opting for the dirtiest, most ragged outfits he could find."

Conduct disorder is a behavioral and emotional disability present in many children across the globe. Those children who suffer from conduct disorder often have trouble following rules or showing empathy and do not respect the rights of others. They also have difficulty reading social cues. As a result of this struggle with social cues those with conduct disorder often misinterpret the words and actions of others and respond in a socially unacceptable manner; therefore, the situation results in conflict. This disorder, which is also present at home, will more likely cause impairment in a child's social and academic functioning[43] as the parents and family members have learned over the years how to negotiate social scenarios.

Researchers believe that conduct disorder is a result of both genetic and environmental factors.[44] In other words, although many children exhibit conduct disorder while young, there are other environmental variables that may aid in the development of conduct disorder throughout a child's life. Those environmental factors are brain damage, school failure, traumatic life experiences, and child abuse or neglect.[45]

Symptoms of conduct disorder are present in 6 to 16 percent of boys and 2 to 9 percent of girls; hence conduct disorder is one of the most diagnosed disorders by mental health professionals.[46] Signs of conduct disorder include aggressive behaviors toward people and animals and the destruction of property. Those who suffer from this disability may also be deceitful and lie or steal from others; therefore, these individuals also often do not follow the rules set forth by authority figures or society.

Within the school setting the symptoms of conduct disorder may be displayed by a child bullying another, a student who initiates physical fights, or by one not showing remorse after an aggressive episode. Students with this disorder may also destroy the property of their classmates, vandalize school property, or steal from others within this environment. A major indicator of conduct disorder for teens in the school setting is truancy, the act of not attending school without reason.[47]

If children with conduct disorder do not receive treatment early in their lives, it is likely they will continue to have ongoing problems into adulthood. One type of treatment for those with this disability is cognitive-behavioral therapy. Through this therapy children learn how to better communicate with others while also learning how to manage their anger and control their negative behaviors. In some cases, special education may be helpful in treating this disability. The majority of treatments for conduct disorder are not short term since it takes time to establish new attitudes and behaviors.

At the University of Alabama on February 12, 2010, a biology professor killed three other professors during a biology department meeting. After the shooting occurred, previous incidents of violence in which she had been involved were reevaluated. These incidents included the killing of her brother in 1986 (officially having been ruled as an accident) and a pipe-bomb incident that had occurred in 1993 toward her direct lab supervisor.

Many children who exhibit traits of conduct disorder suffer from mood disorders, anxiety, and thought disorders. In fact, conduct disorder is very likely to be comorbid with ODD and ADHD.[48]

Depression

"Sometimes, you don't feel like you deserve to be considered a person when you're dealing with stuff like this."

A common but serious mood disorder that affects many school-age children, teens, and college students is clinical depression (depression). As displayed in Table 5.3, depression is documented in various countries. Clinical depression affects the way one feels and thinks and has an impact on daily activities. Sleeping, eating, working, and social interactions are some of the many daily activities that may be affected when a person is suffering from this disorder. This mood disorder may take different forms in people and may arise as a result of multiple unique stimuli.[49]

Some of the more common forms of depression seen within the school environment are persistent depressive disorder, seasonal affective disorder, and bipolar disorder. Persistent depressive disorder is a depressed form in which one is stuck in for at least two years. Someone who suffers from persistent depressive disorder may have periods of extreme depression along with phases of less serious feelings. A major form of depression that students on college campuses are diagnosed with is seasonal affective disorder. Seasonal affective disorder begins at the onset of the winter months when there is less sunlight and fades away during the spring and summer. Symptoms of this form of depression are increased sleep in winter months, social withdrawal,

Table 5.3. Depression throughout Countries

Country	Percentage of Population with Depression
Australia	4.95%
Brazil	3.72%
Canada	4.00%
China	3.68%
Russia	4.06%
South Africa	4.16%
United Kingdom	4.30%
United States	5.17%

On February 14, 2008, a twenty-seven-year-old student opened fire into a crowd of students on the campus of Northern Illinois University. The result was five students killed. The perpetrator had been prescribed medications for anxiety and depression but had stopped taking the prescriptions about three weeks prior to the shooting.

and weight gain, which present year after year. Lastly, bipolar disorder is included within these depressive disorders in the form of bipolar depression. Although different from depression, bipolar disorder may be included as it results in periods of extreme low moods, which is where the bipolar depression is diagnosed, along with extreme highs.

Research suggests that depression is one of the most common mental disorders and may be caused by biological, environmental, and psychological factors. A key biological factor that plays a part in the likelihood of one having this disorder is family history of depression. In reference to environmental factors, major life changes, trauma, or stressful periods of time are considered variables that correlate with depression. For example, with children and adolescents, there are many changes taking place in their brain and body that affect the way they think and feel. Also, when one leaves home for the first time to attend a university, a student must learn to live independently, take challenging classes, and socialize with people they do not know all at once. All of these environmental factors may increase the likelihood that a student becomes depressed. Psychological factors that impact one's likelihood of becoming depressed are certain physical illnesses or even medications.[50]

Symptoms of depression may vary based upon the severity of each diagnoses. Common symptoms include episodes of extreme sadness, feelings of hopelessness, and high irritability. Feeling helpless and the loss of interest in hobbies are also key components reported when considering if a person may be suffering from depression. Depression may present at the same time as various other medical problems such as anxiety, substance abuse, or an eating disorder.

As displayed previously, depression is present in all populations. Within the school environment symptoms may present themselves as a student having decreased energy, moving more slowly than normal, or having trouble sitting still in their seat. Visible changes in one's weight, loss of appetite, and difficulty concentrating are also major signs one may be suffering from depression. One of the most extreme violent outcomes of this mental illness is suicide.

According to the National Association of School Psychologists, suicide is the second leading reason of death among school-age children.[51] Suicide

"As a ten-year-old with that kind of sadness, and desire to not be around, you're separate from society, even though you're in a class with twenty other kids, you're by yourself. The adults don't understand you, and the kids don't understand you."

is the act of inflicting violence on oneself with the intent to end one's life and dying because of this action, whereas a suicide attempt is when one harms oneself with the intent to end one's life but does not die because of this action.

One type of treatment for those suffering from depression is cognitive-behavioral therapy. Through this therapy children learn how to better understand their thoughts, behaviors, and feelings that result from their disability. For those who exhibit self-harming behaviors as a symptom of depression, dialectical behavior therapy may be especially beneficial. Dialectical behavior therapy focuses on regulating extreme emotions and decreasing the result those emotions have on the person's behaviors. By learning how to handle these emotions and becoming equipped with new skills that aid in this, those suffering from depression may notice a decrease in the severity of their symptoms. In reference to the college atmosphere in particular, the majority of university campuses provide mental health counseling services through their health centers for students who may be struggling with this disorder. Finally, as displayed in Table 5.4, aside from therapy, medications may also be prescribed to those suffering from depression as well.

Table 5.4.   Pre-Incident Suicide Warnings

Suicide Warning Signs	Suicide Resources
• Talking about wanting to die	National Suicide Prevention Lifeline
• Talking about feeling hopeless	1 800–273–TALK (8255)
• Stating they have no reason to live	https://suicidepreventionlifeline.org/
• Statements about feeling unbearable pain	
• Talking about being a burden to others	Crisis Text Line
• Reckless behavior	Text "HOME" to 741741
• Expressing feelings of others being better off without them	https://www.crisistextline.org/
• Social isolation	
• Increasing use of drugs and alcohol	
• Giving away possessions of importance	
• Irregular sleep patterns	

(National Association of School Psychologists, 2015)

Generalized Anxiety Disorder

"I had to give 'believable' reasons for my panic attacks because saying that your teachers scare you isn't a good enough excuse."

Although sporadic anxiety is a regular part of our lives as a result of changes in health, financial status, or relationships, people who feel particularly worried or nervous about these types of things, as well as other things, when there are little to or no reason at all to worry about them suffer from an illness called generalized anxiety disorder (GAD). Those who suffer from GAD find it difficult to stay focused on daily tasks as a result of their inability to calm their worried or nervous feelings.[52]

It is suggested that GAD is one of the most common mental disorders within the school environment and may be caused by biological, environmental, and psychological factors. GAD may be passed down from generation to generation, although researchers are unsure as to why some family members present symptoms of the disorder while others do not. As our society has learned more about the mind and body, researchers have also begun to explore the correlation between stress and environmental factors and one's likelihood of having GAD.[53] As diplayed in Table 5.5, anxiety is a global problem.

Like depression, symptoms of GAD may vary based upon the severity of each diagnoses. The majority of those who suffer from this disorder show symptoms of excessive worrying about everyday things, have trouble controlling their nervousness, and often have trouble relaxing. These individuals may also be easily startled or have trouble falling asleep and staying asleep. Physical indicators of GAD may be presented as sweating a lot or excessive trembling.

Table 5.5. **Anxiety throughout Countries**

Country	Percentage of Population with Anxiety
Australia	6.61%
Brazil	6.14%
Canada	5.55%
China	3.2%
Russia	2.97%
South Africa	3.82%
United Kingdom	5.01%
United States	6.08%

On December 14, 2012, the deadliest mass shooting at a K–12 school in US history occurred at Sandy Hook Elementary School in Newtown, Connecticut. The twenty-year-old perpetrator had been diagnosed with Asperger's syndrome and suffered from depression, anxiety, and obsessive-compulsive disorder as a teenager.

Within the school environment, children or teens who suffer from GAD may present as one who has a hard time concentrating, is seeming to be overly tired, or has excessive bathroom use. Children who suffer from this disorder within the K–12 school environment often worry about their performance in school or sports and will talk about tragedies that are unlikely to happen, such as wars or environmental disasters. In reference to college students, those with GAD usually display nervousness surrounding job security or performance upon graduation, health, being late, or finances. Those who suffer from extreme GAD may even exhibit physical symptoms that can decrease productivity within their daily life.

GAD is most commonly treated through cognitive-behavioral therapy. Through this therapy individuals learn how to better understand their emotions and are able to acquire skills that may aid in decreasing their excessive worrying habits. Medications may also be prescribed to those suffering from GAD as well.[54]

Antisocial Personality Disorder (ASPD)

"Even though I always had plenty of friends and was popular at school, inside I felt I didn't fit properly."

Although unable to be diagnosed before the age eighteen, antisocial personality disorder is a mental illness that may be seen among those within the college or university setting. It is diagnosed when a person has long-lasting patterns of disrespect for other people's rights. Those who suffer from this disorder often cross the line and violate others' rights while also feeling little or no empathy for others as a result of their actions. ASPD also may make one vulnerable to breaking laws as those with this disorder likely do not see a problem with violating the rules set forth by authority figures. ASPD is more prevalent in males than females and is seen at extremely high rates within prisons.[55]

Research shows that there ae both biological and environmental factors that may contribute to one's likelihood of being diagnosed with ASPD. A person's genes may contribute to developing this condition while having an antisocial or alcoholic parent may increase the likelihood as well. ASPD is a mental illness that will not be diagnosed in children under the age of eighteen because under that age one's brain and personality are still developing.[56]

Symptoms of ASPD may present as one being unable to conform to social norms, deceitful actions, lack of remorse, and reckless behavior. Those who suffer from this illness may also be impulsive or come off as excessively angry or irritable. These individuals may also have an extremely arrogant personality or may come off to others as highly opinionated. Serious symptoms of ASPD are the use of superficial charm and the use of technical jargon when discussing topics unfamiliar to others.[57]

Although unable to be diagnosed before age eighteen, signs of ASPD such as arson and animal cruelty within childhood are indicators that one may develop this mental illness. Arson is the deliberate setting of fire to property. Within the university setting symptoms of ASPD may present as a student who does not abide by school rules or excessive warnings from campus safety or deans on a campus. Physical fights and reckless behaviors are also examples of signs one may be suffering from ASPD on a college campus. Students who suffer from this mental illness may also fail to complete assignments or attend scheduled events.

This disorder is considered one of the hardest to treat as the majority of those who suffer from this mental illness will not seek treatment on their own. Behavioral treatments that focus on rewarding positive behaviors may work for some people who suffer from ASPD, but those who have ASPD usually have other disorders that should be treated as well.

Internet Addiction Disorder

A more recent explanation for violence in the school setting is internet addiction disorder. Internet addiction disorder (hereafter IAD) or problematic internet use is a result of extensive internet use to the point that it interferes with daily life. As adolescents and young adults are the most active age groups utilizing the internet, they are the cohort most likely to suffer from IAD. These individuals are also the age cohort less likely to identify illegal activities that occur on the internet[58] and more likely to play violent online games.

A research project on high schools in China suggested that individuals with IAD were more than two times more likely to develop depression than teens without IAD.[59] In addition, teens who spend hours each day with instant messaging, downloading music, updating Facebook pages, and visiting gaming cites often fail to create actual social relationships, experience declines in school performance, and suffer in relationships with their families.[60]

In terms of physical problems, individuals with IAD often suffer from a weak immune system due to a lack of sleep, a lack of exercise, and little or no fresh air or sunshine exposure. Other physical symptoms of IAD include eye strain, wrist strain, neck and shoulder pain, migraines, and the potential for carpal tunnel syndrome. In addition, the overuse of the internet often leads to neglected personal hygiene and the choices of unhealthy foods that may be easily eaten while playing games in the virtual world. Finally, neurological research suggests that long hours of video gaming as often occurs with IAD changes not only how the brain performs but also the brain's structure, including sustained attention levels.[61]

Whereas there is no direct correlation between IAD and school violence, symptoms of withdrawal include anger, depression, and agitation.[62] In addition, when individuals spend excessive amounts of time in virtual worlds, which often occurs with online gaming, the line between reality and virtual reality may become blurred.[63] Therefore, students who see themselves as excellent marksmen in a virtual reality may assume themselves true marksmen in true reality.

TEEN CONSEQUENCES

Three of the more common outcomes of mental health problems or mental illness in teens are consequences of eating disorders. Those consequences include anorexia, bulimia, and binge eating.

Anorexia Nervosa

"Too many things were out of control, so I thought, I can control my eating."

As the most frequent diagnoses during the adolescent years, anorexia nervosa is becoming more frequently prevalent in children and older adults as well. Anorexia nervosa (anorexia) is an eating disorder that is "characterized by weight loss (or lack of appropriate weight gain in growing children); difficulties maintaining an appropriate body weight for height, age, and stature; and, in many individuals, distorted body image."[64] According to research published in 2016, young people between the ages of fifteen and twenty-four who are diagnosed with anorexia have a ten times increased risk of dying compared to their peers.[65] More specifically, between 1 to 2 percent of the female population will develop anorexia during adolescence, with males representing 25 percent of those diagnosed.[66] In addition, males are also considered to be at an increased risk to die because of anorexia as a result of often not being diagnosed early enough since many people do not assume men would suffer from an eating disorder.[67]

The two most common features that society thinks about when they hear about this illness are that those with the illness are likely to limit the number of calories they ingest or the types of food they eat, and that these individuals will also exercise on impulse. Although these are common thoughts we have when hearing about this disorder and we usually picture these individuals as extremely thin, studies have found that heavier individuals may also suffer from anorexia. In fact, heavier individuals who suffer from anorexia are less likely to be diagnosed as a result of the generalized stereotype connected to this disorder.[68]

There are many emotional and behavioral warning signs of anorexia, a major one being extreme weight loss, but many other symptoms of anorexia may also be helpful to look out for. For example, obsession with weight or certain foods, denial of feeling hungry, comments after eating concerning the need to go work off the calories that were just ingested, and the inability to maintain a healthy weight for their age, height, and build are other common warning signs of a person who may be suffering from anorexia. Emotional and behavioral signs that may indicate anorexia are an individual expressing an extreme fear of gaining weight and also an individual holding a worrisome viewpoint on self-evaluation or hazardous amounts of denial about their low body weight. There are also many physical indicators that may be exhibited by one who is suffering from anorexia. Feeling cold a lot, sleeping difficulties, thinning of hair, and muscle weakness are some of the most common physical warning signs of this illness. In girls who have begun their menstrual cycle, irregularities in their period are also a likely physical indicator of anorexia.[69]

In reference to the school setting, those suffering from anorexia may show emotional and behavioral indicators including dressing in layers in an effort to stay warm or hide weight loss from others, recurrent expression of thought pertaining to believing they are overweight, and seeming to be anxious about eating in public. Those with anorexia may also make excuses not to eat during scheduled mealtimes while also exhibiting strict thinking on the need for control. Within the school environment it is likely that physical warning signs of anorexia will be exhibited through difficulty concentrating, dizziness, or fainting.

As a result of the constant lack of eating and self-starvation, individuals with anorexia are unable to provide their body nutrients that are essential to normal functioning. The consequence of the lack of nutrition forces the body to slow down all of its functions in an effort to preserve energy. In turn, serious medical consequences can arise, and even death in the most severe cases.

Bulimia Nervosa

"You see, bulimia became a sort of coping mechanism for me. It ended up not being so much about food as it did about control. I was dealing with a lot of stress later on in high school. I had started touring colleges, I was taking the SATs, and I had a boyfriend who cheated on me. There were lots of things in my life that I just wasn't able to manage. I'd binge and get a rush from eating so much food. Then I'd get an even bigger, better rush after getting rid of it all."

Similar to anorexia nervosa, bulimia nervosa is a severe, potentially lethal eating disorder. According to the National Eating Disorders Association, bulimia nervosa (bulimia) is "a cycle of binging and compensatory behaviors such as self-induced vomiting designed to undo or compensate for the effects of binge eating." In general, those who are diagnosed with bulimia exhibit these behaviors, on average, at least once a week for three months. These individuals often exhibit behaviors and attitudes indicating that weight loss and food control are a main focus and concern of theirs. Evidence of binge eating and purging behaviors are also evident.[70] It is estimated that between 1 to 5 percent of females will become bulimic within their lifetime.[71]

Binge eating behaviors may be indicated by the disappearance of large amounts of food or many food containers becoming completely empty within a short period of time. Evidence of purging may be exhibited by repeated trips to the bathroom after food consumption, smells of vomit, or the presence of laxatives or diuretics.[72] Aside from the common binge eating and purging behaviors previously discussed, emotional and behavioral warning signs of bulimia include disappearance after eating and hoarding food.

Physical indicators may be present in a student suffering from bulimia that can be identified by a school staff member or another student. For example, noticeable variations in weight both low and high are one of the most common indicators of bulimia that may be observed within the school environment. Individuals may also suffer from visible swelling around the salivary gland, slow healing of wounds, and a weakened immune system. Bulimics may also have tooth discoloration and cuts or calluses across the tops of their finger joints as a result of their recurrent, prompted vomiting.[73]

The persistent binge-and-purge cycle of bulimia can have lasting impacts on the entire digestive system. This cycle may also lead to electrolyte and chemical imbalances throughout the body that can end up affecting the heart and other major organ-functioning processes. Many of those who suffer from bulimia may also struggle with other co-occurring conditions. A co-occurring condition is a condition or disability that occurs simultaneously with another condition or disorder. Common co-occurring conditions with bulimia are self-harm, substance abuse, diabulimia (intentional misuse of insulin for type 1 diabetes), and impulsivity.

Binge Eating Disorder

"I felt like I can't tell anyone I suffer from depression, anxiety, and an eating disorder because everyone automatically start[s] assuming I'm lying and over-reacting about my situation."

(MakeItOK.org)

Although one of the newest eating disorders to be recognized by the DSM-5, according to the National Eating Disorders Association, binge eating disorder is considered to be the most common eating disorder within the United States. Binge eating disorder (BED) is characterized by recurrent episodes of eating large quantities of food (often very quickly and to the point of discomfort); a feeling of a loss of control during the binge; experiencing shame, distress, or guilt afterwards; and not regularly using unhealthy compensatory measures (e.g., purging) to counter the binge eating.[74] Although similar to that of bulimia nervosa, the key component differentiating BED from bulimia is the absence of unhealthy compensatory actions taken after the food binge.[75] It is suggested that between 0.2 percent and 3.5 percent of females and between 0.9 percent and 2.0 percent of males will develop BED within their lifetime with "subthreshold" BED occurring in 1.6 percent of adolescent females.[76]

BED has many similar emotional and behavioral indicators as bulimia, such as a fear of eating in public, low self-esteem, and feeling guilty after eating, but it also has characteristics that make it distinguishable from the other. For example, an individual suffering from BED is likely to create schedules in an effort to make time for their binge eating, as well as constantly checking the mirror for flaws in their appearance.[77]

Within the school setting one may be able to identify an individual with BED if the person begins to withdraw from their usual friends and activities, or they begin to eat alone because they are embarrassed about the amount of food they will be ingesting. Difficulties when trying to concentrate and complaints about stomach discomfort are also common symptoms of this disorder. Also, as with bulimia, students with BED are likely to experience intense fluctuations in their weight, both up and down, and also exhibit an intense concern with their body shape and weight.

BED can be diagnosed in any person with any weight, although it's most commonly associated with those who suffer from clinical obesity. In fact, of individuals who have been diagnosed with BED, up to two-thirds are labeled clinically obese.[78]

ADDRESSING MENTAL ILLNESS WITHIN
THE SCHOOL ENVIRONMENT

Individuals with dangerous pasts, criminal records, and a history of drug abuse are more likely to commit more violent crimes.[79] When an incident of school violence is perpetrated by a student who has been diagnosed with a mental illness, the question concerning why school personnel are not informed of such information often arises. In reference to the campus or school setting, unless a student makes a threat toward themselves or another person, information is not allowed to be shared. Privacy laws restrict the information that can be shared about a student, including their mental health history, in an effort to make sure those within the environment are not bias toward each other.

The conversation surrounding mental illness in relation to school violence was brought to the public eye after the April 1999 massacre at Columbine High School in Colorado. Once this horrific incident had occurred, people from all educational disciplines began dissecting the case and examining the differing variables within these children's lives that could have influenced their likelihood of becoming violent.

Mental health problems may be influenced by biological factors, life ex perIences, and family histories of mental health problems, which can affect our overall thinking, mood, and behavior. It is suggested that having positive mental health allows for people to appreciate and strive to reach their full potential, cope with the stresses of life in a healthy way, work more efficiently, and make significant contributions to their communities overall.[80] Unfortunately, just as with the case of Adam Lanza, the twenty-year-old shooter at Sandy Hook Elementary School (Connecticut—USA), who mental health professionals concluded was not a risk to himself or others, mental illness is not always recognizable. This shooting, in 2012, resulted in the deaths of twenty-six students and teachers.[81]

CHAPTER QUESTIONS

1. What are some of the most common warning signs that a student may be suffering from a mental illness?
2. What percent of the global population suffers from bipolar disorder?
3. What are the three subtypes of ADHD?
4. What are five suicide warning signs?
5. What are the three most common outcomes of teens who suffer from mental illnesses?

DISCUSSION QUESTIONS

1. Do you believe the rate of mental illness across the globe is on the rise? Explain.
2. Why do you think eating disorders are common among teens? Explain your opinion.
3. Do you think that lifting mental health restrictions such as not allowing teachers to know specific conditions students suffer from could aid in the prevention of school violence? Why or why not?

NOTES

1. Kimberly McCabe and Gregory Martin, *School Violence, the Media and Criminal Justice Responses* (New York: Peter Lang, 2005).

2. Cynthia Crosson-Tower, *Understanding Child Abuse and Neglect*, eighth edition (Boston: Allyn and Bacon, 2010).

3. David Finkelhor, "The International Epidemiology of Child Sexual Abuse," *Child Abuse and Neglect*, 18(5) (1994): 409–17.

4. Kimberly McCabe and Olivia Johnston, "Perceptions on the Legality of Sexting: A Report," *Social Science Computer Review*, 32(6) (2014): 765–68.

5. Kimberly McCabe and Gregory Martin, *School Violence, the Media and Criminal Justice Responses*.

6. Kimberly McCabe, *Protecting Your Children in Cyberspace: What Parents Need to Know* (Lanham, MD: Rowman and Littlefield Publishers, Inc., 2017).

7. US Department of Health and Human Services, "What Is Mental Health?, 2017," MentalHealth.gov., accessed on January 31, 2019, at https://www.mental health.gov/basics/what-is-mental-health.

8. US Department of Health and Human Services, "Adolescent and School Health: Protective Factors, 2017," Centers for Disease Control and Prevention, accessed on January 22, 2019, at https://www.cdc.gov/healthyyouth/protective/index.htm.

9. US Department of Health and Human Services, "What Is Mental Health?, 2017."

10. Bureau of Justice Statistics, *Violence in the Workplace, 1993–1999*, NCJ 190076, December 2001.

11. Bureau of Justice Statistics, *Violent Victimization of College Students, 1995–2000*, NCJ 196143, December 2003.

12. US Department of Health and Human Services, "What Is Mental Health?, 2017."

13. US National Library of Medicine, "Mental Disorders," National Institutes of Health, accessed on January 31, 2019, at https://medlineplus.gov/mentaldisorders.html.

14. US National Library of Medicine, "Mental Disorders."

15. US National Library of Medicine, "Mental Disorders."

16. Michael Shear and Michael Schmidt, "Gunman and 12 Victims Killed at DC Navy Yard," *New York Times*, September 17, 2013, accessed on November 7, 2018, at https://www.nytimes.com/2013/09/17/us/shooting-reported-at-washington-navy-yard.html.

17. World Health Organization, "Risk Factors," World Health Organization, accessed on January 31, 2019, at https://www.who.int/topics/risk_factors/en/.

18. World Health Organization, "Risk Factors."

19. Andrew Brill, "Life with Antisocial Personality Disorder (ASPD)," June 16, 2017, accessed on December 3, 2018, at https://www.mind.org.uk/information-support/your-stories/life-with-antisocial-personality-disorder-aspd/#.XFyN4FVKgdV.

20. Briony Harris, "Half of All Mental Illness Began by the Age of 14," *World Economic Forum*, October 10, 2018, accessed on November 7, 2018, at https://www.weforum.org/agenda/2018/10/half-of-all-mental-illness-begins-by-the-age-of-14/.

21. American Psychiatric Association, "DSM-5: Frequently Asked Questions," American Psychiatric Association, 2018, accessed on January 16, 2019, at https://www.psychiatry.org/psychiatrists/practice/dsm/feedback-and-questions/frequently-asked-questions.

22. American Psychiatric Association, "DSM-5: Frequently Asked Questions."

23. American Psychiatric Association, "DSM-5: Frequently Asked Questions."

24. National Eating Disorders Association, "Anorexia Nervosa," National Eating Disorders Association, 2014, accessed January 31, 2019, at https://www.nationaleatingdisorders.org/learn/by-eating-disorder/anorexia.

25. US Department of Health and Human Services, "Adolescent and School Health: Protective Factors, 2017," Centers for Disease Control and Prevention, accessed on January 22, 2019, at https://www.cdc.gov/healthyyouth/protective/index.htm.

26. Shekhar Saxena, Eva Jane-Llopis, and Clemens Hosman, "Prevention of Mental and Behavioural Disorders: Implications for Policy and Practice," *World Psychiatry*, 5(1) (2006): 5–14.

27. Kimberly McCabe and Gregory Martin, *School Violence, the Media and Criminal Justice Responses*.

28. Kimberly McCabe and Daniel Murphy, *Child Abuse—Today's Issues* (New York: Taylor and Francis Publishing, 2016).

29. National Institute of Mental Health (NIMH), "Generalized Anxiety Disorder: When Worry Gets Out of Control," National Institutes of Health (NIH), accessed January 16, 2019, at https://www.nimh.nih.gov/health/publications/generalized-anxiety -disorder-gad/index.shtml.

30. American Academy of Child and Adolescent Psychiatry, "Oppositional Defiant Disorder," July 2013, accessed January 16, 2019, at https://www.aacap.org/ aacap/families_and_youth/facts_for_families/fff-guide/Children-With-Oppositional -Defiant-Disorder-072.aspx.

31. American Academy of Child and Adolescent Psychiatry, "Oppositional Defiant Disorder."

32. American Academy of Child and Adolescent Psychiatry, "Oppositional Defiant Disorder."

33. American Academy of Child and Adolescent Psychiatry, "Oppositional Defiant Disorder."

34. Johns Hopkins Medicine, "Health Library: Oppositional Defiant Disorder (ODD) in Children, 2018," accessed January 16, 2019, at https://www.hopkins medicine.org/healthlibrary/conditions/mental_health_disorders/oppositional_defiant _disorder_90,p02573.

35. American Academy of Child and Adolescent Psychiatry, "Oppositional Defiant Disorder."

36. Johns Hopkins Medicine, "Health Library: Oppositional Defiant Disorder (ODD) in Children, 2018."

37. Johns Hopkins Medicine, "Health Library: Oppositional Defiant Disorder (ODD) in Children, 2018."

38. Johns Hopkins Medicine, "Health Library: Oppositional Defiant Disorder (ODD) in Children, 2018."

39. Johns Hopkins Medicine, "Health Library: Oppositional Defiant Disorder (ODD) in Children, 2018."

40. *Merriam-Webster Medical Dictionary* (Springfield, MA: G and C Merriam Co., 2016).

41. American Psychiatric Association, "DSM-5: Frequently Asked Questions."

42. Kimberly McCabe and Gregory Martin, *School Violence, the Media and Criminal Justice Responses.*

43. American Academy of Child and Adolescent Psychiatry, "Oppositional Defiant Disorder."

44. American Academy of Child and Adolescent Psychiatry, "Oppositional Defiant Disorder."

45. American Academy of Child and Adolescent Psychiatry, "Oppositional Defiant Disorder."

46. American Psychiatric Association, "DSM-5: Frequently Asked Questions."

47. American Academy of Child and Adolescent Psychiatry, "Oppositional Defiant Disorder."

48. American Academy of Child and Adolescent Psychiatry, "Oppositional Defiant Disorder."

49. US Department of Health and Human Services, "What Is Mental Health?, 2017."

50. US Department of Health and Human Services, "What is Mental Health?, 2017."

51. US Department of Health and Human Services, "What is Mental Health?, 2017."

52. US Department of Health and Human Services, "What is Mental Health?, 2017."

53. US Department of Health and Human Services, "What is Mental Health?, 2017."

54. US Department of Health and Human Services, "What is Mental Health?, 2017."

55. American Psychiatric Association, *Diagnostic and Statistical Manual of Mental Disorders*, fourth edition (Arlington, VA: American Psychiatric Publishing, 1994).

56. American Psychiatric Association, *Diagnostic and Statistical Manual of Mental Disorders*, fourth edition.

57. American Psychiatric Association, *Diagnostic and Statistical Manual of Mental Disorders*, fourth edition.

58. Kimberly McCabe and Olivia Johnston, "Perceptions on the Legality of Sexting: A Report."

59. Lawrence Lam and Zi-Wen Peng, "Effects of Pathological Use of the Internet in Adolescent Mental Health," *Archives of Pediatric and Adolescence Medicine*, 164(10) (2010): 901–6.

60. Stephanie Newman, "Teens and the Internet. How Much Is Too Much?" *Psychology Today*, April 6, 2010, accessed on November 7, 2018, at https://www.psychologytoday.com/us/blog/stepmonster/201004/teens-and-the-internet-how-much-is-too-much.

61. Hannah Nichols, "How Video Games Affect the Brain," Medical News Today, July 10, 2017, accessed on November 7, 2018, at https://www.medicalnewstoday.com/articles/318345.php.

62. Stephanie Newman, "Teens and the Internet. How Much Is Too Much?"

63. Adam Gazzaley and Larry Rosen, *The Distracted Mind* (Cambridge, MA: MIT Press, 2016).

64. National Eating Disorders Association, "Binge Eating Disorder." http://www.nationaleatingdisorders.org/learn/by-eating-disorder/bed.

65. Manford Fichter and Norbert Quadflieg, "Mortality in Eating Disorders—Results of a Large Prospective Clinical Longitudinal Study," *International Journal of Eating Disorders*, accessed on January 3, 2019, at https://www.ncbi.nlm.nih.gov/pubmed/26767344.

66. Eric Stice and Cara Bohon, "Eating Disorders." In Theodore P. Beauchaine and Stephen P. Hinshaw (eds.), *Child and Adolescent Psychopathology*, second edition (New York: Wiley, 2012).

67. Jonathan Mond, Deborah Mitchison, and Phillipa Hay, "Prevalence and Implications of Eating Disordered Behavior in Men." In L. Cohn and R. Lembergs, *Current Findings on Males with Eating Disorders* (Philadelphia: Routledge, 2014).

68. National Eating Disorders Association, 2014, "Anorexia Nervosa," National Eating Disorders Association, accessed January 31, 2019, at https://www.national eatingdisorders.org/learn/by-eating-disorder/anorexia.

69. National Eating Disorders Association, "Anorexia Nervosa."

70. National Eating Disorders Association, "Bulimia Nervosa." http://www.national eatingdisorders.org/learn/by-eating-disorder/bulimia.

71. Eric Stice and Cara Bohon, Eating Disorders. *In Child and Adolescent Psychopathology, second edition.*

72. National Eating Disorders Association, "Bulimia Nervosa."

73. National Eating Disorders Association, "Bulimia Nervosa."

74. National Eating Disorders Association, "Binge Eating Disorder."

75. National Eating Disorders Association, "Binge Eating Disorder."

76. Eric Stice and Cara Bohon, Eating Disorders. *In Child and Adolescent Psychopathology,* second edition.

77. National Eating Disorders Association, "Binge Eating Disorder."

78. National Eating Disorders Association, "Binge Eating Disorder."

79. Carolyn Wolf and Jamie Rosen, "Miss the Mark: Gun Control Is Not the Cure for What Ails the US Mental Health System," *Journal of Criminal Law and Criminology*, 104(4) (2015): 851–78.

80. US Department of Health and Human Services, "What Is Mental Health?, 2017."

81. James Barron, "Nation Reels after Gunman Massacres 20 Children at School in Connecticut," 2012, accessed on November 3, 2019, at https://www.nytimes.com/2012/12/15/nyregion/shooting-reported-at-connecticut-elementary-school.html.

Chapter Six

Warning Factors and Teachers' Perceptions

KEY WORDS

conditional threat	inferred threat	risk factor
direct threat	preventive actions	third-party threat

KEY ACRONYMS

(IACP) International Association of Chiefs of Police

When a school shooting occurs, the reactions from the public, students, and school officials are usually surprise and shock that an event such as this could happen in their community.[1] In addition, there will be many individuals who proclaim that there were no warning signs and that the perpetrator just "snapped" when, in fact, there were probably many signs or clues to the violent destruction that were in place long before the event occurred.[2] Researchers suggest that the perpetrators of the majority of the incidents of severe school violence, such as a school shooting, spend at least a week planning the event and nearly a week preparing for the event (i.e., purchasing guns, ammunition) prior to the actual incident of destruction.[3] Unfortunately, these warning signs are often overlooked or ignored.

In the case of the professor at the University of Alabama, there were certainly indicators for potential violence. In particular, she had a history of anger in reaction to life's disappointments and a history of involvement in

On February 12, 2010, professor Amy Bishop shot and killed three professors during a department meeting at the University of Alabama in Huntsville
(USA). Dr. Bishop had been denied tenure, and this was her last semester of
teaching at the university. After the shooting, her previous incidents of violence were reevaluated. These incidents included reactions of anger to disap-
pointment, the killing of her brother in 1986 (officially having been ruled as
an accident), and a pipe-bomb incident that had occurred in 1993 involving
her immediate lab supervisor.

incidents of severe violence, so her school shooting, although not expected,
should not have been seen as a complete surprise.

In many cases, after victims or observers of a tragic event such as a school
shooting have had time to reflect upon the experience, they will acknowledge
that there were warning signs and/or pre-incident indicators to the shooting.[4]
On average, perpetrators of severe school violence encounter three to four
stressful events in their lives prior to the incident.[5] For clarity in this chapter,
warning factors are defined as general characteristics that exist prior to an incident of school violence, and pre-incident indicators are those specific events
that occurred prior to a particular incident of violence within the school setting.
This chapter will discuss severe school violence or school shootings in terms of
warning factors and teachers' perceptions as well as the roles of a teacher after
a crisis. In addition, this chapter will discuss other categories of school violence
as related to teachers' perspectives and teachers' abilities to intervene.

POTENTIAL SOURCES OF VIOLENCE

In any physical setting there is the potential for tragedy. In the ocean there
is the potential for drowning as well as the potential for an attack by various
marine animals. On the freeway, there is the potential for two vehicles to
collide as well as the potential for a single driver to lose control of his or her
vehicle and crash. On a farm, there is the potential for injuries or death by the
improper use of farm equipment as well as an injury from many of the farm
animals. In the educational setting, although many schools have initiated preventive measures and purchased surveillance equipment in order to address
school security, there is still the potential for victimization and a tragedy such
as a school shooting.

In the school environment, the potential sources for violence are strangers,
employees, and students. As discussed later in the book in the chapter on

adult offenders, strangers or those without social ties to the school are generally adults with the motives of notoriety or revenge or who are on a mission to send a message. In these cases, it is essential that they are not allowed access to the school.

Entry into the School

Research suggests that mass murders, and especially those mass murders executed by teens, occur at locations familiar to the teen.[6] In addition, for many students within the school setting who have contemplated such an event, the notion of a copycat is significant in providing them ideas and plans to execute a mass murder.[7] However, as discussed in this book, some perpetrators of a school shooting are adults without any connection to the school but with simply the motive of rage, power, or revenge. Therefore, one of the first strategies in reducing incidents of school violence is the restriction of entry into the school. The logic, of course, is that without entry of the violent perpetrator into a school, then the risk of violence is eliminated. In the majority of the adult-perpetrated cases of school shootings, a restricted entry would have reduced the severity of many incidents.[8]

In October of 2016, in California, four males waited in a parking lot across from a high school and began shooting students as they exited the school. Although there were no fatalities, many students were injured.

As demonstrated in the provided case example, the perpetrators of that particular incident were not inside the school. Hence, restricting entry into the school would not have eliminated the tragic event, although it may have reduced the severity of the perpetrators' intent to kill and injure.

Strangers

Many strangers perceive a school as a desirable location for violence often due to its proximity to the central components of a community. The restriction of access to a school environment is dependent upon the cooperation of students, parents, school staff, law enforcement, and the community. Some identified measures of restricting access to schools include security measures that lock buildings, limit access to visitors, and restrict movements of students or groups of people within the school environment. Ideally, access-controlling systems should be in place to prohibit a stranger from entering the school building.[9] If security systems are installed that limit access to the school and areas within the school, then the potential stranger with an intent to do harm to the students is limited within the campus setting. If research is correct and strangers select a school because it is perceived as less protected, then a strongly protected entry into the school may reduce the likelihood of the selection of an institution of learning as the location for mass destruction.

School officials should require that all individuals entering a school are identified and, if strangers are allowed access, their purpose is reasonable and their movements monitored. School systems with questions or concerns about policies to restrict the entry of individuals should seek the assistance of their local law enforcement agency as most law enforcement agencies have, in effect, policies related to building access and safety.[10] These police policies, based upon training and experience, will provide school officials the information they need to devise a well-developed protection plan. But, for policies and practices regarding entry into a school setting to be enforced, support is required from everyone within the school setting and within the community.

Employees

As discussed later in this book, adult employees within the school are potential perpetrators of school violence. Teachers, of course, are the largest population of employees within the school. The majority of teachers are dedicated educators with a love of teaching and a love of learning. However, just as some individuals become hostile in the workplace, there exist teachers who have been perpetrators of severe cases of school violence.

In March of 2012, in Florida, a former Spanish teacher brought an AK-47 assault-style rifle into the school and shot and killed the head of the school before killing himself. This teacher had been fired earlier in the day.

The Florida case example provided demonstrates the potential for teachers to be perpetrators of school shootings. In addition, assaults by teachers and other staff may include physical violence, sexual violence, and emotional abuse.[11] Teachers are not only the majority of the staff, but they are also often the first adults to hear from students about any unusual activities or victimizations within the school environment.[12] So teachers may not only be a resource to students but also a resource to other teachers and staff. Through education and training, teachers are taught to identify signs of potential violence.[13] The world of education today, with its emphasis on standards of learning, policies regarding student engagement, and online distractions, is stressful; therefore, it is reasonable to expect that some of these stressed individuals react with violence. Teachers who are provided support are less likely to become frustrated.[14] In many cases, this support may come from other teachers. Teachers who are trained on how to work with problem children may also apply that training to their coworkers. Weekly team meetings to discuss problems and concerns allow teachers to develop strategies for handling their many challenging situations.[15]

In addition, and discussed in this book as related to child victimization, teachers and staff may themselves be the perpetrators of violence against children. These criminal actions include sex, corporal punishment, stalking, cyberstalking, and sexting. Teachers and staff who engage in such activities with students must be removed from the school setting as one case of less severe violence may lead to more severe cases of violence.[16]

Across the globe, those individuals who are employed or volunteer in schools are required to undergo the collection of their social and legal history (i.e., a background check) prior to the beginning of their relationship with the school. These background checks will reveal histories of sexual abuse, domestic violence, and, in some cases, financial problems. For some schools, any indication of a problem on a background check is the rationale for not offering that person employment. Even in cases where only a history of financial problems exists, and not problems of violence, employees may be tempted to profit through the abuse of their students in terms of payments for grades, the production and distribution of child pornography, or extortion.[17] Unfortunately, in most cases background checks are used as only a condition of employment;[18] if a teacher or staff person is arrested for crimes of drugs or violence and the school is not informed, they may continue teaching or working within the school without any repercussions. In the United States, with easy access to handguns for adults, an incident of violence is a possibility.[19]

Just as teachers are in a position within the school to identify problems with students, they are also often in the position to identify problems with their coworkers. A teacher, although not formally responsible for providing support to peers, is often the person to provide informal support to coworkers. So a teacher is one of the people within a school best able to identify the propensity for school violence within peers.

Students

Research suggests that, in most cases, students involved as perpetrators of a school shooting will have a specific target in mind.[20] Since the beginning of the public's awareness of school shootings, researchers have suggested that teachers are critical in the prevention of any form of school violence. Students depend upon their schools and their teachers for their educational and social needs, and in today's world, school staff are placed in the position of providing emotional support to their students. Unfortunately, today's teachers can no longer be focused solely on the education of children[21] as teachers and other school officials must also address the educational, emotional, and social needs of their students. In some cases, with the initiative taken by counselors, students and teachers in the United States are participating in weekly group discussions on subjects of concern for the students such as bullying, abuse, and sexting.[22] In many cases, students attain the skills needed for expressing their emotions positively and successfully solving conflicts among their peers within these group learning sessions.[23]

Countries such as Belgium, Finland, France, Germany, Ireland, Luxembourg, Sweden, and the United Kingdom have legal requirements to prevent violence on the school premises.[24] In many cases, often these requirements are accompanied by whole-school approaches, which provide frameworks and assign responsibilities, to include those responsibilities given to teachers. Through these teacher-to-student sessions, students not only observe appropriate behaviors by their teachers in addressing conflict, they also learn the skills of communication and critical thinking, which helps them navigate the difficulties of the teen and young adult worlds. Some approaches involve well-developed programs that include curriculum and assignments[25] as well as individual initiatives with at-risk students.[26] For example, the Olweus Bullying Prevention Program (discussed in chapter 2) is used throughout Norway and has also been implemented in Austria, Finland, and Germany. Other preventive actions that are led by teachers focus on areas such as social competency, peer mediation, and problem solving as well as discovering ways to increase self-esteem in students.[27] In addition to these teacher-supported group-based efforts, teachers are also often in the best positions within the school setting to identify and address individual behaviors that may be related to an incident of school violence.

Teachers, who are in daily contact with schoolchildren, are the best in dividuals to identify signs of abuse in their students. This is critical in attempting to address violence in the school setting as students with a history of abuse may choose to react to that abuse through violence directed either internally or at others.[28] In cases of physical abuse, bruises on children are instant indicators. Although physical abuse within the home decreases with the age of the child,[29] students are often victims of peer violence and dating violence.[30] A teacher, once recognizing physical symptoms, is in the positon to facilitate help for the student. However, in some cases of physical abuse, especially in cases of child self-harm, the physical injuries go undetected.[31] In those undetected scenarios, the behavioral indicators that are often observed by teachers are the most visible clues of abuse.

Research suggests that there exist certain common behaviors that are seen more often in teens who are being physically abused. Those behaviors include (but are not limited to) tendencies toward aggressiveness with others or directed at themselves, withdrawn personalities, poor social relations with peers and adults, and difficulties in academic learning.[32] In addition, aggressive behaviors such as cruelty toward others, vandalism of property, and stealing may all be observed within the school setting. Actions included under the label of cruelty toward others include pushing, shoving, and hitting, and behaviors such as biting. In many cases, children who are physically abused or dominated believe that they are defenseless against their abuser and feel the need to dominate others outside of their home.[33] Thus victims of child physical abuse may also be perpetrators of child abuse against their peers. Teachers involved in prevention efforts to reduce school violence will often be aware of such actions as related to child abuse.

Teachers may also be in the best positions within a school to identify students who are victims of sexual abuse at home or within the school setting. Unfortunately, in most cases of child sexual abuse there are no physical indicators.[34] Therefore, once again, teachers may observe behavior indicative of sexual abuse. In young children, a child who is sexually abused will often appear depressed, avoid others, become quick to anger, or display a change in appearance and may have trouble sitting (because of physical pain) in the classroom.[35] For adolescent and teen victims of sexual abuse, they may experience academic problems at school, start missing school, begin using sexual language, provide descriptions of sexual acts in conversations, or begin to physically, sexually, or emotionally abuse other students.[36] Some victims of sexual abuse demonstrate an overwhelming fear of everyday activities or an overestimation of world dangers and begin using drugs, run away from home or school, or attempt suicide. Research suggests that many perpetrators of school violence have a history of victimization,[37] and teachers are one of the best sources of help for the victim.

In many cases, a teacher will spend more time with a student than the parent of the child. As the first step in deterring any sort of negative action is identifying the behaviors prior to the action; a teacher, once again, occupies the most significant of those positions filled by adults within the school environment. For many individuals, including teens, perception is reality and, oftentimes, with students, what they view in cyberspace or read on Facebook or Instagram may be perceived as reality. As a five-second clip on YouTube or a picture on Snapchat represents the real world for many students, teachers today must also be aware of the influences of technology on the actions of their students. In addressing the issues of hate and violence with students, teachers will understand that teens will demonstrate a desire to express their ideas and opinions.

In these cases, a teacher may serve as the student's sounding board for questions and thoughts that they may choose not to discuss with their parents. In some cases, the ideas of students may not mirror those of their parents or their questions may cause them embarrassment in discussions with their parents;[38] hence, the teacher is often the adult of choice for a student. Therefore, teachers should be aware of the behavioral indicators of abuse demonstrated by their students as often students who are victim of abuse continue to be victims of abuse or become perpetrators of incidents of severe violence.

IDENTIFYING WARNING SIGNS
OF POTENTIAL VIOLENCE

- History of violent behavior
- Inability to control or manage emotions such as anger
- Befriends others who exhibit problem behaviors
- Utilizes profane or abusive language
- Has brought a weapon to school, or has threatened to
- Makes violent comments when angry
- Excessive use of substances such as drugs or alcohol
- High rates of truancy or expulsion from school
- Expresses a fascination with weapons or violence
- Has a limited number of friends, despite having lived in the area for an extended period of time
- Decreased interest in academics and school activities
- Experience of trauma or loss in home life or within community
- Shows little empathy toward others
- Frightens others
- Has been a victim of intimidation by others
- Blames others for problems within their own life and seems to be resentful
- Expresses a fascination in TV shows, movies, games, books, or music that contains violence or violent/abusive messages
- Communicates angry or violent thoughts and messages through writing assignments
- Exhibits extreme mood swings or extreme sadness spells
- Becomes withdrawn from social interaction
- Voices opinions about sadistic, violent, or prejudicial/intolerant attitudes they may possess
- Has attempted, or threatened to attempt, to commit suicide

As released by the International Association of Chiefs of Police (IACP) (1999), the box on the previous page lists some of the behavioral indicators that teachers may observe when working with abused students. These warning signs are either part of the student's background or displayed by the student within the school setting and may be indicators of future acts of violence by students.

Lastly, teachers who often feel responsible for the actions of their students must learn to release themselves from that responsibility in some situations. Over and over again, a teacher will hear that if they had only addressed the student's risk factor that the tragedy within the school could have been avoided. Quite simply that is not the case. A "risk factor" is a concept from biological or physical science and should be used with extreme caution.[39] In behavioral research, a risk factor is a behavior or demographic that researchers have identified in association with some outcome. The idea that a particular risk factor will cause a certain behavior totally ignores the person's ability of choice. Given that not everyone with a particular risk factor chooses violence, risks are not direct causes of violence.[40] Unfortunately, by focusing on specific risks factors, teachers and school staff often ignore other behaviors that may precipitate violence. The resulting problem is that focusing on so-called risk factors may lead to an inappropriate and unsuccessful response to youth violence.[41] The same can be said for threats of violence within the school setting. By focusing on only specific actions or backgrounds, teachers and other school staff may overlook significant individual indicators of violence.

TYPES OF THREATS

In the school environment, as is in most environments conducive to human interactions, threats occur.[42] In considering acts of violence within the school, research suggests that actions and threats are often observed or heard days, weeks, and even months before an incident.[43] However, school staff are rarely trained on the detection of verbal threats. In general, there are four different categories of threats, all of which exist within the school setting. Specifically, threats may be: (1) direct; (2) conditional; (3) inferred; or (4) a third party.

Many governments are attempting to address threats with a school through legislative actions and police efforts. For the most part, governments have adopted legislation similar to the language provided below in the state of Virginia's (USA) definition of a threat with penalties according to the potential level of violence. (In the United States, felony crimes receive more sanctions than misdemeanor crimes.)

§ 18.2-60. Threats of death or bodily injury to a person or member of his family; threats to commit serious bodily harm to persons on school property; penalty. (Virginia—USA)

A. 1. Any person who knowingly communicates, in a writing, including an electronically transmitted communication producing a visual or electronic message, a threat to kill or do bodily injury to a person, regarding that person or any member of his family, and the threat places such person in reasonable apprehension of death or bodily injury to himself or his family member, is guilty of a Class 6 felony. However, any person who violates this subsection with the intent to commit an act of terrorism as defined in § 18.2-46.4 is guilty of a Class 5 felony.

2. Any person who communicates a threat, in a writing, including an electronically transmitted communication producing a visual or electronic message, to kill or do bodily harm, (i) on the grounds or premises of any elementary, middle or secondary school property, (ii) at any elementary, middle or secondary school-sponsored event or (iii) on a school bus to any person or persons, regardless of whether the person who is the object of the threat actually receives the threat, and the threat would place the person who is the object of the threat in reasonable apprehension of death or bodily harm, is guilty of a Class 6 felony.

B. Any person who orally makes a threat to any employee of any elementary, middle or secondary school, while on a school bus, on school property or at a school-sponsored activity, to kill or to do bodily injury to such person, is guilty of a Class 1 misdemeanor.

Direct Threats

Direct threats require an explicit one-to-one relationship between the student being threatened or victimized and the student (i.e., perpetrator) threatening. Direct threats may be in the form of verbal abuse or bullying and may occur in the school environment after two individuals at one time involved in a relationship have terminated that relationship. A direct threat leaves little ambiguity in terms of context. Examples of direct threats include statements such as "I will kill you," "I will hurt you," and "I will hurt your boyfriend."

In October of 2016, in Utah (USA), two teen males (ages fourteen and sixteen) were involved in a confrontation and argument where direct threats of violence were made by both parties. Later the argument resulted in a shooting when the fourteen-year-old shot and injured the sixteen-year-old.

Conditional Threats

Conditional threats, also often found in conjunction with dating or peer rela-tionships, in the school setting are also of concern to staff. Conditional threats are made under the umbrella of providing the victim a choice (although the choice is not always in the victim's control). A conditional threat such as "your money or your life" provides the victim the choice of bodily harm or surrendering any money in their possession. Although this crime (classified as a robbery in the United States) does exist in the school environment, a more common conditional threat would be "leave my boyfriend alone or I'll beat you." The fact that the perpetrator would have harmed the victim if the condition had not been met is enough to generate the required intent of violence. It is this type of threat that often provides the perpetrators of vio-lence within the school setting the justification to carry out their attack. In the perpetrator's mind, if the victim had not wanted to be assaulted, then they would have stopped interacting with the person identified in the threat. These indirect threats are also present in incidents of school shootings.

In January of 2016, in Pennsylvania (USA), a gunshot rang out during a fight on a stairway. There were no injuries, but three people were detained when a threat to "leave (another person) alone or else" was made.

Inferred Threats

Inferred threats are often found within the contents of a group or gang rival in that as one of the members of a group feels threatened by a rival group member and the other members assume the threat to also be against them. In a school with a large presence of gang activities, vandalisms or the tagging of areas within the school send the inferred message to rival gangs that the area belongs to the gang identified by the tagging and, therefore, the potential for violence is a reality if their area or territory within the school experiences a trespass.

On April 16, 2007, thirty-two people were killed and seventeen injured by one student utilizing two semi-automatic pistols on the campus of Virginia Tech, while many more students were injured as a result of jumping from windows to escape the assailant. The gunman, Seung-Hui Cho, was a senior studying English who had a history of disturbing writings (submitted as as-signments in his writing class) and who ultimately committed suicide as law enforcement entered a residence hall in an effort to arrest him.

In addition, inferred threats can manifest themselves in the form of violent writings. Eric Harris, one of the gunmen involved in Columbine's 1999 tragedy, turned in themes of violence of mass murder to his teachers prior to the Columbine shootings.[44]

Third-Party Threats

Finally, and also common in school settings across the globe, is the third-party threat. With cliques and gossip abundant in the school setting, the "he said if you ever . . ." conversations are certain to take place during teens' interactions.[45] These third-party threats are often ignored by students and educational staff. Unfortunately, as in the 2014 case noted below, these third-party threats are not only associated with violence against other students but also violence against teachers.

> In April of 2014, a fifteen-year-old boy in London who had threatened to kill his teacher stabbed her to death and asked a classmate to video the attack. Most of the student's classmates did not believe he was serious when he announced he planned to kill their Spanish teacher so the other students did not report the threats.

In the school environment, where peer acknowledgment is coveted, one cannot discount the impact of third-party threats. Often the perpetrators of violence will follow through on another's threat to remain in good standing with their peers. Teachers are often in the position to hear the news of most threats within a school setting. Unfortunately, they are also in the position to receive threats by students in the school setting.

THREATS AGAINST TEACHERS

> In 2014, a student in Northern Ireland was ordered to spend one year in prison after posing online as several people to extort money from her teacher. The student, an honor student, through threats of violence directed at the teacher's unborn child, forced the teacher to send sexually explicit pictures over the internet.

Unfortunately, oftentimes those who are attempting to help individuals become the targets of violence by those individuals. In the school setting, students will often target teachers. In May of 2000, in New York, a seventh-grade boy killed his teacher on the last day of school after he had been sent home for throwing water balloons in class. The boy returned at the close of the last period of the school year and shot the teacher.[46]

In the United Kingdom, more teachers are reporting threats by their students.[47] In the West Midlands, a teaching assistant reported being punched, kicked, sworn at, insulted, and bitten all within her first week of teaching.[48] Another teacher in London reported threats, not from students, but rather their parents, who threatened to beat the teacher for correcting their son.[49] And a teacher in Northern Ireland reported a student attempting to slap her, hitting her with furniture, and attempting to choke her.[50]

Explaining why a student or parent would want to cause harm to the teacher, who only attempts to offer help, is difficult. A 2018 study in Alberta, Canada, found that between 41 to 90 percent of surveyed teachers had experienced or witnessed violence directed toward teachers from either students or parents.[51] In this study violence was classified as everything from verbal harassment and swearing, to physical threats and assault. In addition, the study concluded that female teachers experience higher rates of violence than male teachers, but that male teachers are more likely to be targets of physical violence. Lastly, when 2018 was reported as the worst year in the United States for school shootings,[52] it was concluded that elementary teachers were more likely to experience violence than secondary teachers.[53]

Across the globe and before Columbine, researchers have attempted to explain why students kill teachers.[54] In the United States, often the rationale for a student killing a teacher is related to the availability of guns; however, when these incidents occur in non-gun-affiliated countries, the answer is moot. Other researchers suggest that students are influenced by the online availability of information on not only guns but also explosives[55] or the violence in television, movies, and video games. In addition, some research indicates that the breakdown of the family and an absence of a moral compass is responsible for these incidents of violence.[56] Lastly, these violent indicators are explained by the tendency for teens to seek violent cliques and gangs for a sense of belonging.[57] Unfortunately, just as there is no one risk factor for explaining violence in young people, there is no one reason for students injuring or killing their teachers. Therefore, just as teachers and school officials initiated preventive measures to reduce school violence, they must also plan for an incident of school violence.

AFTER A CRISIS

Unfortunately, sometimes even with the best preventive measures in place, an incident of severe violence such as a school shooting will occur. In these cases, the students, faculty, and community are in shock and fear.[58] The community will be addressed by law enforcement officials and the administrative personnel, the faculty will receive counseling from employee assistance programs, and the fears of the students will be addressed by the school counselors and teachers. In most schools, the number of teaching staff significantly outnumber the counselors and, as students often already have stronger bonds established with their teachers, much of a teacher's role after a crisis is dedicated to the needs of the students.

The first role for a teacher after a severe incident of violence such as a school shooting is cooperating with law enforcement.[59] Given that the majority of school shooters are themselves students,[60] they are usually known by others within the school. In events such as a school shooting, investigators with the local law enforcement agency will conduct an after-event investigation. In the majority of the cases, teachers as well as other students will be able to provide the most detailed background on the shooter. A teacher, while cooperating with law enforcement by providing information on the student shooter, is also helping to alleviate the fears of surviving students as they observe the teacher actively working to provide an explanation for the tragedy; thus, attempting to address the factors that contributed to the event and reduce the risk of more shootings. In addition, as students observe their teachers cooperating with law enforcement, they are more likely to cooperate with law enforcement with the post-event investigation.

The second role for a teacher is to help victims.[61] Although teachers do not possess medical training or, in many cases, mental health training, they are still able to help victims. For most students, the majority of their awakened hours are spent at school and with their teachers. Consequently, the teacher, in many cases, serves as a surrogate parent to the child. Just as children are comforted by the presence of their parent after a tragedy, many students are comforted by the presence of their teachers after a violent event. This presence includes their availability during a class, as occurred prior to the incident, and their availability on the school campus.

The third role for a teacher is to provide accurate information to students.[62] After an event, students will want to know the details of the incident as well as the conditions that may have existed prior to the incident. The teacher will know the maturity levels of the students. They will know what information is significant and what information is insignificant. Therefore, a teacher, through their experiences in interacting with their students prior to the shooting, will, in many ways, be one of the best people to communicate accurate information regarding the tragedy to the students.

The fourth role for a teacher is to provide activity for the students to reduce stress.[63] For many teachers, the activities may simply include course work to help the students to resume their studies and focus their concentrations on the course subjects. For other teachers, assignments based upon the event, such as writing assignments or art assignments, often help students cope with and accept the consequences of the tragedy.

The fifth role for a teacher is to alter the curricula.[64] After a tragedy such as a school shooting, many students, and particularly those students who were directly victimized in the event, often will require some extra time to process what they have experienced. Teachers, by altering curricula and rescheduling tests and/or assignments, are in the position to alleviate some of the pressure on student survivors.

The sixth role for a teacher is to ensure that information is available to students to address the crisis.[65] For the majority of students in this current age of technology use, this includes links to articles, statistics on school violence, and blogs that students may utilize as a resource for answers to questions that they may not want to discuss in a face-to-face conversation. In addition, and often overlooked in today's time frame, is the availability of books on the subjects of victimization and survival. A teacher is in the position to help ensure that librarians have books available to address a crisis.

The seventh role for a teacher is training.[66] After a crisis such as a school shooting, students will be more dependent upon teachers than before the incident. Hence, a teacher should receive training of detecting signs of grief and depression in their students. Unfortunately, in events of school violence, one action often leads to another.[67] Students who survive may have feelings of survivor guilt, anxiety, and thoughts of self-harm.[68] A teacher trained to identify the behaviors manifested by these feelings is in the position to provide the student the quickest response and, therefore, the most efficient avenue for mental health assistance.

Finally, the role for a teacher may be to discuss funeral procedures.[69] In most cases, a student's exposure to death and funerals will be only in regard to a death of an older relative or family friend. Few students have an experience with death of a peer. Teachers may be able to not only communicate the logistics of time and place for a funeral, but they may also be able to answer students' questions prior to the funeral about what they should wear, where they should sit, and what they might say. A teacher's role after a crisis is often critical for the school that has experienced an incident of severe violence such as a school shooting.

In the school environment, violence from strangers, school employees, or students is a concern for everyone across the globe. In most cases, denying the access of strangers to the school will significantly reduce actions of severe violence such as a school shooting. Threats by employees within the school are also potentially violent and, again, teachers may be able to detect and address some of those potential conflicts. Lastly, as most incidents of school violence are perpetrated by students, teachers, through their daily interactions and histories with students, are central to the prevention of school violence. Teachers, who are often victimized by their students, may be the savior for the students. Thus, education, training, and teacher-involved prevention programs may help to reduce incidents of school violence.

CHAPTER QUESTIONS

1. What are some measures that have been identified within the school environment as ways to restrict access to the campus/school by strangers?
2. Name three identifiable warning signs of potential violence?
3. What are the four types of threats that exist in schools?
4. What type of person/people may target or threaten the safety of a teacher?

DISCUSSION QUESTIONS

1. If you were a teacher, what are some measures you would take in an effort to reduce the victimization of students within your classroom?
2. In your opinion, what topics do you believe should be of primary focus in discussions on group-based preventive action efforts within the school environment?
3. Explain how you would handle the aftermath of an extreme act of school violence, for example, a school shooting, if you were a school administrator? Why would you handle it in this manner?

NOTES

1. Kimberly McCabe and Gregory Martin, *School Violence, the Media and Criminal Justice Responses* (New York: Peter Lang, 2005).
2. Mark Follman and Becca Andrews, "How Columbine Spawned Dozens of Copy Cats," *Mother Jones*, October 15, 2015, accessed on February 5, 2019, at https://www.motherjones.com/politics/2015/10/columbine-effect-mass-shootings-copycat-data/.

3. James Silver, Andre Simons, and Sarah Craun, *A Study of the Pre-attack Behaviors of Active Shooters in the United States between 2000 and 2017* (Washington, DC: US Dept. of Justice, 2018).

4. Thomas Gullotta and Sandra McElhaney, *Violence in the Homes and Communities: Prevention, Intervention and Treatment* (Thousand Oaks, CA: Sage, 1999).

5. James Silver, Andre Simons, and Sarah Craun, *A Study of the Pre-attack Behaviors of Active Shooters in the United States between 2000 and 2017.*

6. Kimberly McCabe and Daniel Murphy, *Child Abuse—Today's Issues* (New York: Taylor and Francis Publishing, 2016).

7. Kimberly McCabe and Gregory Martin, *School Violence, the Media and Criminal Justice Responses.*

8. Kimberly McCabe and Gregory Martin, *School Violence, the Media and Criminal Justice Responses.*

9. Mike Kennedy, "School Security: Ensuring Control," 2012, *American School and University,* accessed on January 31, 2019, at https://www.asumag.com/access -controlvisitor-management/school-security-ensuring-access-control.

10. K. McCabe and Robin Fajardo, "Law Enforcement Accreditation: A National Comparison of Accredited versus Non-Accredited Agencies," *Journal of Criminal Justice,* 29(1) (2001): 127–35.

11. Kimberly McCabe and Daniel Murphy, *Child Abuse—Today's Issues.*

12. Kimberly McCabe and Gregory Martin, *School Violence, the Media and Criminal Justice Responses.*

13. Peter Smith, *Violence in Schools: The European Response* (London: Routledge, 2003).

14. Kimberly McCabe and Gregory Martin, *School Violence, the Media and Criminal Justice Responses.*

15. Meri Wallace, "Six Steps for Schools to End School Violence, 2018," *Psychology Today,* accessed on February, 3, 2019, at https://www.psychologytoday.com/ us/blog/how-raise-happy-cooperative-child/201808/six-steps-schools-end-school -violence.

16. Katie Hesketh and Sara Alcorn, "Workplace Violence in Alberta and British Columbia Hospitals," *Health Policy,* 63(3) (2003): 311–21.

17. Kimberly McCabe, *Protecting Your Children in Cyberspace: What Parents Need to Know* (Lanham, MD: Rowman and Littlefield Publishers, Inc., 2017).

18. K. McCabe and Robin Fajardo, "Law Enforcement Accreditation: A National Comparison of Accredited versus Non-Accredited Agencies."

19. Mark Follman and Becca Andrews, "How Columbine Spawned Dozens of Copy Cats."

20. James Silver, Andre Simons, and Sarah Craun, *A Study of the Pre-attack Behaviors of Active Shooters in the United States between 2000 and 2017.*

21. Meri Wallace, "Six Steps for Schools to End School Violence, 2018."

22. Kimberly McCabe, *Protecting Your Children in Cyberspace: What Parents Need to Know.*

23. Meri Wallace, "Six Steps for Schools to End School Violence, 2018."

24. Kateina Ananiadou and Peter Smith, "Legal Requirements and Nationally Circulated Materials against School Bullying European Countries," *Criminology and Criminal Justice*, 2(4) (2002): 471–91.

25. Kateina Ananiadou and Peter Smith, "Legal Requirements and Nationally Circulated Materials against School Bullying European Countries."

26. James Silver, Andre Simons, and Sarah Craun, *A Study of the Pre-attack Behaviors of Active Shooters in the United States between 2000 and 2017.*

27. Peter Smith, *Violence in Schools: A European Perspective* (London: University of London, 2004).

28. Kimberly McCabe and Gregory Martin, *School Violence, the Media and Criminal Justice Responses.*

29. Kimberly McCabe, *Child Abuse and the Criminal Justice System* (New York: Peter Lang, 2003).

30. Kimberly McCabe and Daniel Murphy, *Child Abuse—Today's Issues.*

31. Kimberly McCabe and Daniel Murphy, *Child Abuse—Today's Issues.*

32. Harvey Wallace and Cliff Roberson, *Family Violence: Legal, Medical, and Social Perspectives*, sixth edition (Boston, MA: Pearson, 2010).

33. Wesley Jennings, Mirang Park, Elizabeth Tomsich, Angela Glover, and Rachel Powers, "Exploring the Relationship between Child Physical Abuse and Adult Dating Violence Using a Causal Inference Approach in an Emerging Adult Population in South Korea," *Child Abuse and Neglect*, 38(12) (2014): 1902–13.

34. Cynthia Crosson-Tower, *Understanding Child Abuse and Neglect*, eighth edition (Boston: Allyn and Bacon, 2010).

35. Kimberly McCabe, *Child Abuse and the Criminal Justice System.*

36. Kimberly McCabe and Gregory Martin, *School Violence, the Media and Criminal Justice Responses.*

37. Daniel Victor, "Mass Shootings Are All Different Except for One Thing—Most Are Men," *New York Times*, February 17, 2018, accessed on January 3, 2019, at https://www.nytimes.com/2018/02/17/us/mass-murderers.html.

38. Kimberly McCabe, *Protecting Your Children in Cyberspace: What Parents Need to Know.*

39. Queensland Government, *Working Together. Understanding School Violence in Schools* (Queensland Government, Australia: Schools Alliance against Violence, 2010), 1–45

40. Gale Morrison and Russell Skiba, "Predicting Violence from School Misbehaviors: Promises and Perils," *Psychology in the Schools*, 38(1) (2001): 173–84.

41. Queensland Government, *Working Together. Understanding School Violence in Schools.*

42. Kimberly McCabe and Gregory Martin, *School Violence, the Media and Criminal Justice Responses.*

43. Kimberly McCabe, *Protecting Your Children in Cyberspace: What Parents Need to Know.*

44. Kimberly McCabe and Gregory Martin, *School Violence, the Media and Criminal Justice Responses.*

45. Kimberly McCabe and Gregory Martin, *School Violence, the Media and Criminal Justice Responses.*

46. Jon Nordheimer, "Seventh Grade Boy Held in Killing of Teacher," *New York Times*, 2000, accessed on February 3, 2019, at https://www.nytimes.com/2000/05/27/us/seventh-grade-boy-held-in-killing-of-a-teacher.html.

47. Jonathan Owen, "Ann Maquire Killing: Teachers Reveal Horrifying Tales of Classroom Violence," *Independent*, 2014, accessed on January 3, 2019, at https://www.independent.co.uk/news/education/schools/ann-maguire-killing-teachers-across-britain-reveal-horrifying-tales-of-classroom-violence-9303146.html.

48. Jonathan Owen, "Ann Maquire Killing: Teachers Reveal Horrifying Tales of Classroom Violence."

49. Jonathan Owen, "Ann Maquire Killing: Teachers Reveal Horrifying Tales of Classroom Violence."

50. Jonathan Owen, "Ann Maquire Killing: Teachers Reveal Horrifying Tales of Classroom Violence."

51. CBC News, "Classroom Violence on the Rise Teachers Tell Canadian Teachers' Federation, " *CBC Junos*, accessed on February 3, 2019, at https://www.cbc.ca/news/canada/edmonton/classroom-violence-on-the-rise-teachers-tell-canadian-teachers-federation-1.4739869.

52. Sean Counghlan, "2018 Worse Year for US School Shootings," BBC News, 2018, accessed on February 3, 2019, at https://www.bbc.com/news/business-46507514.

53. CBC News, "Classroom Violence on the Rise Teachers Tell Canadian Teachers' Federation."

54. Kimberly McCabe and Gregory Martin, *School Violence, the Media and Criminal Justice Responses.*

55. Kimberly McCabe, *Protecting Your Children in Cyberspace: What Parents Need to Know.*

56. Leonard Holmes, "Why Do Young People Commit Murder?" *Very Well Mind*, 2018, accessed on January 31, 2019, at https://www.verywellmind.com/why-do-young-people-murder-2330565.

57. Kimberly McCabe and Gregory Martin, *School Violence, the Media and Criminal Justice Responses.*

58. Kimberly McCabe and Gregory Martin, *School Violence, the Media and Criminal Justice Responses.*

59. Alissa Kramen, Kelly Massey, and Howard Tunn, *Guide for Preventing and Responding to School Violence* (Alexandria, VA: International Association of Chiefs of Police [PSLC027.T99], 1999).

60. Anne Garrett, *Keeping American Schools Safe* (Jefferson, NC: McFarland, 2001).

61. Alissa Kramen, Kelly Massey, and Howard Tunn, *Guide for Preventing and Responding to School Violence.*

62. Alissa Kramen, Kelly Massey, and Howard Tunn, *Guide for Preventing and Responding to School Violence.*

63. Alissa Kramen, Kelly Massey, and Howard Tunn, *Guide for Preventing and Responding to School Violence.*

64. Alissa Kramen, Kelly Massey, and Howard Tunn, *Guide for Preventing and Responding to School Violence.*

65. Alissa Kramen, Kelly Massey, and Howard Tunn, *Guide for Preventing and Responding to School Violence.*

66. Alissa Kramen, Kelly Massey, and Howard Tunn, *Guide for Preventing and Responding to School Violence.*

67. Kimberly McCabe and Gregory Martin, *School Violence, the Media and Criminal Justice Responses.*

68. Kimberly McCabe and Daniel Murphy, *Child Abuse—Today's Issues.*

69. Alissa Kramen, Kelly Massey, and Howard Tunn, *Guide for Preventing and Responding to School Violence.*

Chapter Seven

Adult Offenders

KEY WORDS

Corporal punishment	Educator sexual mis-	Pornography
Corrupting	conduct	Sexting
Coworkers	Emotional abuse	Sextortion
Customers	Grooming	Sexual abuse
Cyberstalker	Ignoring	Strangers
Cyberstalking	Motives	Suicide
Domestic violence of-	Neglect	Suicide attempt
fenders	Nonverbal abuse	Supervision neglect
Educational neglect	Physical abuse	Verbal abuse

KEY ACRONYMS

(NIH) National Institutes of Health
(WHO) World Health Organization

As school violence began to receive widespread attention from the media, researchers throughout the globe began focusing on peer-on-peer violence in their attempts to explain bullying, physical assaults, and, most often—school shootings.[1] However, peer-on-peer violence does not explain the school shootings that occurred in Scotland in 1996, in France in 2012, and in California (USA) in 2017. These school shootings were all perpetrated by an adult without a history of attendance or employment within the specific schools. Therefore, peer-on-peer violence does not explain all school shootings.

Since the mass shooting at Columbine in 1999, there has been little attention focused on school shootings or the victimization of students by school staff or other adults. This chapter focuses on those adult perpetrators of school violence. Although the global definition of an adult is an individual of the age eighteen or older, in this chapter adults are defined as those individuals of the age of nineteen or older in an attempt to avoid the cases of eighteen-year-old shooters still attending secondary or high schools.

On March 13, 1996, Thomas Hamilton arrived at Dunblane Primary School near Stirling, Scotland, where he killed sixteen children and one teacher before ending his own life. Although the motivation behind this act is unknown, prior to this event several complaints had been made to police regarding Hamilton's behavior toward young boys within a youth club he had directed. This incident is still considered the deadliest mass shooting in British history.[2] Thomas Hamilton was not a teen; he was forty-three years old, white, and male without an affiliation to the primary school.

On March 19, 2012, a French citizen of Algerian descent named Mohammed Merah shot and killed four people at the Ozar Hatorah Day School in Tolouse. During the attack, the perpetrator proclaimed anti-Semitic motives in his proclamation that "the Jews kill our brothers and sisters in Palestine." In this case, the perpetrator was twenty-three years old.

On October 1, 2015, Chris Harper-Mercer, a twenty-six-year-old white, male student at Umpqua Community College (Oregon—USA) shot and killed nine people. Some accounts of the incident suggest the shooter asked his victims about their religion before killing them, but others point out that his rage was not limited to religious matters and acknowledge his mental health history. On the day of the shooting, Harper-Mercer gave a survivor numerous writings of his, showing he had studied mass killings. Furthermore, these notes expressed his sexual frustration as a result of being a virgin, hostility toward black men, and an absence of fulfillment in his life. This event is considered the deadliest mass shooting in Oregon's modern history.[3]

On April 10, 2017, Cedrick Anderson killed his wife and one student at North Park Elementary School in California (USA) before killing himself. During the after-event investigation, his paranoid and possessive behaviors toward his wife were revealed as well as his history of domestic violence. In this case, the perpetrator was fifty-four years old, African American, and male. Hence, the study of school shooters as well as other adult perpetrators of violence within the school is essential to understanding and reducing incidents of school violence across the globe.

Included within this chapter is a profile of school shootings across the globe within the last two decades as perpetrated by adults as well as discussions on the shooters' motives, the risk factors, and various rationales for selecting a school as the target for their tragic assault. Also included in this chapter are discussions of other crimes of violence by adults who are identified as staff within these educational institutions. For clarity the educational institutions discussed in this chapter include all levels of learning from primary school to colleges and universities. As demonstrated in the following case, adult perpetrators of severe school violence have existed for decades.

In 1927, in Bath Michigan (USA) adult perpetrator Andre Kehoe, age fifty-five, killed forty-three people in a school shooting. This event, explained through the facts that Kehoe had recently lost an election to the school board and that he was angry with the county for raising his taxes, was one of the first cases of a school shooting in the United States that involved an adult offender and elementary-level students.

CATEGORIES OF PERPETRATORS

When discussing the adult perpetrators of school violence, much of the historical research utilizes the environment of the workplace and workplace violence in place of the school.[4] In the workplace, approximately 15 percent of the deaths result from violence.[5] In the schools, approximately 4 percent of the student deaths are from active-shooter scenarios.[6] Therefore, if we consider the school as the workplace for students, the comparison of mass shooters across both locations is reasonable.[7]

After applying the typologies of adult perpetrators of workplace violence to the adult perpetrators of school violence, research suggests that there exist essentially four categories of perpetrators. Those categories are: (1) strangers; (2) customers; (3) coworkers; and (4) domestic violence offenders.

Strangers in incidents of school violence have no previous relationship to the school nor do they have a relationship with anyone currently interacting within the school's environment. An example of such a scenario is demonstrated in the 2015 mass murder of 147 people at Garissa University College in Kenya.[8] In this case four gunmen associated with the Somalia-based Al-Shabaab attacked the university and its students around dawn and continued their rampage for hours before being killed by law enforcement. The shooting at Dunblane Primary School in Scotland (discussed previously in this chapter) is another example of a stranger-perpetrated school shooting.

Customers in incidents of school violence are either involved in a current relationship with the school or have been involved in a previous relationship with the school. An example of this category of perpetrator is demonstrated in the June 1, 2016, shooting of a professor at the University of California-Los Angeles (USA). The perpetrator was a student of the professor's who was unhappy with the professor's critics of his work. In the months prior to the incident, the perpetrator utilized social media to post hostile comments about the professor. This perpetrator killed himself and the professor.

A third category of perpetrators of violence in the school environment is the coworker. In these cases, most similar to those mass shootings in workplace violence incidents, the perpetrator is currently employed by the educational institution. An example of this category of perpetrator is demonstrated in the University of Alabama shooting. In this case, on February 12, 2010, a biology professor at the university shot and killed three other professors during a department meeting.

In many cases, perpetrators of violence in the workplace are also perpetrators of domestic violence. As illustrated earlier in this chapter, in 2017, the shooter at North Park Elementary School in California (USA) also had a history of domestic violence and his current victim (his wife) was a teacher at the school. This incident resulted in the death of his wife and a child.

As demonstrated, in many cases adults are the perpetrators of incidents of severe violence within the school (i.e., school shootings). However, as the adults were not bullied or physically abused within the school, their motives are often different from those motives of the teen shooter.

MOTIVES FOR MASS DESTRUCTION

Current research on school shooters suggests that the notion that "they just snapped" is wrong. In fact, research suggests that adults involved in school shootings had problems with violence at least two years prior to their school shooting incident[9] and, unlike many individuals who commit crimes of violence as a quick reaction,[10] these actions are not spur of the moment. Many adult perpetrators of a school shooting are motivated by anger, rage, and the power that they perceive when planning and executing their action of destruction. When discussing the motives of mass murder in the workplace, much of the research on the perpetrators suggest five general motives.[11] These motives include: (1) to achieve notoriety; (2) revenge or to avenge a wrong; (3) a mission or to bring attention to a problem; (4) to attain a special relationship; and (5) to end personal pain. For many of these motives, rage is an outcome;

however, these emotions of anger or rage are associated with a wide variety of violent acts, including homicide, aggravated assault, rape, domestic violence, child abuse, bullying, torture, and even terrorism.[12]

Achieving Notoriety

In many cases, perpetrators of school violence feel that an action of mass destruction such as a school shooting will provide them the recognition and fame that they have sought but have not been able to attain within their lives. These adult perpetrators, who seek the attention of the media and the public, often feel as though they should be celebrated.[13] For many of the younger school shooters, Columbine inspired them to commit their acts of violence as research suggests that the mass shooting at Columbine has spawned at least seventy-four additional plots or attacks just across the United States.[14] Even for some adult perpetrators, Columbine is a model case. In particular, in at least fourteen cases, the Columbine copycats aimed to attack on the anniversary of the original massacre as individuals in thirteen of these cases suggested that their goal was to outdo the Columbine body count.[15] Thus, the act of imitation to gain notoriety is not limited to teens. Individuals of all ages are hardwired to imitate others.[16] This mode of imitation by an adult to achieve notoriety was demonstrated in the February 2008 shooting at Northern Illinois University. In this case, the perpetrator killed five students before killing himself. According to reports published after the event, the perpetrator of this mass shooting was believed to have studied the actions of the perpetrator of the 2007 school shooting at Virginia Tech. So copycat events, as discussed previously, also apply to adult school shooters.[17]

Revenge or Avenging a Wrong

Within any type of social connection comes the possibility of conflict. Often within a conflict is the notion that one part has caused the other part harm, and the term *revenge* often becomes a reality. Revenge, by definition, is the action of hurting or harming someone in return for an injury or wrong suffered at their hands. For the most part, revenge is an individual one-on-one reaction; however, in some cases these injuries or wrongs were inflicted upon another with the party feeling they must avenge those actions for the other person. Thus, by definition, avenge means to take vengeance for or on behalf of another. Many incidents of mass school shooting by adults are motivated by avenging a wrong. This likelihood of an adult avenging a wrong is increased with the adult's ability to obtain firearms and other explosive materials legally.[18]

An example of this category of perpetrator is demonstrated in the April 2, 2012, Oikos University (California—USA) shooting. In this case, the forty-three-year-old perpetrator was arrested after firing shots during a nursing class on the campus. The perpetrator was a former student who was said to have returned to the campus in an effort to locate one of the school's administrators who had denied his request for a prorated tuition fee reversal. Upon realizing the administrator was not there, the perpetrator began firing at random.

Another example was demonstrated in Germany in the April 26, 2002, killing of sixteen people by a nineteen-year-old expelled student from the Gutenberg-Gymnasium. Lastly, the Episcopal High School (Florida—USA) shooting in March of 2012 involved a former teacher who shot and killed the head of the school before killing himself. The perpetrator had been fired from his teaching job earlier in the day. Research suggests that when a single death occurs (especially the death of a child), the victim and the perpetrator usually know each other;[19] however, when a mass murder occurs, the perpetrator usually has more of a connection to the location. Adult perpetrators wishing to avenge a wrong may select a school to right the wrong for themselves as well as others.

Mission or Attention to a Problem

Typically, most mass shootings to demonstrate a commitment to a mission or to draw attention to a perceived problem do not target schools. In fact, the 2019 shooting at a Pittsburgh synagogue that left eleven people dead as the shooter proclaimed "All Jews must die!"[20] is more the norm for adult offenders; however, as with cases such as the attacks by the Boko Haram at the University of Maiduguri in Nigeria and the Taliban's attack at Pakistan's Bachakhan University discussed in a later chapter, mission-oriented incidents of mass shooting do sometimes include school targets.

Specifically, the March 2012 shooting in France involved a perpetrator who killed four people to draw attention to the religious war in the Middle East. During the siege, the perpetrator proclaimed the violence in his statement that "the Jews kill our brothers and sisters in Palestine." This shooting was in a religion-based school, and it was orchestrated to send a message or threat.

Attain a Special Relationship

Incidents of violence that occur in an attempt by the adult perpetrator to attain a special relationship are rare in the school setting,[21] with most attributed to lone gunmen seeking the attentions of one person such as was the case in the 1980 shooting of then US President Ronald Reagan by John Hinckley in order to gain the romantic attention of movie star Jodie Foster. However, they do occasionally occur in the school setting as demonstrated by the teen shooter in the May 2018 shooting in the Santa Fe high school (New Mexico—USA). The perpetrator, who killed ten people, spared his friends so they could later tell his story.

The school setting also occurred in the Brazilian shooting in 2011. On the morning of April 7, twelve children were killed when the twenty-three-year-old perpetrator entered the school claiming he was a lecturer for the day. Although police found no concrete evidence of religious or political motives for the perpetrator's actions, it was felt that he wanted to be recognized for his dedication to Islam after having been a Jehovah's Witness. In his last wishes, as his final action was a suicide, he requested to be buried following Islamic traditions and asked Jesus for eternal life and God's forgiveness.

End Personal Pain

One of the more common motives for a school shooting is to end the perpetrator's personal pain.[22] For many adult perpetrators of incidents of mass murders in schools, their goal is to end their pain; for most perpetrators, that end is a suicide. Unfortunately, as research on school violence indicates, if the perpetrator's final planned act is suicide, the number of fatalities and injuries will be large. This is the case both for young school shooters and adults. This goal to "end pain" is demonstrated over and over again with mass casualties in the school setting.

One example of this motive for mass shootings within a school setting is the Virginia Tech shooting. On April 16, 2007, thirty-two people were killed by one student utilizing two semi-automatic pistols on the campus of Virginia Tech, while many more students were injured as a result of jumping from windows to escape the assailant. The gunman, twenty-three-year-old Seung-Hui Cho, was a senior studying English, and he ultimately shot and killed himself as police stormed a residence hall in an effort to arrest him. Cho's history included depression, anger, and writings of mass murder as his response to his life. To date, this massacre is known as the deadliest school shooting in the history of the United States.[23]

Another example occurred five years later at an elementary school in Connecticut. On December 14, 2012, the deadliest mass shooting at a K–12 school in US history occurred at Sandy Hook Elementary School and resulted in twenty-six murders. It is reported that the twenty-year-old perpetrator had a learning disability and suffered from depression, anxiety, and obsessive-compulsive disorder. Furthermore, it was reported that his severe and deteriorating internalized mental health problems, combined with a lifetime of pain, were the foundation for his behaviors.

As demonstrated, the motives for mass destruction as well as the categories of perpetrators as referenced in research on workplace violence are also applicable to the educational setting of a school, regardless of the academic level. In these cases of school violence, researchers continue to seek commonalities among cases in order to address the victimization.[24]

Table 7.1 shows data from eighteen incidents of severe violence perpetrated by adults within school environments. More specifically, these incidents are school shootings around the world between the years of 1996 and 2017. In terms of the demographics of the adult offenders examined, the minimum age of offender was nineteen and the maximum was fifty-four, with an average offender age of thirty-one. Furthermore, the majority (89 percent) of the adult perpetrators were male, and the majority (78 percent) ended their killing spree by committing suicide.

As research supports, the majority (78 percent) of the incidents occurred within the United States, with all of the incidents analyzed carried out by one perpetrator. The most common months were April, February, and March. Fatalities ranged from one to thirty-two, with an average of nine fatalities per shooting. More specifically, 22 percent of incidents had one fatality and 50 percent were considered *true* (by definition) mass murders with four or more victims. The number of injured individuals ranged from zero to twenty-three, with an average of six individuals injured per incident. Furthermore, 28 percent of the incidents resulted in zero injuries; however, 34 percent resulted in five or more injured victims.

WHY SELECT A SCHOOL

Research suggests that there are a variety of reasons why adult shooters select a school as the target location for their reign of terror.[25] Some researchers suggest the offenders want to ensure that their actions will be noticed by all.[26] Others suggest that a school is selected as it is the least protected.[27] Lastly, there are those researchers who suggest that a school location is selected because of its close proximity and its large number of potential victims. Therefore, for perpetrators of a mass shooting, the location of school is not random but selected—and this also applies to adult offenders.

In a school shooting intended to raise awareness on an issue or in response to a perceived injustice, perpetrators select a particular educational institution based upon their perceived reaction by the society as a whole.

Table 7.1. Incidents of Severe School Violence (1996–2017)

Year	Location	Number of Perpetrators	Age of Perpetrator	Sex of Perpetrator	Number of Fatalities	Number of Injuries	End Result
1996	Scotland	1	43	Male	17	15	Suicide
2002	Germany	1	19	Male	16	1	Suicide
2002	USA	1	41	Male	3	0	Suicide
2006	USA	1	27	Male	2	2	Arrest
2007	USA	1	23	Male	32	23	Suicide
2008	USA	1	23	Female	2	0	Suicide
2008	USA	1	28	Male	5	21	Suicide
2010	USA	1	44	Female	3	3	Arrest
2011	Brazil	1	23	Male	12	22	Suicide
2011	USA	1	22	Male	1	0	Suicide
2012	USA	1	28	Male	1	0	Suicide
2012	USA	1	23	Male	4	5	Suicide
2012	USA	1	43	Male	7	3	Arrest
2012	USA	1	20	Male	26	2	Suicide
2014	USA	1	26	Male	1	2	Arrest
2015	USA	1	26	Male	9	9	Suicide
2016	USA	1	38	Male	1	0	Suicide
2017	USA	1	54	Male	2	1	Suicide

On April 2, 2015, multiple gunmen affiliated with Somalia's al-Shabab jihad-
ist terror group entered Garissa University College (Kenya). The result was
147 fatalities.

This assault on Garissa University demonstrated a current shift in modern
terror tactics. In these cases, attention has turned from attacks on subways,
cafes, and airports to institutions of learning.[28] When one considers that an
attack on public transportation, with its ease of entry and exit, requires much
less planning than an attack on a school, it must be acknowledged that a
shooting based on the choice of an educational institution as a target will
certainly gain the attention of the public.

In the attacks on Umpqua Community College (2015), Ozar Hatirah
School in France (2012), and Virginia Tech (2007), these perpetrators chose
schools as opposed to courthouses, police stations, or airport terminals. The
logic behind their choices is the ease of the target.[29] These adult perpetrators,
for fear of return gunfire, chose the educational setting as their soft targets.

Therefore, the school setting, which may be extremely convenient for
the young teen shooter, requires extra effort from the adult perpetrator. The
school, a location they may not normally visit, is accessible with some planning. In addition, the number of victims is limited only by the size of the
student body. Hence, a school setting, for an adult wishing to gain the focus
of his or her community or the world, is a logical choice.

Finally, schools are often centrally located and filled with hundreds of defenseless victims. Gunmen choose schools because schools embody a sense
of safety and secure experimentations of life.[30] For individuals with a history
of difficulties in their kid-learning world and inadequate socialization skills,
the school environment is the convenient target with the promise of multiple
victims.

For many, it is easier to understand school violence if it is seen as a random
act from a stranger; however, when cases involve adults within the school,
individuals across the globe take notice. These internal perpetrators have
been provided access to students with the expectation that they will better
these young people.

ABUSES WITHIN THE SCHOOL

Adults within the school environment are supposed to be students' immediate
source of help when they are faced with problems or feel unsafe. Through

their interactions with educators, students are able to learn important life skills in empathy, respect for others, and conflict resolution. The victimization of students by the adults in this setting therefore may have severe, long-term consequences. For the purposes of this chapter, an educator includes teachers within the classroom as well as coaches, counselors, administrators, tutors, aides, and other adult staff members within the school.

As described, on February 12, 2010, one professor shot and killed three other professors during a biology department meeting at the University of Alabama in Huntsville. In March of 2012, a former Spanish teacher at Episcopal High School shot and killed the head of the school before killing himself.[31] Again, in both of these cases, the perpetrators were adults and employed by the school.

Adults within the school environment are supposed to be students' immediate source of enlightenment and assistance when they feel as though they are in danger or have been threatened. Although violence perpetrated by school officials may not always be as common as portrayed by the media,[32] one event often leaves students, parents, and the public with increased hesitation and the fear of victimization within the school setting. These types of victimization, as related to the categories of child abuse, are physical abuse, sexual abuse, emotional abuse, and neglect.

Physical Abuse

In June of 2018, a fifteen-year-old Jewish girl was physically assaulted by three male students;[33] thus, this type of teen-on-teen violence is what is expected in the school setting. However, not all physical assaults that occur within a school are perpetrated by students.

In general, child physical abuse is defined as a non-accidental physical injury that results from punching, beating, kicking, slapping, biting, shaking, throwing, stabbing, choking, hitting, burning, or otherwise harming a child by a parent or other person who has the responsibility of the care of that child.[34] For the purpose of this section, the *other person* is an employee of the school setting. It is noted that some of the actions listed under the definition of child physical abuse (e.g., slapping or hitting) are often associated with spanking as forms of corporal punishment as used as discipline within some schools.

For the purposes of this chapter, physical abuse may be described as intentional and accepted corporal punishment. Corporal punishment in schools is defined as the infliction of pain or confinement as a penalty for an offense committed by a student.[35] Throughout the world there has been a shift in the acceptance of corporal punishment in schools; however, in the past teachers used paddles, rubber hoses, leather straps, belts, rods, sticks, and more to discipline students.[36] Furthermore, research has described similar methods having been used within British public schools during the 1950s.[37]

Although considered to have been an everyday punishment at one time, physical punishment in the form of corporal punishment has been eliminated from the majority of educational policies worldwide. Hence, staff may react to violations within this environment with disciplining students using various degrees of force. Pushing, shoving, slapping, pinching, and kicking are some of the ways in which school officials may react as a result.[38] Controversies continue to be debated on the use of corporal punishment for corrective purposes in the school setting[39] as many researchers assert that physical punishment is associated with adverse outcomes such as mental illness, long-term injury, and violence across the lifetime.[40] Corporal punishment, most often cited as a form of child physical abuse in the school setting, is prohibited in many European countries, with Sweden identified as the first country to forbid spanking in schools as early as the 1960s.

Research has suggested that child physical abuse by school officials decreases with the age of the child.[41] However, there are other demographic characteristics of children that places them at risk factors for physical abuse within the school setting.[42] Some of those demographic characteristics include gender, as it is more likely the victims are females within the school,[43] and mental disabilities. In the school system, these mental disabilities are more associated with delayed or diminished learning capabilities.[44] For students with delayed learning abilities, the risk for physical abuse by peers and school staff is increased.[45]

Corporal punishment continues to be allowed in nearly 40 percent of the K–12 schools in the United States, in many Middle Eastern countries, Malesia, and in the private schools in Australia.[46] In addition, although prohibited by law, there still exist cases of physical abuse, maiming, and death as a result of corporal punishment in some schools in South Africa. When considering the fact that countries in the regions of Africa, the Middle East, Asia, and Latin America report that at least 80 percent of the children between the ages of two and fourteen have experienced violent discipline at either home and/or school,[47] one must acknowledge that much of the physical abuse that exists within schools today is at the hands of teachers and administrators within the school setting. Child physical abuse in the school is an international concern.

In reference to the adult perpetrators, research has concluded that male teachers were more supportive of corporal punishment. In addition, research also suggests that physical punishment is more frequently perpetrated by a male adult within the school toward a male victim.[48] Lastly, male teachers who reside in areas with patriarchal roots are more likely to use corporal punishment as a means of discipline in their classrooms.[49]

Sexual Abuse

The sexual abuse of students by an adult within the school setting is another tragedy that brings to the public's attention the notion of victimization and violence within the school setting. In 2004, a twenty-six-year-old reading teacher in the United States was charged with two counts of a lewd and lascivious battery with a fourteen-year-old boy.[50] A little over a decade later, a twenty-four-year-old English teacher was arrested on child sexual abuse charges as a result of a nine-month relationship she had with a thirteen-year-old student who is said to have impregnated her. More recently, in February of 2018, middle-school science teacher Stephanie Peterson was arrested for engaging in a sexual relationship with one of her fourteen-year-old students.[51]

The World Health Organization defines child sexual abuse as the involvement of a child in a sexual activity that he or she does not fully comprehend and is unable to give informed consent to, or that violates the laws of society.[52] When considering sexual abuse of school-aged children, approximately 50 percent involve children between the ages of six and fourteen.[53] For the purposes of this chapter, educator sexual misconduct is defined as behavior by an educator that is directed at a student and intended to sexually arouse the educator or the child.[54] This may take a physical, verbal, or visual form that is considered to be sexual behavior between the educator and student.

The majority of the perpetrators of traditional cases of child abuse are family members or *familia*, but this is not the case for those incidents of child sexual abuse that occur within the school setting. For the most part, the sexual abuse of a child in a school setting involves a male teacher or coach and a female student.[55] For these cases, those abusers often report romantic feelings toward the victim. The same justification is often cited in the relationship of adult females and students. However, intercourse, although the most mentioned in media reports of sexual abuse in the schools, is usually the end result to a variety of other sexual abuses, many of which utilize technology, in a school setting.[56]

Research suggests that today's child pornography is often the result of peer-to-peer contact or networks.[57] In addition, research suggests that pedophiles (individuals who act upon their sexual attractions to the physical characteristics of children) aggressively target specific victim types today and often place themselves in locations (such as schools) frequented by children. In cases of child pornography, adult offenders will not only victimize the child during the initial time of the photo, but they may also utilize the online community to victimize the child indirectly in the distribution of child pornography.[58]

Another crime of sexual abuse that may be facilitated by an adult in the school environment is the act of child solicitation. These perpetrators, trained in communicating with students, may use an array of strategies to engage in sexual contact with a minor.[59] In the school system, these are the cases that often involve an employee requesting a sexual relationship with a student. In some cases, these requests are made online. Historically, these cases, thought to be restricted to the university setting and in the scenario of sex for a grade, may also occur in the secondary school setting as society now places much more of an emphasis on academic achievement in high school to facilitate a student's entry into a selected college.

Cyberstalking is also a concern as related to school violence. By definition, cyberstalking is the repeated use of technology to monitor, harass, intimidate, coerce, or frighten someone into an unwilling action.[60] Unlike physical stalking, which has resulted in a variety of laws for prevention, cyberstalking relies upon the anonymity of the internet and the online community to protect the perpetrator. In the school system, the adult stalker is usually known to the student as they have engaged in other personal as well as technology-based conversations. Thus, the apprehension of a cyberstalker, and especially a stalker in the role of a teacher, is much easier to hide and therefore often continues without repercussions.

Sexting is another crime of concern within the school environment. Statistics indicate that more than 80 percent of all US teens have their own cell phones and that the majority of those with cell phones send text messages.[61] For many teens, those text messages are sometimes considered sext messages,[62] and in some cases they are received and sent by adults within the school. Sexting is vaguely defined to include the sending or receiving of sexual images. Those teens who generally send the original sext messages are females. It is these cases that most often involve an adult male receiver. In general, teens who participate in sexting place themselves at risk for other forms of victimization. In particular, teens who have sexted a message may also find themselves victims of harassment, cyberstalking, or sextortion by the adult.

The crime of sextortion involves the use of a computer to obtain through coercion sexual dialogues or pornography from another. In many cases, the victims are teens and the perpetrators are adults. In some cases these adults are employed within the school system. Unlike consensual sexual activities, with cases of sextortion, an offender, who essentially enters the home of a child or teen electronically or through interactions via cell phones, demands the production of sexual materials such as videos or images by the victim. According to the US Justice Department, sextortion is one of the most significantly growing threats against children within the online community.[63]

While there exists no clear indicators of risk for child sexual abuse, some researchers suggest that some factors are associated with an increase in risk.[64] Some of those factors are related to the child's cultural background,[65] the presence of domestic violence in the home,[66] and opportunity of the abuse.[67] In extrafamilial (i.e., outside the family) abuse, the perpetrator usually has a history of approaching students and, over the course of time, they have learned from their mistakes. These perpetrators often target children under the context of a social relationship with the child.[68]

Teachers and other educational staff are in prime positions for these potential relationships. As these adults create special circumstances to place themselves in the proximity of children, they easily gain the confidence of the child or teen.[69] Before sexual abuse occurs, actions may be taken by the educator that are seen as marginally inappropriate. By partaking in such acts, the adult is able to desensitize the child to the initiation of more explicit sexual activities. A key component for the adults who initiate this type of relationship with students is referred to as grooming. Grooming is described as the process in which an offender lures in a victim in an effort to sexually abuse them in the end.[70] As a result of the high levels of interaction and accessibility the adults within a school setting have to children, children are likely to feel as though they must partake in any actions asked of them. An example of grooming may be the increase in attention to a particular student while slowly initiating physical contact that could be seen as inappropriate. Another example would be the asking of questions in relation to the student's sexuality. The point of these actions is to aid in the attachment between the child and the teacher, while the behaviors exhibited by the adult also test the student's likelihood of keeping the interactions a secret.

Emotional Abuse

It has been suggested that emotional abuse is the most common form of child abuse.[71] However, since emotional abuse often is accompanied by a more "severe" form of abuse (i.e., physical or sexual), it is often overlooked as abuse and is allowed to continue in the home and school setting.[72] For clarity in this section, emotional (or psychological) abuse is defined, based upon a chronic behavior, as the ongoing maltreatment of a child. In this chapter, emotional abuse is perpetrated by adults in the educational setting and includes not only verbal acts of aggression toward a child, but also the deliberate attempts to humiliate, scare, ignore, or isolate a child.

Emotional abuse within the school setting addresses a variety of actions. In the school setting, the two more common categories of emotional abuse are ignoring and corrupting.[73]

To ignore someone is to fail to notice them. For clarity, ignoring a child's basic needs of food and shelter may be referred to as neglect;[74] however, in the school setting ignoring refers to depriving a child of social stimulation and responsiveness.[75] Children learn through their relationships with others. Teachers who ignore their students fail to provide these children the social interactions required for healthy mental and educational development. Many students who are ignored by their teachers will fail to advance in their academic studies. Teachers, just as parents, may ignore one student if the majority of their time is devoted to the attention of another student. In these cases, one child, the better student, is labeled as the teacher's *pet* while another is ignored.[76] This also occurs in situations where a problem emerges with one child such as a disciplinary problem; thus, the teacher may feel forced to provide the "problem child" more attention. Unfortunately, for the child without the issue, he or she becomes the ignored child. Unfortunately, the ignoring of a child creates consequences for that child. Just as adults seek and desire social relationships, children also seek and desire such relationships. If a child is ignored in the school, the child will often not feel socially connected to the school.

The other category of emotional abuse by some adults in the educational setting is corruption. The act of corrupting destroys the trust among students and educational staff. The corruption of a child involves engaging the child in self-destructive and sometime criminal behaviors.[77] These behaviors include providing the child with alcohol or drugs and enticing the child into participating in criminal activity. Generally, adults corrupt children for one of two reasons: individual pleasure or economic gain.[78] The child who wishes for that attention of his or her teacher or coach will do whatever is asked to receive that positive reinforcement. The adult who provides a child alcohol or drugs does so to gain the favor of that child; that favor obliges the child to act as the adult desires. Whether the adult desires to be seen as a leader by the child or desires a sexual relationship with the child, the action of corruption is illegal and is a form of emotional abuse.

A study conducted in Israel stated that 29 percent of elementary students in grades four to six had reported at least one type of emotional abuse by a teacher.[79] More recently, a school-based study revealed that approximately 18 percent of the students had experienced at least one example of emotional abuse by teachers. The instances ranged in severity, with teachers having insulted, mocked, or referred to the students using humiliating labels during the previous academic year.[80]

For the purpose of this chapter, emotional abuse by a teacher is defined as a pattern of verbal or nonverbal behaviors that do not include any physical contact, but result in emotional, social, cognitive, and somatic consequences for the student's functioning and adjustment.[81] Research suggests that emotional abuse by teachers has been examined through a range of both verbal and nonverbal behaviors.[82] Verbal abuse is described as the use of sarcasm, ridicule, or demeaning statements, yelling, name-calling, insulting, making comments in reference to a student's appearance or disabilities, or making negative comments about a child's family.[83] Nonverbal abuse may include neglect such as ignoring the student and other behaviors such as assigning homework as a disciplinary action or punishment and the use of assignments as a result of not responding correctly to a question.[84]

Emotional abuse by teachers may have a damaging effect on children's well-being. It is suggested that this form of abuse is likely to reduce children's views of self-worth and decrease their confidence.[85]

Neglect

In general, neglect is defined as a failure to provide attention to certain areas or circumstances within a child's life. Neglect is usually related to age-appropriate care.[86] In the school setting, neglect is most related to education and supervision and this neglect is from teachers, coaches, and staff within the educational setting.

Educational neglect refers to the caretaker's failure to provide an education or a means to obtain an education for the child.[87] Included in this category of neglect are chronic school truancy, a failure to enroll the child in school, and inattention by the parents or caretakers to a child's special education programs. Children throughout the world are required to attend school. Educators who do not follow up on students when they miss school or classes are failing to provide for the educational needs of the child. From an educational standpoint, a child who does not perceive attending school as a priority will not attend. These children place little effort into their assignments; however, they are often simply passed from grade to grade until the time in which they can decide for themselves if they would like to continue their education.

Supervision neglect is the failure to adequately supervise children by leaving them alone, leaving them in the care of an inadequate guardian, or ejecting them from the home. Supervision neglect also may occur within the school structure. Teachers who fail to supervise their students not only fail to provide an education for those students but also provide an avenue for victimization of those students by peers. A student who is unsupervised may be assaulted or bullied while within the school setting. As the school staff fail to recognize these actions, they also fail to end these actions.

THE ROLE OF MENTAL HEALTH
IN ADULT PERPETRATORS

In the majority of the more recent incidents of school shooting that involved an adult perpetrator, a history of mental health problems or mental illness was mentioned. In particular, many adult perpetrators of severe school violence exhibit paranoid behaviors, depression, and anger.[88] In addition these adults, similar to younger shooters, have difficulties with interpersonal communications and narcissism.[89]

In February of 2008, twenty-seven-year-old student Steven Kazmierczak opened fire into a crowd of students on the campus of Northern Illinois University and killed five and injured seventeen before killing himself that same day. It is noted that Kazmierczak was prescribed medications by a psychiatrist for anxiety, depression, and sleep aid, although it is said that he had stopped taking the prescriptions about three weeks prior to the shooting.[90] Four years later, On December 14, 2012, the deadliest mass shooting at a K–12 school in United States history occurred at Sandy Hook Elementary School in Newtown, Connecticut. A report issued by the Office of the Child Advocate in November 2014 stated that shooter Adam Lanza had Asperger's syndrome, while also having suffered from depression, anxiety, and obsessive-compulsive disorder as a teenager, but concluded that they had "neither caused nor led to his murderous acts." Furthermore, the report stated that Lanza's severe and deteriorating internalized mental health problems, combined with an atypical preoccupation with violence and access to deadly weapons, provided for a disaster.[91] Hence, the mental health of adult offenders is critical when discussing adult perpetrators of severe violence within a school environment.

In many cases, perpetrators of school violence have not been diagnosed with a mental illness, although they may be suffering from an undiagnosed mental illness. Specifically, many attackers exhibit a history of suicidal thoughts or extreme sadness. Also, a significant life change such as the death of a loved one, public humiliation, or a breakup may spark an emotional response from someone suffering from a mental illness, which may in turn lead to their involvement in violence within the school.[92] Suicide, an outcome to the majority of school shootings perpetrated by an adult, is a very real concern when associated with school violence.

Suicide, the thought of wanting to end one's own life, is a common symptom of many mental illnesses, although the reasons to want to take such an action may vary. For example, in February of 2008 gunshots were fired at Louisiana Technical College in Baton Rouge. The offender was identified as twenty-three-year-old nursing student Latina Williams. Williams shot and killed two of her classmates before killing herself in a classroom on the school's campus.[93] Three years later, part-time Radford University student Ross Truett Ashley shot and killed a Virginia Tech university police officer in a parking lot on the campus of Virginia Tech before killing himself. Although the motive for this incident is unclear as Ashley was not a Virginia Tech student and no connections between him and the university officer were ever discovered, Radford Police were able to identify Ashley as the suspect in the case of a 2011 Mercedes SUV that was stolen at gunpoint from a real estate office a few days prior.[94]

In June of 2014 one student was killed and two injured during a shooting on the campus of Seattle Pacific University. Twenty-six-year-old Aaron Ybarra was arrested and admitted to having planned a mass shooting to kill as many people as possible before he had planned to kill himself.[95] The act of inflicting violence on oneself with the intent to end one's life and dying because of this action is known as suicide.[96] A suicide attempt is when a person harms themselves with the intent to end their life, but they do not die because of this action.[97]

On April 26, 2002, a nineteen-year-old, expelled student of Gutenberg-Gymnasium (Germany), Robert Steinhäuser, shot sixteen people before committing suicide. Although his motive is unknown, it is assumed that it was related to his school expulsion. Steinhäuser had been expelled as a result of forging a mandatory medical certificate that was required of him in reference to previous absences from school.[98] In October of 2002, forty-one-year-old Robert Flores Jr. shot three professors before killing himself at the University of Arizona. The victims were three of Flores's nursing professors, which police noted as having been specifically targeted by the offender.[99]

On June 1, 2016, thirty-eight-year-old former PhD student Mainak Sarkar, of the University of California, shot and killed an associate professor in a murder-suicide at an engineering building on the university campus. The associate professor who was the victim was Sarkar's thesis adviser from when he was a student attending UCLA, and it was even noted that he had been making hostile comments about the professor on social media in the months having led up to the event.[100] A common theme among all of these cases is mental illness.

In the school setting, adults are, in some cases, the perpetrators of violence. Although most media accounts emphasize school shootings, adults may also be involved in physical abuse, sexual abuse, emotional abuse, and neglect. As suggested by the application of *Broken Windows*[101] to the school environment, in some cases, less severe violence facilitates severe violence.[102]

Adult perpetrators of school shootings account for less than one-half of all the shootings that have occurred within the last two decades and less than 20 percent of the school shootings that have occurred within the K–12 environment; however, they still are significant factors in discussions of severe violence with a school setting. Adults, as related to their age, often have a more extensive history of violence and mental health problems. In addition, adults who kill children are often motivated by revenge or anger.[103] Furthermore, adults are more likely to select a school when planning an attack, not because of familiarity with the environment but because a K–12 school is often close and less protected. Therefore, adult perpetrators of school violence are a concern for everyone regardless of location within the world.

CHAPTER QUESTIONS

1. What are the four categories of adult perpetrators?
2. What are the five most common motives behind mass destruction?
3. What is educator sexual misconduct?
4. What are the two major types of emotional abuse discussed in reference to the school setting?
5. What are some characteristics that an adult perpetrator of school violence may be identified by?

DISCUSSION QUESTIONS

1. In your opinion, which category of adult perpetrator is the most harmful?
2. What type of abuse do you think is most prevalent in schools as perpetrated by an adult?
3. In your opinion, which motive behind mass destruction would create the most controversy on a school campus?

NOTES

1. Kimberly McCabe and Gregory Martin, *School Violence, the Media and Criminal Justice Responses* (New York: Peter Lang, 2005).

2. Alastair Jamieson, "Dunblane's Snowdrops: How a School Shooting Changed British Gun Laws," NBC News, March 13, 2016, accessed on November 15, 2018, at https://www.nbcnews.com.

3. Eli Saslow, Sarah Kaplan, and Joseph Hoyt, "Oregon Shooter Said to Have Singled Out Christians for Killing in 'Horrific Act of Cowardice,'" *Washington Post*, October 2, 2015, accessed on December 20, 2018, at https://www.washingtonpost.com.

4. Louise Fitzgerald, "Sexual Harassment: Violence against Women in the Workplace," *American Psychologist*, 48(10) (1993): 1070–76.

5. US National Safety Council, *Workplace Fatalities* (Washington, DC: US National Safety Council, 2019).

6. Stephen Satterly, "Report of Relative Risk of Death in US K–12 Schools," April 15, 2014, SafeHavensInternational.org, accessed on December 12, 2018, at https://safehavensinternational.org/wp-content/uploads/2014/06/Relative_Risks_of_ Death_in_US_K-12_Schools.pdf.

7. Kimberly McCabe and Gregory Martin, *School Violence, the Media and Criminal Justice Responses*.

8. Josh Levs and Holly Yan, "147 Dead, Islamist Gunmen Killed after Attack at Kenya College," CNN.com, 2015, accessed on February 3, 2019, at https://www.cnn .com/2015/04/02/africa/kenya-university-attack/index.html.

9. Mark Follman, "New FBI Study Shows Mass Shooters Aren't Loners Who Just Snap," *Mother Jones*, June 20, 2018, https://www.motherjones.com/crime-justice/ 2018/06/active-shooters-fbi-research-warning-signs/. Accessed on February 3, 2019.

10. Joy Lyneham, "Violence in New South Wales Emergency Department," *Australian Journal of Advanced Nursing*, 18(2) (2000): 8–16.

11. Kimberly McCabe and Gregory Martin, *School Violence, the Media and Criminal Justice Responses*.

12. Scott Bonn, "Fear-based Anger Is the Primary Motive for Violence," *Psychology Today*, July 17, 2017, accessed on December 7, 2018, at https://www.psychology today.com/us/blog/wicked-deeds/201707/fear-based-anger-is-the-primary-motive -violence on January 31, 2019.

13. Daniel Victor, "Mass Shootings Are All Different Except for One Thing— Most Are Men," *New York Times*, February 17, 2018, accessed on December 20, 2018, at https://www.nytimes.com/2018/02/17/us/mass-murderers.html.

14. Mark Follman and Becca Andrews, "How Columbine Spawned Dozens of Copy Cats," *Mother Jones*, October 15, 2015, accessed on February 5, 2019, at https://www.motherjones.com/politics/2015/10/columbine-effect-mass-shootings -copycat-data/.

15. Mark Follman and Becca Andrews, "How Columbine Spawned Dozens of Copy Cats."

16. Kimberly McCabe, *Protecting Your Children in Cyberspace: What Parents Need to Know* (Lanham, MD: Rowman and Littlefield Publishers, Inc., 2017).

17. Kimberly McCabe, *Protecting Your Children in Cyberspace: What Parents Need to Know*.

18. Mark Follman and Becca Andrews, "How Columbine Spawned Dozens of Copy Cats."

19. Kimberly McCabe and Daniel Murphy, *Child Abuse—Today's Issues* (New York: Taylor and Francis Publishing, 2016).

20. USAToday, "What We Know about the Shooting at the Tree of Life Synagogue in Pittsburgh," October 27, 2018, accessed on February 5, 2019, at https:// www.usatoday.com/story/news/nation/2018/10/27/pittsburgh-shooting-what-we -know-shooter-tree-life-synagogue-and-victims/1789247002/.

21. Kimberly McCabe and Gregory Martin, *School Violence, the Media and Criminal Justice Responses.*

22. Kimberly McCabe and Gregory Martin, *School Violence, the Media and Criminal Justice Responses.*

23. Sean Alfano, "At Least 33 Killed in Va. Tech Massacre," CBS News, April 16, 2007, accessed on November 17, 2018, at https://www.cbsnews.com.

24. Josh Elliott, "FBI Flags Easy Warning Signs for Potential Mass Shooters," Global News, June 22, 2018, accessed on December 20, 2018, at https://globalnews .ca/news/4290607/fbi-active-mass-shooter-guns-warning-signs/.

25. Kimberly McCabe and Gregory Martin, *School Violence, the Media and Criminal Justice Responses.*

26. Daniel Victor, "Mass Shootings Are All Different Except for One Thing—Most Are Men."

27. Carol Shakeshaft, *Educator Sexual Misconduct: A Synthesis of Existing Literature* (Washington, DC: US Department of Education, 2004).

28. Bill Shackelford, "There's a Reason Shooters Target Schools. It's Simple," February 22, 2018, accessed on December 20, 2018, at https://www.desmoines register.com/story/opinion/readers/2018/02/22/theres-reason-shooters-target -schools-its-simple/361105002/.

29. Bill Shackelford, "There's a Reason Shooters Target Schools. It's Simple."

30. Michael Reist, "Why Schools Are a Target of Choice," *The Globe and Mail*, December 15, 2012, accessed on December 20, 2018, at https://www.theglobe andmail.com/opinion/why-schools-are-a-target-of-choice/article6441362/.

31. Jim Schoettler, "Episcopal School Head Dale Regan Killed by Fired Teacher, Who Then Kills Himself," *Florida Times-Union*, March 6, 2012, accessed on November 24, 2018, at https://www.jacksonville.com.

32. Kimberly McCabe and Gregory Martin, S*chool Violence, the Media and Criminal Justice Responses.*

33. Jewish Telegraph Agency, "French Girl Assaulted Inside Jewish School near Paris," June 15, 2018, Jewish Telegraphic Agency (JTA.org), accessed on December 3, 2018, at http://www.israelnationalnews.com/News/News.aspx/247513.

34. Child Welfare Information Gateway, *What Is Child Abuse? Recognizing the Signs and Symptoms* (Washington, DC: US Department of Health and Human Services, Children's Bureau, 2013).

35. Irwin Hyman, *Reading, Writing, and the Hickory Stick (*Lexington, MA: Lexington Books, 1990).

36. Irwin Hyman, *Reading, Writing, and the Hickory Stick.*

37. Jonathan Benthall, "Invisible Wounds: Corporal Punishment in British Schools as a Form of Ritual," *Child Abuse and Neglect*, 15 (1991): 377–88.

38. Irwin Hyman and Pamela Snook, "Dangerous Schools and What You Can Do about Them," *Phi Delta Kappan*, 81 (2000): 489–501.

39. Dinan Baumrind, Robert Larzelere, and Philip Lowan, "Ordinary Physical Punishment: Is It Harmful?" *Psychological Bulletin*, 128(4) (2002): 580–89.

40. Traci Afifi, Natalie Mota, Harriet MacMillan, and Jitender Sareen, "Harsh Physical Punishment in Childhood and Adult Physical Health," *Pediatrics*, 132(2) (2002): 333–40.

41. Kimberly McCabe and Gregory Martin, *School Violence, the Media and Criminal Justice Responses.*

42. US Department of Health and Human Services, *Child Maltreatment 2006* (Washington, DC: US Government Printing Office, 2008).

43. Kimberly McCabe, *Child Abuse and the Criminal Justice System* (New York: Peter Lang, 2003).

44. Robert Ammerman, "The Role of the Child in Physical Abuse: A Reappraisal," *Violence and Victims*, 6(2) (1991): 87–102.

45. Kimberly McCabe and Gregory Martin, *School Violence, the Media and Criminal Justice Responses.*

46. Matthew Willis, "Non-Disclosure of Violence in Australian Indigenous Communities," *Trends and Issues in Crime and Criminal Justice, No. 405* (Australian Government: Australian Institute of Criminology, 2011).

47. Kimberly McCabe and Daniel Murphy, *Child Abuse—Today's Issues.*

48. Forrest Parkay and Colleen Conoley, "Characteristics of Educators Who Advocate Corporal Punishment: A Brief Report," *Journal of Humanistic Education and Development*, 21(1) (1982): 1–9.

49. Kimberly McCabe and Gregory Martin, *School Violence, the Media and Criminal Justice Responses.*

50. CBS News, *Protecting Students from Sexual Abuse by Teachers*, June 20, 2015, accessed on November 3, 2018, at https://www.cbsnews.com/video/protecting-students-from-sexual-abuse-by-teachers-and-coaches/.

51. Alex Sundby, "Female Teacher Accused of Sexual Relationship with 14 Year Old Boy," CBS News, March 2, 2018, accessed on January 3, 2019, at https://www.cbsnews.com/news/stephanie-peterson-teacher-sexual-relationship-boy-arrested-florida/.

52. World Health Organization (WHO), *Eliminating Female Genital Mutilation* (Geneva, Switzerland: WHO Press, 2008).

53. Children's Bureau, *Child Maltreatment 2013* (Washington, DC: US Department of Health and Human Services, Administration for Children and Families, 2014).

54. Carol Shakeshaft, *Educator Sexual Misconduct: A Synthesis of Existing Literature.*

55. Kimberly McCabe, *Child Abuse and the Criminal Justice System.*

56. Kimberly McCabe and Gregory Martin, *School Violence, the Media and Criminal Justice Responses.*

57. Kimberly McCabe and Olivia Johnston "Perceptions on the Legality of Sexting: A Report," *Social Science Computer Review*, 32(6) (2014): 765–68.

58. Kimberly McCabe, *Protecting Your Children in Cyberspace: What Parents Need to Know.*

59. Kimberly McCabe, *Protecting Your Children in Cyberspace: What Parents Need to Know.*

60. Kimberly McCabe, *Protecting Your Children in Cyberspace: What Parents Need to Know.*

61. Kimberly McCabe, *Protecting Your Children in Cyberspace: What Parents Need to Know.*

62. Amanda Lenhart, "Teens and Sexting," Pew Internet and American Life Project, December 15, 2009, accessed July 11, 2018, at https://www.pewinternet.org/REports/2009/Teens-and-sexting.aspx.

63. Janis Wolak and David Finkelhor, *Sextortion: Findings from a Survey of 1631 Victims* (Durham: University of New Hampshire, Crimes against Children Research Center, 2016), 5–7.

64. Cynthia Crosson-Tower, *Understanding Child Abuse and Neglect*, eighth edition (Boston: Allyn and Bacon, 2010).

65. Andrea Sedlak, Jane Mettenburg, Monica Basena, Ian Petta, Karla McPherson, Angela Greene, and Spencer Li, *National Incidence Study of Child Abuse and Neglect (NIS-4): Report to Congress Executive Summary* (Washington, DC: U.S. Department of Health and Human Services, Administration for Children and Families, 2010).

66. Maureen Kenny and Adriana McEachern, "Racial, Ethnic, and Cultural Factors of Childhood Sexual Abuse," *Clinical Psychological Review*, 20(7) (2000): 905–22.

67. Kimberly McCabe, *Child Abuse and the Criminal Justice System*.

68. Harry Wallace and Cliff Roberson, *Family Violence: Legal, Medical, and Social Perspectives*, sixth edition (Boston: Pearson, 2010).

69. Kimberly McCabe and Daniel Murphy, *Child Abuse—Today's Issues*.

70. Kimberly McCabe, *Child Abuse and the Criminal Justice System*.

71. Kimberly McCabe, *Child Abuse and the Criminal Justice System*.

72. Kimberly McCabe and Daniel Murphy, *Child Abuse—Today's Issues*.

73. Kimberly McCabe and Gregory Martin, *School Violence, the Media and Criminal Justice Responses*.

74. Harry Wallace, *Family Violence. Legal, Medical, and Social Perspectives*, second edition (Boston: Allyn and Bacon, 1999).

75. Cynthia Crosson-Tower, *Understanding Child Abuse and Neglect*.

76. Kimberly McCabe and Daniel Murphy, *Child Abuse—Today's Issues*.

77. Cynthia Crosson-Tower, *Understanding Child Abuse and Neglect*.

78. Kimberly McCabe, *Child Abuse and the Criminal Justice System*.

79. Rami Benbenishty, Anat Zeira, Ron Avi Astor, and Mona Khoury-Kassabri, "Maltreatment of Primary School Students by Educational Staff in Israel," *Child Abuse and Neglect*, 26 (2002): 1291–1309.

80. Kristina Lee, "Prevalence and Predictors of Self-reported Student Maltreatment by Teachers in South Korea," *Child Abuse and Neglect*, 46 (2015): 113–20.

81. Finiki Nearchou, "Resilience Following Emotional Abuse by Teachers: Insights from a Cross-Sectional Study with Greek Students," *Child Abuse and Neglect*, 78 (2018): 96–106.

82. Oyaziwo Aluede, "Psychological Maltreatment of Students: A Form of Child Abuse and School Violence," *Journal of Human Ecology*, 16 (2004): 265–70.

83. Adriana McEachern, Oyaziwo Aluede, and Maureen Kenny, "Emotional Abuse in the Classroom: Implications and Interventions for Counselors," *Journal of Counseling and Development*, 86 (2008): 3–10.

84. Adriana McEachern, Oyaziwo Aluede, and Maureen Kenny, "Emotional Abuse in the Classroom: Implications and Interventions for Counselors."

85. Stuart Twemlow and Peter Fonagy, "The Prevalence of Teachers Who Bully Students in Schools with Differing Levels of Behavioral Problems," *American Journal of Psychiatry*, 162 (2005): 2387–89.

86. Psychology Today, *Child Neglect* (New York: Sussex, 2014).

87. Cynthia Crosson-Tower, *Understanding Child Abuse and Neglect*.

88. Mark Follman, "New FBI Study Shows Mass Shooters Aren't Loners Who Just Snap."

89. Mark Follman and Becca Andrews, "How Columbine Spawned Dozens of Copy Cats."

90. Mike Nizza, "Gunman Was Once 'Revered' on Campus," *New York Times*, February 15, 2008, accessed on December 20, 2018, at https://www.nytimes.com.

91. Aaron Katersky and Susanna Kim, "5 Disturbing Things We Learned Today about Sandy Hook Shooter Adam Lanza," ABC News, November 21, 2014, accessed on December 7, 2018, at https://abcnews.go.com.

92. Kimberly McCabe and Gregory Martin, *School Violence, the Media and Criminal Justice Responses*.

93. Jeremy Alford, "Student Kills 2 and Herself at a Louisiana College," *New York Times*, February 9, 2008, accessed on November 7, 2018, at https://www.nytimes.com.

94. Mark Gangloff, "Police Identify Virginia Tech Shooter as Radford University Student," *Roanoke Times*, December 8, 2011, accessed on December 13, 2018, at https://www.roanoke.com.

95. *Seattle Times*, "1 Dead, Others Hurt in Shooting at Seattle Pacific University before Student Tackles Gunman," *Seattle Times*, June 6, 2014, accessed on November 7, 2018, at https://www.seattletimes.com.

96. National Institute of Mental Health (NIMH), "Suicide in America: Frequently Asked Questions," 2018, National Institutes of Health (NIH), accessed January 17, 2019, at https://www.nimh.nih.gov/health/publications/suicide-faq/index.shtml#pub1.

97. National Institute of Mental Health (NIMH), "Suicide in America: Frequently Asked Questions."

98. Edmund Andrews, "Shooting Rampage at German School," *New York Times*, April 27, 2002, accessed on December 3, 2018, at https://www.nytimes.com.

99. Jamie Holguin, "4 Dead in Univ. of Arizona Shooting," CBS News, October 29, 2002, accessed on November 25, 2018, at https://www.cbsnews.com/news/4-dead-in-univ-of-arizona-shooting/.

100. Susan Svrluga, Mark Berman, and Sarah Larimer, "UCLA Attack: Gunman Who Shot Former Professor Has 'Kill List,' Connected to Estranged Wife's Death," *Washington Post*, June 2, 2016, accessed on December 3, 2018, at https://www.washingtonpost.com.

101. James Wilson and George Kelling, "Broken Windows: The Police and Neighborhood Safety," *Atlantic Monthly*, March (1982): 29–38.

102. Katie Hesketh and Sara Acorn, "Workplace Violence in Alberta and British Columbia Hospitals," *Health Policy*, 63(3) (2003): 311–21.

103. Kimberly McCabe and Daniel Murphy, *Child Abuse—Today's Issues*.

Chapter Eight

Violence in Higher Education

KEY WORDS

ACPA Presidential Task Force on Sexual Violence Prevention in Higher Education
American College Personnel Association Statement of Ethical Principles and Standards
Boko Haram
Bullying
Closed campus
Consent
Cybercrime
Cyberstalking
Dating violence
Dear Colleague Letter
First Amendment
Harassment
Hate crime
Hate model
Hazing
Incompetent stalker
Internet troll
Intimacy-seeking stalker
Irrational hate
Ivory Tower
Not Alone
Open campus
Predatory stalker
Rape
Rational hate
Rejected stalker
Resentful stalker
Sexual assault
Stalker
Stalking
Terrorism
The Campus SaVE Act
The Jeanne Clery Disclosure of Campus Security Policy and Campus Crime Statistics Act
White House Task Force to Protect Students from Sexual Assault

KEY ACRONYMS

(ACPA) American College Personnel Association
(VAWA) Violence Against Women Act

In 1840, the first documented school shooting occurred at the University of Virginia in the United States. The shooter was a student at the time and the one fatality was a professor, who died at the scene. Hence, school violence occurred prior to the shootings at Dunblane Primary School (Scotland) in 1986 and Columbine High School (USA) in 1999; however, school shootings and school violence were only recognized as a significant public concern over the last two decades when the type of location changed from institutions of higher education to K–12 schools.[1]

Today, estimates suggest that thousands of colleges and universities exist throughout the world. In particular, in the United States, there exists approximately five thousand institutions of higher education, in Europe there exists approximately four thousand institutions, and in Latin America, approximately three thousand institutions. For the overwhelming majority of these colleges and universities, there has never been a recorded incident of severe violence; however, within the twenty-first century, the media has highlighted numerous incidents of violent attacks on college and university campuses. These attacks have varied in location, severity, and presumed nature of cause, but they are common in their outcomes of concern and fear by the public. One central theme that seems to be inferred by students, faculty, and institutions is the increasing number of these tragedies. For the purpose of this chapter, and for clarity throughout the international community, the terms college and university will be used interchangeably and will simply represent any educational institution beyond the K–12 educational units.

University campuses experience the same types of violent crimes present on K–12 campuses in addition to increased incidents of sexual assaults, hazing, and harassment.[2] For most part, those violent crimes that occur on university campuses include shootings, rape, physical assault, hazing, dating violence, self-harm, and stalking. The critical question—Are these crimes present because of the culture surrounding the campus lifestyle or because institutions of higher education are viewed by many as symbols of authority or freedom of expression? When explanations for such events are sought, responses often revolve around the risks by students on these campuses. In other responses, researchers suggest that these attacks in higher education are related to the external global crisis of conflict around their communities and within the world.[3] This chapter discusses school violence in higher education as a result of not only the internal risk factors for violence, but also the external factors that facilitate violence. Multiple *causes* may be proposed, but that does not solve the issue of the increasing prevalence of these events throughout the world.

INTERNAL RISKS

Although many theories may be proposed as to why one commits a violent act, research has shown that there is no single cause of violence. This lack of a definitive answer carries over to the campus communities of universities as there are many possible influences that promote individual acts of violence. Individual factors that may influence one to act violently are the attitudes of the faculty, the staff, and the other students. An example of an interpersonal factor leading to violence would be group norms regarding appropriate behavior on the campus.[4] Alcohol consumption at high levels and campus policies and procedures are also considered to be risk factors that may influence violence within a campus setting.[5] Others suggest that the extent of involvement by law enforcement is related to risk factors. Finally, influences from subgroups, technology, and the media coverage of previous tragedies are also often considered risk factors for violence within the educational setting.[6]

Regardless of the possible influences present on a college campus, a violent event requires the combination of a person with an inclination toward violent behavior, a situation in which elements are present that create the risk of a violent event, and, in most cases, a significant life event that activates the individual to partake in some sort of violence.[7] As a result, universities must begin to consider if there are factors within their control that might contribute to the likelihood of a violent incident occurring on their campus. Some of those internal factors include the structure of the university's campus and the presence of guns, mental illness, hate crimes, bullying, harassment, and cyberbullying.

Open Campuses

One major factor that differentiates the university setting from a K–12 school setting is the standard layout of the campus. For the most part, schools that make up grades kindergarten through high school are composed of *closed campuses*. A closed campus may be operationalized by having a gate surrounding the entire campus, multiple buildings connected by enclosed walkways, one building, or one entrance to the campus or buildings. However, *open campuses* are those in which there are outdoor walkways from one building to another and multiple entrances to the campus or school buildings, and these types are predominantly represented among the majority of university campuses across the globe.

As a result of the many buildings, high volumes of student traffic, and outsider traffic as well, the open campus layout associated with universities

On August 1, 1966, at the University of Texas, Charles Whitman climbed to the top of the university's tower with multiple firearms. The twenty-five-year-old had murdered his wife and mother earlier in the day and then continued on a ninety-six-minute killing spree during which he shot forty-three people, which resulted in an additional thirteen fatalities that day.

may have a significant correlation to the high incidents of violence that occurs within this specific setting. For a university to ensure that all doors are locked and that they have security staff within all buildings throughout the days and evenings is unreasonable, and essentially structurally impossible.

Historically, many university campuses were constructed with major routes of transportation somewhat close to allow students to migrate back and forth from home to campus as the terms of the academic year continued. Over the years, with the expansion of campus buildings and structures, many universities are now located within walking distance from major transportation routes. Also, as the campus size has increased with the additions of sporting arenas and open lecture halls with public attendance encouraged, more individuals who are not attending the universities as students are entering the campus facilities. As a result, perpetrators outside of the university environment often are allowed an easy access to the campus as well as the students, faculty, and staff.

On April 26, 2002, in Germany, a nineteen-year-old expelled student of Gutenberg-Gymnasium, Robert Steinhäuser, shot and killed sixteen people before committing suicide. Prior to the incident Steinhäuser had been expelled and, therefore, was not to be on campus.

As a result of the open campus structure, institutions of higher education, purposely designed to be open to all individuals, may be facilitating these severe acts of violence. This welcoming design is also welcoming for perpetrators of violence.

Mental Illness

Research shows that the highest rates of mental illness are present in the eighteen to twenty-five age cohort; the same age cohort that generally attends institutions of higher education.[8] Some researchers suggest that many incidents of campus violence are a result of the presence of this age cohort and

In June of 2014 on the campus of Seattle Pacific University (USA), one student was killed during a shooting. The twenty-six-year-old perpetrator had a history of mental illness, had stopped taking his medicine, and had planned a mass shooting to kill as many people as possible.

their propensity for mental health issues.[9] Therefore, simply by the presence of the populations of students, institutions of higher education are at risk for violence victimizations.

As the symptoms of mental illness vary drastically and change over time, the warning signs for an individual suffering from a mental illness also vary and change. Unfortunately, behaviors such as changes in appearance, poor academic behavior, diminishing hygiene, and tiredness or stress are also normally observed in students on college campuses; therefore, these indicators are not the signs to indicate the potential for violence within an institution of higher education. Consequently, these indicators of teen and adolescent mental illness, which may be more easily identified in a K–12 environment, are not often identified on a university campus.

When perpetrators of extreme school violence (school shootings) were questioned about why they had been involved in the incidents many gave responses indicating symptoms related to mental illnesses.[10] Examples of such responses include thoughts of suicide, feeling sorry for themselves, the expectation of being killed in the incident, not caring about their future, feelings of helplessness, feeling as though they do not belong to a group, or finding themselves in a dark place, especially one in which they have felt to have been in for a while and could not escape.[11] The incident at Virginia Tech in 2006 was the most tragic example. Although the discussions around mental illness in relation to violence within higher education have increased, there still remains much to be addressed as this problem continues and is a concern throughout the world.

Conceal Carry

Many countries allow their citizens the right to own firearms. In the United States, firearms within homes are a norm. In addition, in the United States laws have been enacted that permit the carry of a concealed weapon (i.e., guns). Historically, institutions of higher education within the United States were one of the areas in which it was prohibited to carry a firearm; however, in 2018, this law changed and many of the fifty US states now allow individuals to conceal handguns on college campuses. Research suggests that male students exhibit a higher level of approval for the legalization of concealed weapons on campuses than females.[12] They are also more prone to violence with handguns. In addition, students whose parents owned firearms or students who had friends who carry concealed weapons also had a significantly higher level of approval of the legalization of concealed firearms on college campuses as well as those who lived off campus.[13]

In October of 2002, Robert Flores Jr., age forty-one, shot three professors before killing himself at the University of Arizona (USA). Classmates of Flores stated that he had informed them of his concealed weapon permit.

In addition, research suggests that college students in the United States see many advantages of carrying concealed handguns on campuses to include that they felt they would be better able to protect themselves as well as the belief that others may bother them less if they were able to conceal carry on campus.[14] Therefore, violence and, in particular school shootings, may be facilitated in the United States through the presence of handguns on college campuses.

Research suggests that violence in schools may occur in areas with little community violence.[15] In addition, open campuses, access to weapons, and mental illness are not the only factors related to violence on a university campus. However, in some cases, the violence on a university campus is a result of violence within the community. These external factors or risks increase the likelihood of violence on a university campus.

EXTERNAL RISKS

From September of 2016 through August of 2017, there were 257 identified attacks (55 violent) on institutions of higher education (i e , colleges or universities) within thirty-five different countries.[16] These attacks resulted in the deaths of more than forty-five students, faculty, and staff. In addition, and most relevant to this section, many of these violent attacks occurred in countries experiencing armed conflicts or violent extremisms.[17] Universities, which by nature often emphasize free inquiry and expression, are often the targets for these attacks in attempts to deter free speech, political action, and community mobilization. Recently, three of the more targeted countries are Nigeria, Pakistan, and Syria.[18]

In Nigeria, the University of Maiduguri, which has experienced multiple violent attacks, has reported at least fourteen deaths and more than thirty injured persons within a twelve-month period. Unfortunately, the University of Maiduguri has been a target of Boko Haram's terrorist attacks since 2009, including bombings, gun attacks, and suicide attacks.[19] By attacking the university, Boko Haram creates fear among those who disagree with their beliefs and ideologies. As universities often emphasize the questioning of authority, by targeting these universities, the Boko Haram has attempted to eliminate inquiry.

In Pakistan, attacks on institutions of higher learning often represent attacks on symbols of state authority and opposition to radical ideologies.[20] One report on violence toward colleges and universities in Pakistan identified 724 terrorist attacks between 2004 and 2013.[21] Although the majority of the reported attacks were not lethal, one more recent attack in January of 2016 resulted in twenty fatalities at Pakistan's Bacha Khan University by Taliban gunmen.[22] In addition, attacks on institutions of higher learning in Syria have been frequent and, according to one report, more than 50 percent of the schools across Syria have experienced some sort of violence against them.[23] Two explosions at Aleppo University in 2013 killed at least eighty people.[24] Two months later, gunfire in Syria killed at least ten more students at the Damascus University.[25]

In Pakistan, in addition to these actions of mass destruction against individuals within institutions of higher learning, there have also been actions of physical assaults against students participating in protests and kidnappings within these universities.[26] Specifically, in January of 2017, a professor and activist from Fatima Women University was kidnapped. A few weeks later, three other activists were kidnapped. All were returned later, but the identities of the abductors were never announced.[27]

In attempts to obstruct academic freedoms, many countries have imprisoned, prosecuted, and dismissed or expelled students. In particular, in Central and Eastern Europe legislative actions over the last few years have targeted the operations of universities and research centers, especially at the Levada Center (Russia) and the Central European University (Hungary).[28] In these cases, university officials were released from their positions after questioning government laws and regulations. At the same time, students and faculty were imprisoned for being perceived as enemies of the state.[29]

VIOLENT CRIMES ON CAMPUS

As the media's attention to severe violence on university campuses usually focuses on the crimes of murder and mass murder, other crimes that affect college communities often become minimized. For the majority of the victims of violence on a college campus, their victimization is not one through mass destruction and fatalities but those crimes of individualized victimization. Unfortunately, some of these nonlethal crimes of violence may have long-term effects on the victims, including the final outcome of death by suicide. These crimes include bullying, harassment, hazing, hate crimes, dating violence, rape and sexual assault, and cybercrimes.

Bullying, Harassment, and Hazing

For the purpose of this chapter, bullying is defined as an individual or a group of people with more power who repeatedly and intentionally cause hurt or harm to another person or group of people who feel helpless to respond.[30] Although bullying is not as commonly recognized on university campuses, harassment has been recognized as one of the more prevalent issues of concern on college campuses. Harassment includes a range of repeated behaviors that are considered offensive, humiliating, demeaning, or embarrassing to the victim.

On April 2, 2012, forty-three-year-old One L. Goh was arrested after firing shots during a nursing class on the campus of Oikos University. Goh was a former student of the Korean Christian college. It was suggested that a possible motivation for Goh may have been the fact that while he was attending this school classmates mistreated, harassed, and disrespected him.

In college, male students often report being a victim of bullying or harassment more than female students.[31] For clarity, harassment refers to unwanted and consistent verbal or physical attacks that result in fear or humiliation on the part of the victim. In the Swarthmore College (USA) example, one student, who claimed constant harassment by his abuser, shot and killed his abuser.[32] Although bullying within higher education is not commonly discussed, this incident demonstrates the presence of such events within a university setting. Harassment and hazing are other concerns for universities attempting to reduce incidents of school violence. By definition, hazing, regardless of a person's willingness to participate, is any action taken or any situation created intentionally that causes embarrassment, harassment, ridicule, emotional risks, and/or physical harm to members of a group or a team. Most recently, hazing has been associated with Greek student organizations on university campuses.

In the United States, the Campus Violence Prevention Center reported that fraternity members were disproportionately represented among offenders for hazing on university campuses.[33] Concerns to uphold masculinity or femininity, a set group of inclusion and group protection, high consumptions of alcohol, and an importance of self or organization based on superiority may be reasons that members of Greek life are overrepresented among offenders in this setting.

In December of 2013 at Lusofona University (Portugal), six students drowned as the result of an initiation and hazing by a club in the middle of the night off a deserted beach near Lisbon.

Accordingly, large Greek life systems may be one risk factor when referencing bullying, harassment, and hazing on college campuses. In most Greek organizations, before one is a member, participants are made to partake in actions to show they are loyal and dedicated to the clique. Unfortunately, many of these actions may be referred to as actions of hazing. Examples of these activities range from requiring group members to memorize the Greek alphabet to practices in which new members are made to preform sexual acts on animals or other members of the group. Therefore, the university setting, and especially those universities with a large presence of fraternities and sororities, is a place where the actions of bullying, harassment, and hazing are most likely to occur.

Hate Crimes

Approximately 15 percent of hate crimes in the United States occur within a college or university setting.[34] Approximately half of these hate crimes are outcomes of bias based upon either race or ethnicity, approximately 25 percent are outcomes of bias based upon religion, and approximately 25 percent of hate crimes are based upon a bias toward sexual orientation.[35]

When considering the perpetrators of hate crimes, the majority are under the age of twenty-five, with nearly 30 percent of those individuals under the age of eighteen.[36] Thus, young adults, such as those on college campuses, are actively involved in actions of hate that include not only the destruction of property but also the victimization of individuals. Therefore, given the demographics of college campuses, this propensity of hate or extremist groups is often present.

Within recent years there has been an increase in the attention being paid to the diversity within all types of educational institutions of higher learning and especially those at the university level. It is believed that if there is an increase in the diversity of a university then the university's minority populations are more likely to be retained. Although this is intended to better the overall environment of these institutions, acts of violence or bias against certain groups may increase with the diversity of students on campus and, in turn, may lessen the likelihood of acquiring and retaining a diverse population of faculty and students. A student or faculty member may become a victim of a hate crime simply because of a particular characteristic possessed by that individual. This rationale for victimization based upon a demographic or behavioral characteristic is what is called a hate crime.[37] The US Federal Bureau of Investigation defines a hate crime as a criminal offense against a person or property motivated in whole or in part by an offender's bias.[38]

On October 1, 2015, Chris Harper-Mercer, a twenty-six-year-old student at Umpqua Community College (Oregon—USA) shot and killed nine people. Some accounts of the incident suggest the shooter asked his victims about their religious affiliation before killing them. On the day of the shooting, Harper-Mercer gave a survivor numerous writings showing he had studied mass killings, his hostility toward black men, and an absence of fulfillment in his life.

Depending upon the area of the world, hate crimes may be a result of different dynamics. In the United States, many of the crimes of bias (i.e., hate crimes) are based upon race.[39] In Canada, the majority of their hate crimes are based on religion.[40] In addition, as if hate is not enough of a reason for destruction, some researchers suggest that these hate crimes are often correlated with terrorism.[41]

In particular, hate crimes are likely to create an environment of hostility for victims as a result of their victimization for no other reason than their race, ethnicity, or whatever characteristic that was different from the majority that they were targeted for. Once a student or faculty member is a victim of a hate crime on a university campus, it is likely they will not feel safe within the environment anymore. In addition, victims may also report feeling as though their academic freedom has been taken away.[42] Although universities are supposed to be places in which differing thoughts and opinions are welcomed and examined, victims are likely to keep their ideas to themselves and not voice their opinions in classes openly because they are living with the fear of becoming victimized if their ideas are different from those of others. Table 8.1 shows two examples of specific hate crimes that have been reported within the United States.

Across the world, protests occur daily and many occur on college campuses. The subjects of those projects include worker-employer conflicts,

Table 8.1. Violence Examples on College Campuses as a Result of the Political Environment

University	Incident
Iowa State University (IA)	Following the 2016 presidential inauguration: business cards left in campus library that read, "America was 90% white in 1950. It is now 60%. MAKE AMERICA GREAT AGAIN. Trump was first, we're next!"
Lindenwood University (MO)	Following the 2016 presidential election: Latina student returns to dorm and finds her roommate had made a wall between their beds and left a note that read, "Trump won so here is a little preview of what's to come."

racial inequality, and police officer–involved shootings. The majority of these events on college campuses are peaceful and non-confrontational; however, some are not and some result in arrests, injuries, and deaths.

Many countries provide their citizens the right to gather, to protest, and to speak. This right is often observed within the university setting. This protection of speech is one of the most covenanted rights afforded by countries; however, this right is not available to individuals in all countries.

FIRST AMENDMENT:
UNITED STATES CONSTITUTION (ABRIDGED)

Congress shall make no law respecting an establishment of religion, or prohibiting the free exercise thereof; or abridging the freedom of speech, or of the press; or of the right of the people to assembly, and to petition the Government for a redress of grievances.

On college campuses, this right to protest is most often referenced in discussions on free speech, posts on the subjects of hate and violence via the internet, on social blogs, and through social networks, all within cyberspace. Unfortunately, many individuals and, in particular, young educated people find these posts to be interesting and appealing.[43] It is these electronic posts that often attempt to facilitate bias and hate in our society and it is these posts that should be of concern to those universities attempting to address school violence.

According to researchers, hundreds of active hate groups and extremist groups exist today.[44] Many of these group members post messages and recruit new members via the internet and on college campuses. It is these groups that should be of concern to administrators in higher education as it is these groups that actively recruit students into their organizations with the intent of involving new members in actions of destruction. As suggested by researchers, hate, in some cases, may be displayed in protests and extremist violent activities.

Today's hate groups recognize this "search of self" by young people and often utilize the online community to facilitate the exposure of their ideas to this impressionable audience. Therefore, those in higher education must also be aware that, although many groups and organizations are not created to facilitate hate and destruction, members of some of these groups utilize their personal connections and cyberspace to incite violence by group members.

The majority of hate crimes are nonviolent offenses such as the vandalism of property.[45] This trend is also the case in property crimes on college campuses.[46] In addition, when a hate crime is violent, it is most often an assault or a threat(s) of violence against one person; however, when hate crimes are demonstrated on college campuses, the results are often multiple victims.

In the international community, as documented by some of the violent actions toward universities in Nigeria and Pakistan, the outcomes of hate are legendary with the obvious results of mass destruction and mass murder. Unfortunately, when one begins to explain why another hates something or someone, the rational becomes less apparent.[47] Attempts to combat hate or thoughts of hatred are limited and, oftentimes, ignored, as how does one objectively end an action with a subjective, philosophically based dynamic?

Hate is divided into two categories: rational and irrational. In general, rational hate results from acts perceived as unjust whereas irrational hate is demonstrated as a hatred of a demographic or behavioral characteristic of a person or groups of people (i.e., race, religion) often without the experience of personalized victimization. As Canada's law enforcement has reported, their most common hate crimes are the crimes against their Jewish communities.[48]

In explaining rational hate, the focus by the perpetrator (hereafter hater) is usually the unjust action performed against them or another within their subgroup or clique and their inability to effect change.[49] In these cases, an individual is abused by another and as a result feels hate toward their abuser.

Irrational hate, the category of hate involving most actions of mass destruction, is much more difficult to explain. As suggested in the research on child abuse, this behavior or philosophy is passed down from generation to generation as a learned behavior. It is also this category of hate that rarely results from a personal account of abuse or victimization by the target of hate. Within the university setting, irrational hate is often displayed in off-color jokes about certain races, gender, or religions or in actions of discrimination toward an individual based upon appearance. In addition, it is the cases of irrational hate that are also demonstrated in acts of terrorism as crimes of hate and terrorism are often akin.[50]

Irrational hate allows the hater, most often a very insecure individual, to feel elevated above their hated subject. From this vantage point, the hated individual or clique is perceived as less worthy and, therefore, deserving of violence toward them. It is this category of irrational hate that fuels the memberships and actions of those involved in hate groups that facilitate hate and destruction against others within the college campus. It is also this category of hate that will facilitate violence by those nonstudents against universities of higher learning.

Research suggests that hate is not a spontaneous behavior but a learned behavior with a process of steps and stages.[51] In particular, the psychopathology of hate groups suggests a seven-stage model of hate. Through each stage or step, the hatred of a group is identified, solidified, and acted upon.

It is suggested that in the first stage of the hate model, haters, who rarely desire to hate alone, are motivated or driven to gather as individuals into a common group.[52] Our notion of the strength or protection in numbers is demonstrated in this behavior. Individuals, and particularly young people, who are unwilling to demonstrate actions of destruction alone are more likely to participate in these actions if acting in a clique or subgroup within the university environment.

In the second stage, the group begins to form its own identify through the bonds of common thoughts, meanings, or ideas.[53] It is also during this stage that symbols or rituals are introduced as the goals and the mission of the group. Just as is often demonstrated in religious practices, human beings are often uncertain or at a loss when it comes to faith. For many of us, that means that to believe in something, we must be able to visualize or even to touch a symbol of our faith. In the Hebrew Bible, this was demonstrated over and over again and was apparent in the story of Moses leaving his followers only to later return to discover them worshipping a golden calf.[54] Just as that known story illustrates the need for individuals to have something to see before they could believe and follow, in the campus environment symbols or logos are associated with essentially every student organization that exists and help in the bonding experience of these cliques.

The third stage in the hate model is established to specifically identify the person, persons, or organization for hatred.[55] It is during this stage that group members know exactly who they should hate, even if they do not know why they hate them. The hatred of competing Greek organizations on college campuses demonstrates this stage as the members of the two organizations do not like each other; however, the reasons for these feelings are sometimes unclear.

During the fourth stage, the hate group verbally targets the foci of hate.[56] This stage is demonstrated in racial slurs, negative stories, or demeaning jokes that somehow lessen the perceived value by group members of the target. It is during this stage that members use the N-word to address those of African-American descent, the phrase Camel Jockey for individuals of Middle Eastern descent, or the phrase Christ Killer for a person of the Jewish faith.[57] As universities are associated with the freedom of expression, protests, and assemblies, even those with unpopular ideas may be more accepted on these campuses of higher learning.

During the fifth stage, the hater or haters move from verbal abuse to physical abuse or the destruction of property.[58] It is during this stage that the vandalism of campus buildings, the burning of structures, and physical assaults against individuals occur. It is also during this stage that reports are often made to law enforcement and university officials.

During the sixth stage, the hate group attacks the target or targets with weapons.[59] These weapons may include bats, firearms, and explosives. It is during this stage that the destruction of property and the severity of injury are significant. In addition, in this stage law enforcement and/or emergency services officials are involved in reaction to the attacks.

In the final stage of hate, the subgroup destroys the target.[60] Fortunately, this seventh stage of the hate model is an extremely rare occurrence. However, as described in this chapter, these attacks do occur on college campuses. Hence, hate, often expressed initially through speeches on university campuses or online, is often associated with incidents of violence on college campuses.

Dating Violence

There is much research surrounding the topic of dating violence within a college community that points out the fact that the majority of students personally know, or knew, someone involved in a violent dating relationship. The US Center for Disease Control defines dating violence as, "the physical, sexual, psychological, or emotional aggression within a dating relationship, including stalking."[61] In reference to dating violence, Southern states within the United States exhibited a significantly higher rate of dating violence within college campuses than other regions.[62] In Northern Europe, dating

In May of 2010, a University of Virginia (USA) lacrosse player killed his exgirlfriend after pushing his way into her bedroom and repeatedly smashing her head against a wall. Two years later, he was convicted of murder and sentenced to twenty-three years in prison.

violence is often perceived as acceptable if used by females.[63] In addition, dating violence is viewed as acceptable if talking about an issue has failed to resolve the issue.[64] Regardless of popular opinion, this form of violence is affecting both men and women on college campuses.

In dating violence, when gender is considered, low family income is a risk factor of victimization in males, and those who live in urban areas are more likely to be involved in this type of violence.[65] In addition, women are more likely than men to report violence within a relationship and are also more likely to sustain an injury as a result.[66] Therefore, when women are the perpetrators they usually state self-defense as the reason for the violent incident whereas men are more likely to use violence as an intimidation or scare method. A reason for this may be that men and women hold differing beliefs and expectations about what institutes aggression.

This type of violence usually takes the physical form of pushing, punching, striking with an object, and slapping, as well as verbal threats against the other person involved in the relationship.[67] Verbal aggression is a common form of dating violence experienced by college students usually taking the form of yelling, insulting, and refusal to speak to the other. Jealousy and alcohol consumption are major factors that play into the violence within this specific community. When there is physical violence within these relationships, the frequency of the incidents may be lower than if the aggression within the relationship is verbal. Since dating provides a context for establishing meaningful relationships with members of society we may be romantically interested in, it is hypothesized that as a result of the significant number of incidents of violence within dating relationships on college campuses, the number of domestic violence incidents within families in the future will continue to be a problem.[68]

Rape and Sexual Assault

Research at 153 universities in England and Wales reported that 8 percent of female respondents reported being raped at universities.[69] In a similar survey in the United States, 1 percent of females reported being raped.[70]

Sexual assault, no matter the location, can take an immeasurable toll on the victim's physical and mental health. On the college campus without the presence of family, victims are often lost with the emotional and physical results of the assault impacting their academic, social, professional, and personal responsibilities.[71]

As coping plans often recommend steps such as going to a safe place, victims of these types of incidents of school violence, in many cases, are unable to identify those safe places. In addition, and with any type of victimization, victims should contact the authorities, but in a college environment there is often confusion in identifying authorities—is it the campus administration or law enforcement? Lastly, recommended steps in addressing these types of crime include seeking medical and counseling assistance. Again, on a college campus, victims may be unaware of these resources. Consequently, the victimization of sexual assaults on college campuses is not only a reality but a reality oftentimes unaddressed.

There are many ways for a campus to be proactive in the fight against violence within relationships on their campus. Sexuality education can be facilitated by staff and faculty on campus, as well as by students in leadership roles. Campus health centers, counseling centers, or spiritual life centers may also be places that sexuality education may be utilized in an effort to educate students and reduce the amount of violence within relationships on campus.

Expectations of a healthy relationship, sexual health, how to establish personal boundaries, clear communication, consent, and many other topics should be discussed to enhance the institution's understanding of the topic. Other topics that may aid in the education of students on this topic include sexism, roots of violence, and the potential signs of violence within an already existing relationship.

Regardless of what is portrayed by the media, sexual violence on college campuses exists among all racial and ethnic groups, sexual orientations, and gender identities. Within the college setting, the entire community is affected by this type of violence whether it be students, faculty, staff, or administrators. Sexual assault includes any unwelcomed sexual action, which may range from unwanted touching to rape. As of 2013 the US FBI defines a rape as the penetration, no matter how slight, of the vagina or anus with any body part or object, or oral penetration by a sex organ of another person, without the consent of the victim.[72]

As previously stated throughout the chapter, the culture surrounding campus life may be one reason sexual victimizations occur at such an alarming rate within this setting in particular. For example, alcohol and drugs have high levels of prevalence among this setting. These substances have the opportunity to render one's judgment or make one unaware of what is going on, which may increase the likelihood of becoming a victim. Another sector of the college environment that may increase the odds of one being a victim of a sexual assault is peer pressure.[73] As a result of being surrounded by a group of peers the majority of the time, and not having older adults around to judge and influence their actions, college students may feel inclined to attend social events in which they normally would not have, or even try drugs or alcohol because of the societal pressure of their peers.[74] Aside from increasing the likelihood of victimization due to the environmental factors of peer pressure, one may use peer pressure as a way to get someone to partake in a sexual act that the individual may not have participated in if they had not been pressured in such a way.

There are currently a vast number of legislative bills in the United States that are being discussed and introduced at both the federal and state levels addressing sexual assault on college campuses, with the majority revolving around the requirement of these institutions to put resources toward responding to these incidents when they occur. Countries in Europe and Africa are also attempting to address gender violence through laws and law enforcement. Listed in table 8.2 is some significant US legislation that revolves around sexual assault on college campuses.

In an effort to decrease the number of sexual assaults on college campuses, institutions should aim to educate students on topics such as consent, policies and resources that may be utilized if a situation occurs, healthy relationships and sexuality, and origins of sexual violence. For example, things as easy as defining sexual violence and consent may make a difference within the campus setting as students may not be aware of the exact meanings of these words.

The term *consent* within most legislation implies a freely given agreement to the conduct at issue by a competent person.[75] In reference to the misunderstandings around consent, students must be educated on a clear definition of the word as well as knowing when consent is able to be given. For example, consent may not be granted if an individual is under the influence of drugs or alcohol, is unconscious, or has been manipulated into feeling as though they must partake in a sexual act.

Cyber Victimization

A cybercrime may be operationalized as any criminal offense that is carried out by utilizing the internet. This type of victimization has started to increase drastically over the last few years as the uses of technology have become more involved in the lives of people of all ages. Institutions of higher learning have been implementing extensive Wi-Fi networks, online discussion boards, digital libraries, and conferencing via webcam in an effort to keep up with the way the upcoming generations are utilizing different technologies. On college campuses, the internet is a place in which communication and information retrieval may be made easier and quicker. With the significant use of smartphones, tablets, and laptops, students are able to check their emails, view course syllabi, access their institute's webpage, and many other things within minutes. Since the majority of these devices are connected to the internet via unsecured networks, they are susceptible to many security threats.

Table 8.2. Historical Actions to Address University Campus Violence

Date	Historical Movement	Information
1990	The Jeanne Clery Disclosure of Campus Security Policy and Campus Crime Statistics Act	• Federal statute requiring colleges participating in federal financial aid programs to maintain and disclose campus crime statistics and security information
2006	American College Personnel Association (ACPA) Statement of Ethical Principles and Standards	• All college student educators have an ethical responsibility to create and maintain safe and equitable learning environments for all students
April 2011	Dear Colleague Letter	• US Department of Education Office for Civil Rights: ○ Notified campus officials of their responsibility to provide services and reaction to sexual violence ○ Piloted a trend of federal guidance that sought to elucidate institutions' responsibilities with regard to addressing sexual violence
January 2014	White House Task Force to Protect Students from Sexual Assault	• White House issued an initial report describing the prevalence and complexity of sexual violence within schools • White House Task Force to Protect Students from Sexual Assault formed
April 2014	Not Alone	• White House Task Force to Protect Students from Sexual Assault. Second report ○ Highlighted the recommended best practices for campuses in climate assessment, prevention, response and adjudication, and enforcement efforts by the federal government
Spring 2014	ACPA Presidential Task Force on Sexual Violence Prevention in Higher Education	• Provided direction about educating students, developing professional competency, and guiding institutional leadership in reference to sexual violence
October 2014	The Campus SaVE Act	• Department of Education published the Clery Act amendments (the Campus SaVE Act) enacted under the Violence against Women Act Reauthorization of 2013 (VAWA) • Expanded the scope of legislation in terms of: ○ reporting ○ response ○ prevention ○ education requirements around rape, acquaintance rape, domestic violence, dating violence, sexual assault, and stalking

In September 2010, Tyler Clement, an eighteen-year-old Rutgers (Princeton, New Jersey—USA) freshman jumped to his death from a local bridge. The student decided to end his life after a video capturing himself and another male kissing was released on the internet. In this case, the student's roommate placed a hidden webcam in their dorm room and recorded the encounter. The roommate then posted the sexual encounter on Twitter. Three days after the encounter, the student jumped to his death after leaving behind a suicide note.

With increased accessibility to cyber networks also comes the increased vulnerability of one being victimized through the internet. Many institutions are turning to "clouds" on their campuses as a way to share and save information more quickly and easily than in the past. Although using a cloud to deliver information will reduce the cost and stress related to managing this information, it also increases the risk for the information to be utilized by outside networks. When using a cloud, the information being input is sent to a global data. This escalates the likelihood that information provided be shared with someone who is not in the specific cloud in which the original information was shared and may lead to breaches in confidential information.

As far as the institution's overall data, all universities have a database that contains confidential information on students and faculty. This information includes data such as their date of birth, social security number, income, family income, and so on. As a result of the increasing number of identity thefts via the internet, it is necessary that universities protect this information through encryption and other methods so their students and faculty can't be victimized in this way.[76]

The US Department of Homeland Security suggests that people using public computer networks, such as those in place on university campuses, should change their passwords every few months, download and keep antivirus and firewall software up to date, be aware of spyware threats, and also think before clicking on links.[77]

Many individuals suggest that the constant fear of being observed, harmed, followed, embarrassed, or killed is more paralyzing than the actual act itself.[78] These actions, as related to the victimization by another, would result in fear from a reasonable person and are not unusual occurrences on a college campus. They are often referred to as the actions associated with stalking. By definition, stalking is the obsessive and unwanted attention by an individual or groups of individuals toward another person.[79] Victims of stalking often report a fear of not knowing what will happen next, and they fear the stalking will never end. Many victims of stalking on a college campus will transfer schools to be free of their stalker. Cyberstalking, simply stated, is online stalking or stalking in cyberspace. The goal of the cyberstalker, just as the goal for a traditional stalker, is to leave the victim feeling fearful, humiliated, and powerless.[80]

According to the Bureau of Justice statistics, more than seven million people are stalked annually in the United States; in the world, it is estimated that the number exceeds twenty million. Young college-age (i.e., age eighteen to twenty-five) individuals experience stalking at higher rates than any other age cohort. In addition, more than one-fourth of stalking victims are also victims of cyberstalking.[81]

In the college community, stalking is not a new concept. With the assimilation of the internet in the daily lives of individuals, cyberstalking, or the use of technology to facilitate stalking, is a very real concern on university campuses across the world.

In August of 2016, a British teen from Sussex, Shana Grice, age nineteen, was killed in her family home despite her previous and numerous calls to the police that she was being stalked and cyberstalked. The twenty-seven-year-old man, a former boyfriend, whom she claimed was her stalker, was later arrested and convicted of her murder.

Although the term "stalker" has been used since the 1500s to describe a type of prowler in criminal law, the twentieth-century definition better describes what we imagine with the act of stalking today—an individual who participates in the willful and repeated intrusions and communications with their targeted victim to the point of intimidation or producing fear.[82]

Both cyberstalkers and internet trolls are individuals who utilize computer technology and cyberspace to identify victims.[83] In many cases thee victims and perpetrators are located on college campuses. The difference between the two perpetrators is simple—the cyberstalkers usually know their victims from class or by associations on campus, while the internet trolls have rarely met their victims but seek a sense of power over their victims that is related to the amount of anger and distress they can produce within the online community [84]

Today, within the international community, there exists the debate in both public conversations and legal hearings as to what constitutes stalking.[85] The assertion by many is that stalking is a perception on the part of the victim, and that many cases that are termed stalking are not actually cases of stalking, but rather cases of infatuation. Where one crosses the line from attraction and infatuation to stalking is often explained in terms of length of interactions and, in many cases, is clearly demonstrated.

There exist essentially five categories of stalkers. Those categories are: (1) the rejected; (2) the intimacy-seeking; (3) the incompetent; (4) the resentful; and (5) the predatory.[86] The first and most common category of stalking is the rejected stalkers. These are the individuals who usually have been in a relationship with the victim and are often referred to as the "crazy ex." These stalkers are angry or upset about the end of the relationship and want either the victim to return to their relationship or for the victim to be punished for the pain that they have caused them. On college campuses, there are many individuals who have been in relationships, so there are many potential victims of stalking or cyberstalking within all universities.

The intimacy-seeking stalker, often received as the rejected stalker, usually wants the same outcome as the rejected stalker—either the victim to come back to them or for their victim to be unhappy. In addition, these individuals will often utilize the online community to gain information about their target (or victim) such as their likes and dislikes prior to their first face-to-face meeting.[87] However, critical in the distinguishing between these two categories is the fact that with the intimacy-seeking stalker, there was no actual relationship (and perhaps minimal contact) between the two parties; thus, there is no relationship for return. Unfortunately, for many individuals, and especially college students, perception is reality.[88] Hence, this category of stalker is obsessed with their victim and their victim's daily habits and routine and often utilizes technology to stalk their victims.

The incompetent stalker is another category of stalkers and is quite common in the teen world.[89] These are the individuals that, because of an inability to understand social protocol or a lack of social skills, simply desire to be a part of their victim's world and do not understand that their victim does not want to engage in a relationship with their stalker. They continue to attempt to instant message their victims and to follow their victims through social media.

The resentful stalker, oftentimes associated with hate groups or actions of bias, is the individual who decides to target a person because of some demographic of the victim.[90] The intent of these stalkers is to do damage to the person's character and/or their property.[91] In some cases, a victim may be stalked because of their membership in a racial, ethnic, religious, or homosexual group. If an individual's group affiliation is considered a threat or an annoyance because of an encounter or a bias, then that individual may also become a victim of stalking or cyberstalking.

Finally, the predatory stalker, although not as common as one believes, is the type most likely to receive the attention of the media.[92] These are the stalkers who target someone for violence. These are the individuals most thought to be perceived as the stranger lurking in the darkness, awaiting the opportunity to attack. On a college campus, there are multiple opportunities for predatory stalkers. In terms of cyberstalking, these cases are rare in that the predatory stalker's desired outcome is the physical abuse of their victim; thus, cyberstalking does not provide that end result. However, in cases involving sexual exploitation through cyberspace, this category of stalking may exist in conjunction with the other internet crimes.[93]

In the majority of stalking or cyberstalking cases, the stalker is known to their victim and most stalkers have had some degree of involvement in their victim's lives.[94] On a university campus, many individuals *know* each other (or at least have seen one another on campus). Just as in cases of cyberbullying, the anonymity of the online world and cyberspace often facilitates individuals and their abilities to cyberstalk their victims. On a college campus, stalkers and cyberstalkers often have no fear of repercussion as victimization continues.[95]

ADDRESSING SCHOOL VIOLENCE IN HIGHER EDUCATION

As a result of violence, students may experience a variety of physical and emotional consequences, which may lead to social and academic complications. When victimization on a university campus occurs, the overall quality of life for students may decrease as the students may fear for their safety. For the university as a whole, violence on their campus increases the costs of the university to operate. High levels of violence also lower the retention of faculty and students.

In addition, as a result of the increased presence of violence within higher education, academic freedoms are being restricted.[96] In addition, students who wish to travel abroad are facing travel restrictions on the entry and exit of differing countries as a result of the increasing number of violent incidents. Although universities are designed to be places in which differing thoughts and opinions are welcomed and examined, victims are likely to keep their ideas to themselves and not voice their opinions in classes openly because they are living with the fear of becoming victimized if their ideas are different from others again. Therefore, universities must address school violence.

Since the nineteenth century, colleges and universities have been referred to as the Ivory Tower.[97] This is in part due to its protective environment for intellectual pursuits and its disconnection from the practical concerns of daily life. Unfortunately, as evidence suggests, institutions of higher learning are not immune to incidents of violence.

In the campus community, individuals, interpersonal or clique processes, institutional factors, community factors, and policy and social actions all influence incidents of violence.[98] The victimization of students is often viewed as the responsibility of the universities.[99] Most recently, in a 2016 case within the United States involving a stabbing within a class at the University of California (Los Angeles), the California Supreme Court ruled that public colleges must protect students from foreseeable violence during curricular activities.[100] Therefore, the prevention of the victimizations of individuals within the educational setting, more than ever, is essential for administrators.

In an effort to reduce the amount of violence present on college campuses because of the open campus layout, it is recommended that university security officers keep regular watch of students and faculty, take note of suspicious persons or vehicles, and set up a notification system that informs all students, staff, and faculty if a violent or suspicious incident occurs.

In addition, in an effort to reduce the number of violent acts that occur on a campus as a result of mental illness, university leaders should learn to recognize the warning signs of mental illness, inform students of any counseling services offered at the university, provide students with local community mental health resources, and also report any signs they observe as strange to campus mental health personnel in an effort to help someone before a possibly violent outbreak.

Research suggests that there exist essential principles for the design of an effective plan to prevent campus violence,[101] and these principles should be comprehensive, strategic, and coordinated. In addition, the preventive plans should be implemented across all areas of a campus and must involve students, faculty, staff, and the community.

Specifically, a campus plan to prevent violence should ensure that programs are coordinated and sustainable to prohibit one-time-only efforts. In addition, the campus plan should engage in problem analysis to access local programs as well as local resources.[102] Finally, campus plans should draw on existing research on school violence and evaluations of school violence-prevention programs as well as partnerships and collaborations among all campus entities and the surrounding community.[103]

Campus violence takes many forms, some of which include rape, assault, hazing, dating violence, self-harm, stalking, and property crimes. Within the campus community there are many possible influences that may incline one to act violently. Influences may be drawn from community factors, institutional factors, or other types of interactions one faces within the institution. Regardless of the possible influences present on a campus, a violent event requires the combination of a person with some sort of inclining likelihood for violent behavior, a situation in which elements are present that create the risk of a violent event, and, in most cases, a significant event that activates the individual to partake in some sort of violence. If we want to prevent violence and promote campus safety as a nation, we must dedicate time, resources, commitment, and investment of ideas from all sectors of society.

CHAPTER QUESTIONS

1. What are two major dynamics that differentiate the college school setting from that of K–12 schools?
2. When asked why they had partaken in extreme acts of school violence on college campuses, what were some of the responses perpetrators had given as explanations?
3. What was the total number of documented attacks from September 2016 to August 2017 on university campuses around the globe?
4. What are the seven stages of the hate model?
5. What are the five categories of stalkers (explain)?

DISCUSSION QUESTIONS

1. In your opinion, what do you feel the indicators for school violence are on a college campus that may be different than those present at a K–12 school? Explain.
2. Do you believe dating violence, sexual assault, and rape are adequately investigated on the majority of university campuses across the globe? Explain.
3. What methods do you think should be utilized on college campuses by university staff in an effort to assist in deterring stalking and cyberstalking within this environment?

NOTES

1. Kimberly McCabe and Gregory Martin, *School Violence, the Media and Criminal Justice Responses* (New York: Peter Lang, 2005).
2. Kimberly McCabe and Gregory Martin, *School Violence, the Media and Criminal Justice Responses*.
3. Brendan O'Malley, "Global Crisis of Violence against Higher Education," September 26, 2017, University World News, accessed on January 3, 2019, at https://www.universityworldnews.com/post.php?story=20170926151443689.
4. Gordon Crews, "School Violence Perpetrators Speak: An Examination of Perpetrators Views on School Violence Offenses," *Journal of the Institute of Justice and International Studies*, (14) (2014): 41–52.

5. Emily Reynolds, "Universities Are Having a Rape Epidemic. Here's What They Can Do," Guardian.com, March 2, 2018, accessed on January 3, 2019, at https://www.theguardian.com/commentisfree/2018/mar/02/universities-rape-epidemic-sexual-assault-students.

6. Kimberly McCabe and Gregory Martin, *School Violence, the Media and Criminal Justice Responses.*

7. Kimberly McCabe and Gregory Martin, *School Violence, the Media and Criminal Justice Responses.*

8. Substance Abuse and Mental Health Services Administration, *Alcohol Use. In: Results from the 2001 National Household Survey on Drug Abuse: Volume I. Summary of National Findings* (Rockville, MD: Office of Applied Studies, 2002), 25–32, accessed on April 16, 2018, at: http://oas.samhsa.gov/nhsda/2k1nhsda/PDF/01SOFchp3W.pdf; E. Swedlund, "I Killed My Tormenter, Says UA Prf.," *Arizona Daily Star*, November 19, 2004. Accessed on January 3, 2019.

9. Substance Abuse and Mental Health Services Administration, *Alcohol Use. In: Results from the 2001 National Household Survey on Drug Abuse: Volume I. Summary of National Findings.*

10. Gordon Crews, "School Violence Perpetrators Speak: An Examination of Perpetrators Views on School Violence Offenses."

11. Gordon Crews, "School Violence Perpetrators Speak: An Examination of Perpetrators Views on School Violence Offenses."

12. Jaymi Elsass, Jaclyn Schildkraut, and Mark Stafford, "Studying School Shootings: Challenges and Considerations for Research," *American Journal of Criminal Justice*, 41(3) (2016): 444–64.

13. Jaymi Elsass, Jaclyn Schildkraut, and Mark Stafford, "Studying School Shootings: Challenges and Considerations for Research."

14. Amy Thompson, J. Price, Joseph Dake, Karen Teeple, Sara Bassler, Jagdish Khubchandani, and Chris Stratton, "Student Perceptions and Practices Regarding Carrying Concealed Handguns on University Campuses," *Journal of American College Health*, 61(5) (2013): 243–53.

15. Kimberly McCabe and Gregory Martin, *School Violence, the Media and Criminal Justice Responses.*

16. Scholars at Risk, *Free to Think. Academic Freedom Monitoring Project* (New York: New York University Press, 2017).

17. Brendan O'Malley, "Global Crisis of Violence against Higher Education."

18. Brendan O'Malley, "Global Crisis of Violence against Higher Education."

19. Bayo Wahab, "UNIMAID Remains Resolute in the Face of Terrorists' Attacks," November 8, 2017, Pulse.org, accessed on December 3, 2018, at https://www.pulse.ng/communities/student/pulse-opinion-unimaid-remains-resolute-in-the-face-of-terrorists-attacks/176xbm5.

20. Brendan O'Malley, "Global Crisis of Violence against Higher Education."

21. Global Coalition to Protect Education from Attack, "Education under Attack," 2014, accessed on December 3, 2018, at https://www.google.com/search?sourceid=navclient&aq=&oq=Global+Coalition+to+Protect+Education+From+Attack%2c+Education+under+Attack&ie=UTF-8&rlz=1T4RVEB_enUS848US849&q=Global+

Coalition+to+Protect+Education+From+Attack%2c+Education+under+Attack&gs_
l=hp...0i22i30.0.0.1.860028...........0.hkoyzfNnHDA.

22. Elizabeth Redden, "Attack at a Pakistani University," January 21, 2016, Inside Higher Education, accessed on January 3, 2019, at https://www.insidehighered.com/news/2016/01/21/attack-pakistans-bacha-khan-university-kills-20.

23. Save the Children, *Childhood under Siege: Living and Dying in Besieged Areas of Syria*, 2016, London: Save the Children, accessed on January 4, 2019, at https://www.google.com/search?sourceid=navclient&aq=&oq=Childhood+Under+Siege%3a+Living+and+Dying+in+Besieged+Areas+of+Syria&ie=UTF-8&rlz=1T4RVEB_enUS848US849&q=Childhood+Under+Siege%3a+Living+and+Dying+in+Besieged+Areas+of+Syria&gs_l=hp....0.0.9.141097...........0.AedpV2fOOIM.

24. Mariam Karouny, "Syria Crisis: Dozens Killed by Aleppo University Blasts," BBC News, January 15, 2013, accessed on January 3, 2019, at https://www.bbc.com/news/world-middle-east-21029034.

25. Anne Barnard, "Syria's War Invades—Syria Education Crisis," *New York Times*, April 14, 2017, accessed on October 3, 2018, at https://www.nytimes.com/2017/04/21/sunday-review/one-countrys-war-changed-the-world.html.

26. Brendan O'Malley, "Global Crisis of Violence against Higher Education."

27. Brendan O'Malley, "Global Crisis of Violence against Higher Education."

28. Brendan O'Malley, "Global Crisis of Violence against Higher Education."

29. Brendan O'Malley, "Global Crisis of Violence against Higher Education."

30. Kimberly McCabe, *Protecting Your Children in Cyberspace: What Parents Need to Know* (Lanham, MD: Rowman and Littlefield Publishers, Inc., 2017).

31. Mark Chapell, Stephanie Hasselman, Theresa Kitchin, Safiya Lomon, Kenneth MacIver, and Partick Sarulla, "Bullying in Elementary School, High School and College," *Adolescence*, 41(164) (2006): 633–48.

32. Mark Chapell, Stephanie Hasselman, Theresa Kitchin, Safiya Lomon, Kenneth MacIver, and Partick Sarulla, "Bullying in Elementary School, High School and College."

33. R. Barker Bausell, Carole Bausell, and Dorothy Siegel, *The Links among Alcohol, Drugs and Crime on American College Campuses: A National Follow-up Study* (Towson, MD: Campus Violence Prevention Center, Towson State University, 1991).

34. Walter Bouman, "Best Practices of Hate/Bias Crime Investigations," *Law Enforcement Bulletin*, 72(3) (2003): 21–25.

35. National Crime Prevention Council, "Tolerance for Teens," National Crime Prevention Council, Maryland, 2016, accessed on October 23, 2016, at http://www.ncpc.org/topics/hate-crime/tolerance.

36. Kimberly McCabe, *Protecting Your Children in Cyberspace: What Parents Need to Know*.

37. Michelle Stacey, Kristin Carbone-Lopez, and Richard Rosenfeld, "Demographic Changes and Ethnically Motivated Crime: The Impact of Immigration on anti-Hispanic Hate Crime in the United States," *Journal of Contemporary Criminal Justice*, 27(3) (2011): 76–89.

38. Federal Bureau of Investigation, "Hate Crimes," August 16, 2018, accessed on October 3, 2018, at https://www.fbi.gov/investigate/civil-rights/hate-crimes.

39. Michelle Stacey, "The Effect of Law on Hate Crime Reporting: The Case of Racial and Ethnic Violence," *American Journal of Criminal Justice*, 40(4) (2015): 876–900.

40. Cara Dowden and Shannon Brennan, *Police-reported Hate Crime in Canada, 2010, Juristat* (Ottawa: Canadian Centre for Justice Statistics, 2012).

41. Colleen Mills, Joshua Freilich, and Steven Chermak, "Extreme Hatred: Revisiting the Hate Crime and Terrorism Relationship to Determine Whether They Are Close Cousins or Distant Relatives," *Crime and Delinquency*, 63(10) (2017): 1191–1223.

42. Michelle Stacey, Kristin Carbone-Lopez, and Richard Rosenfeld, "Demographic Changes and Ethnically Motivated Crime: The Impact of Immigration on anti-Hispanic Hate Crime in the United States."

43. Kimberly McCabe, *Protecting Your Children in Cyberspace: What Parents Need to Know*.

44. Kimberly McCabe, *Protecting Your Children in Cyberspace: What Parents Need to Know.*

45. Kimberly McCabe, *Protecting Your Children in Cyberspace: What Parents Need to Know.*

46. Kimberly McCabe and Daniel Murphy, *Child Abuse—Today's Issues* (New York: Taylor and Francis Publishing, 2016).

47. Ann Burgess, Cheryl Regehr, and Albert Roberts, *Victimology: Theories and Applications*, second edition (Burlington, MA: Jones and Bartlett Learning, 2013).

48. Cara Dowden and Shannon Brennan, *Police-reported Hate Crime in Canada, 2010, Juristat.*

49. Kimberly McCabe, *Protecting Your Children in Cyberspace: What Parents Need to Know*.

50. Colleen Mills, Joshua Freilich, and Steven Chermak, "Extreme Hatred: Revisiting the Hate Crime and Terrorism Relationship to Determine Whether They Are Close Cousins or Distant Relatives."

51. John Schafer and Joe Navarro, "The Seven Stage Hate Model," *Law Enforcement Bulletin*, 72(3) (2003): 1–9.

52. John Schafer and Joe Navarro, "The Seven Stage Hate Model."

53. John Schafer and Joe Navarro, "The Seven Stage Hate Model."

54. Kimberly McCabe, *Child Abuse and the Criminal Justice System* (New York: Peter Lang, 2003).

55. John Schafer and Joe Navarro, "The Seven Stage Hate Model."

56. John Schafer and Joe Navarro, "The Seven Stage Hate Model."

57. Kimberly McCabe, *Protecting Your Children in Cyberspace: What Parents Need to Know.*

58. John Schafer and Joe Navarro, "The Seven Stage Hate Model."

59. John Schafer and Joe Navarro, "The Seven Stage Hate Model."

60. John Schafer and Joe Navarro, "The Seven Stage Hate Model."

61. US Department of Health and Human Services. Centers for Disease Control and Prevention, 2018, accessed on January 22, 2019, at https://www.cdc.gov/healthyyouth/protective/index.htm.

62. Jacquelyn White and Mary Koss, "Courtship Violence: Incidence in a National Sample of Higher Education Students," *Violence and Victims*, 6(4) (1991): 247–56.

63. Nina Fredland, Izabel Ricardo, Jaquelyn Campbell, P. Sharps, J. Kub, and Michael Yonasm, "The Meaning of Dating Violence in the Lives of Middle School Adolescents," *Journal of School Violence*, 4 (2005): 95–114.

64. Nina Fredland, Izabel Ricardo, Jaquelyn Campbell, P. Sharps, J. Kub, and Michael Yonasm, "The Meaning of Dating Violence in the Lives of Middle School Adolescents."

65. Jacquelyn White and Mary Koss, "Courtship Violence: Incidence in a National Sample of Higher Education Students."

66. Jacquelyn White and Mary Koss, "Courtship Violence: Incidence in a National Sample of Higher Education Students."

67. Kimberly McCabe and Gregory Martin, *School Violence, the Media and Criminal Justice Responses*.

68. Jacquelyn White and Mary Koss, "Courtship Violence: Incidence in a National Sample of Higher Education Students."

69. Emily Reynolds, "Universities Are Having a Rape Epidemic. Here's What They Can Do."

70. Alexandra King, "Campus Rape Statistics Misleading Says Author of New Book," CNN, January 28, 2017, accessed on January 3, 2019, at https://www.cnn.com/2017/01/28/health/campus-rape-book-author-cnntv/index.html.

71. Best Colleges, "The Realities of Sexual Assaults on Campus," 2017, accessed on February 27, 2019, at https://www.bestcolleges.com/resources/preventing-sexual-assault/.

72. 10 U.S. Code § 920–Art. 120. *Rape and Sexual Assault Generally, 2015*, accessed on December 3, 2018, at https://www.law.cornell.edu/uscode/text/10/920.

73. Kimberly McCabe and Gregory Martin, *School Violence, the Media and Criminal Justice Responses*.

74. Kimberly McCabe and Gregory Martin, *School Violence, the Media and Criminal Justice Responses*.

75. 10 U.S. Code § 920–Art. 120. *Rape and Sexual Assault Generally, 2015*.

76. Kimberly McCabe, *Protecting Your Children in Cyberspace: What Parents Need to Know*.

77. US Department of Homeland Security, *Stop. Think. Connect. Toolkit*, September 26, 2018, accessed on December 3, 2018, at https://www.dhs.gov/stopthink connect-toolkit.

78. Kimberly McCabe, *Child Abuse and the Criminal Justice System*.

79. Jenna Strawhun, Natasha Adams, and Matthew Huss, "The Assessment of Cyberstalking," *Violence and Victims*, 28(4) (2013): 715–30.

80. Robert D'Ovidio and James Doyle, "A Study on Cyberstalking," *FBI Enforcement Bulletin*, 72(3) (2003): 10–18.

81. Robert D'Ovidio and James Doyle, "A Study on Cyberstalking."

82. Benjamin Wittes, Cody Poplin, Quinta Jurecic, and Clara Spera, "Sextortion: Cybersecurity, Teenagers, and Remote Sexual Assault," *Center for Technology Innovation at Brookings* (May 2016): 1–3.

83. Kimberly McCabe, *Protecting Your Children in Cyberspace: What Parents Need to Know*.

84. Stalking Resource Center, *Summary of Changes from VAWA 2013 Related to Stalking* (Washington, DC: Stalking Resource Center, 2014), accessed on October 11, 2016, at www.ncvc.org.

85. Kimberly McCabe and Daniel Murphy, *Child Abuse—Today's Issues*.

86. Stalking Resource Center, *Summary of Changes from VAWA 2013 Related to Stalking*.

87. Kimberly McCabe, *Protecting Your Children in Cyberspace: What Parents Need to Know*.

88. Benjamin Wittes, Cody Poplin, Quinta Jurecic, and Clara Spera "Sextortion: Cybersecurity, Teenagers, and Remote Sexual Assault."

89. Benjamin Wittes, Cody Poplin, Quinta Jurecic, and Clara Spera "Sextortion: Cybersecurity, Teenagers, and Remote Sexual Assault."

90. Robert D'Ovidio and James Doyle, "A Study on Cyberstalking."

91. Kimberly McCabe, *Protecting Your Children in Cyberspace: What Parents Need to Know*.

92. Kimberly McCabe and Gregory Martin, *School Violence, the Media and Criminal Justice Responses*.

93. Protect.org, "What Is the Magnitude of Child Exploitation?" accessed on November 23, 2016, http://www.protect.org/articles/what-is-the-magnitude-of-child-exploitation.

94. Robert D'Ovidio and James Doyle, "A Study on Cyberstalking."

95. David Finkelhor, Kimberly Mitchell, and Janis Wolak, *Online Victimization: A Report on the Nation's Youth* (Washington, DC: National Center for Missing and Exploited Children, 2000).

96. Bayo Wahab, "UNIMAID Remains Resolute in the Face of Terrorists' Attacks."

97. Steven Shapin, "The Ivory Tower: A History of a Figure of Speech and Its Cultural Uses," *British Society for the History of Science*, 54(1) (2012): 1–27.

98. Linda Langford, *Preventing Violence and Promoting Safety in High Education Settings. Overview of Comprehensive Approaches* (Washington, DC: Center for Alcohol and Other Drug Abuse and Violence Prevention, 2004).

99. Steven Shapin, "The Ivory Tower: A History of a Figure of Speech and Its Cultural Uses."

100. Eric Kelderman, "Court Decision May Signal More Legal Liability for Colleges over Violent Crimes," *The Chronical of High Education*, March 23, 2018, accessed on January 3, 2019, at https://www.chronicle.com/article/Court-Decision-May-Signal-More/242915.

101. Linda Langford, *Preventing Violence and Promoting Safety in High Education Settings. Overview of Comprehensive Approaches*.

102. Linda Langford, *Preventing Violence and Promoting Safety in High Education Settings. Overview of Comprehensive Approaches*.

103. Kimberly McCabe and Gregory Martin, *School Violence, the Media and Criminal Justice Responses*.

Chapter Nine

Controlling the School Environment

Criminal Justice Responses

KEY WORDS

2002 Education Act
2006 Education and
  Inspections Act
Anti-Bullying Manifesto
attachment
belief
Child Friendly Schools
  initiative
commitment
conflict resolution
control theory
counselors
cycle of violence
Drug Abuse Resistance
  Education
Gun Free School Zones
  Act

I Can Problem Solve
*Indicators of School
  Crime and Safety*
Internet Crimes against
  Children
involvement
No Child Left Behind
Olweus Bullying Pre-
  vention Programme
Positive Ways Program
probable cause
rational choice theory
Resolving Conflict Cre-
  ativity Program
Responsible Citizen-
  ship Program
routine activities theory

Safe and Drug-Free
  Schools and Com-
  munities Act
school resource officer
social capital
Student, Teacher, and
  Officers Prevention
  (STOP) School Vio-
  lence Act of 2018
The Children Act
The Firearms Act
Weapons Act of 2002
Win-Win Resolutions
zero tolerance

Both the Dunblane Primary School shooting in Scotland and Columbine High School shooting in the United States had the effect of exposing individuals and society to the vulnerabilities of school violence. Citizens across the globe will never forget the tragedies of these school shootings or the fear they produced. In response, both proactive and reactive initiatives were implemented

215

KEY ACRONYMS

(DARE) Drug Abuse Resistance Education
(ICAC) Internet Crimes against Children
(NCES) National Center for Education Statistics
(SDFSCA) Safe and Drug-Free Schools and Community Act
(SRO) School Resource Officer
(UN) United Nations
(UNICEF) United Nations International Children's Emergency Fund

worldwide to help ensure that these events are never repeated. In the United States, preventive programs such as GREAT (Gang Resistance Education and Training) were expanded and more school resource officers and school security were added to the daily fabric of educational institutions. In Sweden and Norway, anti-bullying legislation was passed.[1] In the United Kingdom, the Home Office provided £10 million to reduce gang-related violence in the schools.[2] In many instances, these initiatives, which include laws to prevent school violence, prevention programs, metal detectors at the entrances of schools, surveillance cameras on campuses, training on risk assessment for teachers, the incorporation of school safety officers into the educational staff, and limited access to the schools, have been successful.

Based upon the US Department of Education's Annual Report on School Safety (2018), there has been a decline in school crime with rates lower than any year since the 1999–2000 school year. This decline is consistent within the international community as police and prevention efforts have resulted in significant declines in severe school violence.[3] Although media attention often focuses on the deaths by mass shootings within the school environment, teen deaths while attending school or school functions are rare. For the most part, students are extremely safe while attending school; however, teachers in the United States, Canada,[4] and the United Kingdom[5] report increases in threats and violence toward them by students. If teachers do not feel safe in the school environment, it is only a matter of time before their fears of victimization extend to the students. Therefore, regardless of the statistics and whether the incidents of school violence increase or decrease, school violence remains a concern for everyone and it is a concern that deserves and demands constant attention. Essentially, all parents and members of society want children to be safe; therefore, school safety and school violence is a topic worthy of attention by everyone.

IDENTIFYING ACTIONS OF CONCERN

Just as with any attempt to reduce criminal behavior and promote public safety, the first challenge is to identify the behavior(s) of interest. This is first accomplished by recognizing the various criminal actions that are included under the phrase "school violence." Although it is asserted by some researchers that school officials do not want these incidents identified,[6] throughout this book, specific incidents of school violence have been identified and explored. Therefore, to address that challenge, many global school research centers established to combat violence within schools suggest that the phrase *school violence* is any behavior that violates a school's mission.[7]

Over the last decade, the definition of school violence has changed from its focus on the more severe forms of violence (e.g., shootings, assaults) to a spectrum of behaviors ranging from emotional abuse to homicide.[8] Therefore, the definition is not limited to murders or rapes, but also includes threats and intimidation. In addition, many researchers in the area of school crime and violence recognize that oftentimes incidents of school violence are aftereffects of previous incidents of school violence and suggest an examination beyond the individuals who directly caused the event. They further suggest that these examinations include the conditions that may have existed prior to the violence[9] and be examined in more of a cycle of actions and reactions.[10] From a theoretical perspective, Travis Hirschi's control theory (1969)[11] may aid in the explanations of school violence, as well as Lawrence Cohen and Marcus Felson's (1978) routine activities theory,[12] which suggests that by establishing patterns of daily routines, students and school personnel may contribute to their likelihood of victimization.

Criminologists and criminal justice practitioners across the globe are interested in the issue of control as an explanation for criminal behavior, and as early as the 1950s theories of social control were offered as explanations as to why more crime did not exist.[13] Research also has suggested that social control could be maintained by direct control with physical punishments imposed, by indirect control with the possible disappointments of others imposed, and by internal controls by a sense of guilt.[14] However, Hirschi, in 1969, offered a version of control theory, which is most popular today and empirically tested explanations as to why more people did not commit crimes. In particular, whereas most theories of crime attempt to explain criminal behavior, control theories attempt to explain the absence of criminal behavior.

Hirschi inferred that, by nature, humans are evil and prone to criminal activity, and he suggested that there must exist elements of bond to society that prohibit an individual from committing acts of delinquency or crime.[15]

In effect, Hirschi specified four elements of social bond to be directly related to an individual's propensity to commit crimes; those four elements were attachment, commitment, involvement, and belief.[16]

Attachment refers to an individual's ability to be sensitive to the feelings of others. For example, students who do not enjoy the company of their peers or students who develop a disliking of their peers will not have strong feelings of attachment. In these cases, students may be more likely to commit acts of violence against those peers.

Hirschi's second element of social bond is commitment as it suggests that individuals demonstrate commitment to a society by conforming to the rules of the society.[17] A student who supports a violence-free school environment will be more likely to participate in verbal resolutions and will be less likely to behave violently within the school environment.

Involvement is the condition of participation in an event or activity, and it suggests the opportunity for a social bond.[18] As suggested, people are involved in the daily activities of their society, then they will not desire the opportunity for delinquency.[19] Students who are involved in their school's environment (i.e., studying, athletics, and socializing) will not have the desire, time, or opportunity for violence.

Lastly, belief refers to the extent to which individuals believe that they should observe or conform to the rules of a society. Without the belief that a rule of law is just, individuals will often not observe the law. A student who does not support the rules of the school may be more inclined to not follow those rules. This is especially relevant to school violence as the rules prohibit violent actions.

In studies of victims, the conditions that produce victim risk are often identified. For many, these conditions exist daily and without change. Cohen and Felson, in their historical examinations of crime trends, assert that the motivation to commit crime is consistent.[20] In particular, in every society there will always be some individuals who are willing to break the law or, in the case of school violence, some students willing to disobey the rules of the school. In addition, there will always be suitable targets (such as students for bullying or empty buildings for vandalism). The absence of capable guardians such as a teacher or a school resource officer will facilitate the victimization.

As related to routine activities and the prevention of school violence, the presence of guardians within the school environment is essential. With school resource officers, teachers trained to be aware of risk factors for school violence, and parents educated on the dangers of the internet-facilitated victimization of children, guardians are in place and the risk for school violence is reduced. Accordingly, these elements of social control and routine activities are the foundation for many of the reactive and proactive measures taken by the schools, the community, and criminal justice agencies to reduce school violence.[21]

LEGAL RESPONSES TO SCHOOL VIOLENCE

In most societies, the effectiveness of prevention initiatives is increased with the support of legal policies. Unfortunately, most laws or policies to reduce school violence are in response to a school shooting or a teen suicide.[22] These efforts for reducing incidents of school violence or youth violence across the globe support the role of law enforcement and prosecutors. For most countries, their children's acts consolidate laws as related to child protection, which is applied to the school environment. However, countries such as the United States, the United Kingdom, Canada, and Germany, who have experienced their share of school violence-related incidents (i.e., shootings or suicides), have enacted specific legislation to address school violence.

THE CHILDREN ACT

The Children Act 1989, enacted by the House of Lords (United Kingdom), allocates duties to local authorities, courts, parents, and other agencies in the United Kingdom to ensure children are safeguarded and their welfare is promoted. Central to the Children's Act is that children are best cared for by their families. Included in this act is that local authorities have a duty to safeguard and promote the welfare of all children.

United States

In the United States there are several federal and state laws that focus on preventing school violence. However, most of the state legislation was not initiated until the mid-1980s, and most of the major federal efforts were enacted in the mid-1990s.[23] The laws and policies, enacted from the late 1980s to 2018, demonstrate the country's attention to the subject of school violence.

In the 1985 case New Jersey v. T.L.O., the US Supreme Court ruled that school officials do not require a warrant to conduct a student search. In fact, based upon this case, the only requirement to conduct a search of a student's property or the student on school grounds in the United States is probable cause. For clarity, probable cause is a reasonable belief that a person has committed or will commit a crime based upon knowledge of facts to warrant the belief that a suspect is committing or may commit a crime. In 1990, and in reaction to firearms discovered in the schools, the Gun Free School Zones Act prohibited the possession or discharge of a firearm in a school zone as well as one thousand feet from the grounds of the school. However, one analysis of mass shootings between 2009 and 2016 found that 10 percent of the shootings occurred in gun-free zones.[24] Although invalidated in 1995 by the case of *U.S. v. Lopez*, this act was the foundation for many of the state- and federal-sponsored efforts that followed.

SAFE AND DRUG-FREE SCHOOLS AND COMMUNITIES ACT

The Safe and Drug-Free Schools and Communities Act (SDFSCA) State and Local Grants Program, authorized in 1994, was initiated by the US government in an effort to encourage the creation of safe, disciplined, and drug-free learning environments that will help all children meet challenging academic standards.

In 1994, the Safe and Drug-Free Schools and Communities Act required that the National Center for Educational Statistics (NCES) collect data to determine the severity and frequency of incidents of violence in elementary and secondary schools across the country. From these statistics, data on school crime and school violence are provided on an annual basis and called *Indicators of School Crime and Safety*. By defining and tracking these incidents of school crime, law enforcement and other public officials are better able to monitor and combat the problems of school violence.

In 1994, to address violence in the classroom, then President Clinton signed the 1994 Gun-Free Schools Act, which mandated a one-year expulsion to students who bring weapons to school. In an effort to reduce the number of

GUN-FREE SCHOOLS ACT

The Gun-Free Schools Act of 1994 was part of the US effort to improve American schools. The act encouraged each state receiving federal funds for education to follow suit and introduce their own laws to address school violence. For the most part, these laws are referred to as zero tolerance laws. To address violence in the schools, the act requires each state to expel, for at least one year, any student who is determined to have brought a weapon to school.

weapons in school, the policy of zero tolerance (to be discussed later in this chapter) was established throughout American schools. This policy attempted to eliminate all violence in the school environment. The act targeted specifically injurious weapons such as knives and firearms.[25]

The United States further extended zero tolerance to drugs in cases such as *Verona School District 47J v. Acton* (1995) as the US Supreme Court held that a school's policy of random drug testing for athletes was not unconstitutional and that there would be no tolerance for drug use in schools. In addition, and in an effort to prevent school bullying, the state of Georgia led the anti-bullying efforts with their 1999 anti-bullying legislation. By June of 2016, all fifty states had legislation in place to address bullying.[26] Although there currently exists no US federally sponsored anti-bullying legislation, the No Child Left Behind Act of 2001 provides support to promote school safety programs.[27]

Lastly, the Student, Teacher, and Officers Prevention (STOP) School Violence Act of 2018 provides grants to states, local governments, and Indian tribes to improve security (through the purchase of metal detectors and other equipment) at school and on school grounds. This legislative effort, in response to thousands of students, parents, and teachers demanding action to prevent school violence, amended the Omnibus Crime Control and Safe Street Act of 1968 to revise and reauthorize the Secure our Schools grant program.

United Kingdom

In the United Kingdom, after the 1996 Dunblane massacre, the Firearms (Amendment) Act of 1997 was passed. This act strengthened the Firearms Act of 1988, which banned the ownership of semi-automatic and pump-action rifles, and it required that all handguns be surrendered to the government through a large-scale buyback program. This program, which continues to be supported, has been associated with a significant reduction in firearms deaths to include those shootings that occur within the school environment.

THE FIREARMS ACT

The Firearms Act of 1968 is one of the United Kingdom's efforts to reduce violence. Following the Dunblane School shooting in 1996, the act was strengthened as the Firearms (Amendment) Act of 1997 was passed. This amended act banned most handguns throughout the country.

In addition, although there is no legal definition of bullying within the United Kingdom, the UK Department of Education has provided guiding policies for all schools. In particular, the 2002 Education Act places a legal duty on local authorities and school administrators to safeguard and promote the welfare of children, and the 2006 Education and Inspections Act states that schools must have measures in place that encourage good behaviors and prevent all forms of bullying. All of these actions demonstrate the United Kingdom's desire to address school violence and to decrease the likelihood of a school shooting.[28]

Canada

After the school shootings in Alberta (1999), Quebec (2006), and Ontario (2007), Bill 212, which modified previously existing disciplinary actions within the Education Act, included bullying as an action that will not be tolerated within the school setting. In addition to policies to modify behaviors, Canada supported a policy of zero tolerance (similar to the US policy) regarding violence in the school setting.[29] Through these additional policies and those that followed, schools are required to provide a healthy and secure environment for their students, free from any form of bullying or violence. Hence, Canada has demonstrated a desire to reduce school violence.

Germany

After the 2002 school shooting in the town of Erfurt, which resulted in the deaths of sixteen individuals, the Weapons Act of 2002 increased the age requirements for the purchase of firearms and required a psychological evaluation for persons under the age of twenty-five. Later amendments to the act in 2008 banned certain weapons such as airsoft guns and imitation firearms in public. After the 2009 school shooting at Winnedin when a seventeen-year-

WEAPONS ACT OF 2002

Germany's Weapons Act of 2002 increased the age requirements to purchase guns for licensed hunters and competition shooters and required psychological evaluation for persons under the age of twenty-five. The first amendment to this act, in 2008, banned weapons such as airsoft guns, imitation firearms, and knives with blades longer than twelve centimeters from public places. The second amendment, in 2009, required routine verifications of safe firearms storage by local firearms control offices at the homes of gun owners.

old boy, utilizing his father's guns, killed fifteen people, gun control policies increased and an amendment that introduced routine verification of safe firearms storage was passed. These changes have accompanied a decrease in the incidents of school shootings in Germany and helped to demonstrate Germany's dedication to reducing incidents of school violence.

ECONOMIC IMPACT OF SCHOOL VIOLENCE

Most research on school violence limits the term *cost* as applied to the ambiguous effect of bullying and abuse on the psychological well-being of the child.[30] However, the economic impact of school violence affects the victim or student as well as society. These areas of impact for the victim include attendance, physical health, and psychological or emotional health.[31] The areas of impact for society often include the cost of social capital (i.e., delinquency) and the overall economy.

Educational Attendance

Research on bullying and child abuse concludes that when students are victimized at school, they are less likely to attend regularly.[32] When students are not in school, they do not learn, and, therefore, they are rarely successful in their educational achievements. Researchers in the areas of bullying and cyberbullying have suggested that bullying not only affects the victim, but also the entire school environment.[33] A teacher who spends the majority of his or her day addressing the distractions created by one student is simply unable to provide the remaining students their necessary time of instruction. Bullying disrupts classes and redirects the attention of both the students and the teachers. In particular, students who are bullied or who are distracted by the bullying of another student are not focusing on their education. If students are oftentimes not currently the target of the bully, the fact that they may someday become the target distracts those students from the process of learning. In addition, a teacher who must constantly monitor the activities of one student is not focused upon the teaching of the remaining students.[34] In many cases of bullying, the victims display behaviors of anxiousness, nervousness, and worry; therefore, the victim is not able to focus on learning. In other cases, victims, in an attempt to regain some level of control and self-esteem, will themselves become aggressive toward other non-bullied students,[35] thereby continuing the cycle of abuse within the school environment.

Unfortunately, students who are victims of bullying spend much of the time during their school day planning how not to be a victim. A student who is concerned about being victimized in the bathroom may choose not to eat or drink during the day for fear of having to go to the bathroom or may request permission to go to the bathroom during class time and thus is missing more instruction while the other students remain in the classroom. Also, a student worried about victimization on the playground may act out in class to avoid being allowed to go outside; therefore, the student remains inside and under the supervision and protection of the teacher.

Lastly, for many of these victims of violence, attending school just is not worth the trouble, and absenteeism becomes an issue.[36] In fact, in the 1990s approximately 15 percent of students in schools within the United States reported bullying as their initial reason for missing school.[37] Nearly two decades later, more than 20 percent of the students in the United States and across Europe report missing school because of the victimization of bullying.[38]

In the short-term, globally, schools receive their funding levels based upon the number of students in attendance. With students not attending, the funding for schools, based upon student enrollments and attendance, is reduced; therefore, the school budgets are reduced. These reductions in budgets affect those students still in attendance and the school overall.[39]

Physical Health

A victim of school violence may be a victim of physical violence and/or sexual violence. In some cases, bullying escalates to physical confrontations. In these cases injuries may occur that require medical treatment. A child injured in an incident of school victimization suffers not only the immediate pain of the injury but also the pain associated with the treatment of the injury and the pain associated with the healing of the injury. In some extreme cases, these injuries prohibit a student from participating in other school activities. Hence, an incident such as a physical assault at school may have more consequences to the physical health of the victim beyond that of the initial injury. Unfortunately, although the majority of the research that focuses on child sexual abuse emphasizes that most abuse occurs within the home or by a family member, sexual abuse may also occur within the school environment. The perpetrators of child sexual abuse within the school environment may include teachers, coaches, staff, and peers. Therefore, parents wishing to protect their child from sexual abuse at school must discuss the actions with their children to include the potential perpetrators.[40] Without the knowledge of the actions associated with the phrase "sexual abuse," students may be unaware of the severity of these actions; as a result, a child may be a victim of sexual abuse within the school environment without notifying those in the position to end the abuse.[41]

In addition, children with disabilities (physical or emotional) are especially at risk for sexual abuse.[42] In these cases of sexual abuse within the school environment, the child may be unable to verbalize the abuse, therefore, the behavior of the child may be the first indicator of the abuse. In most cases of child sexual abuse, there are no physical indicators; however, this abuse may also affect the physical well-being of the child.[43] For a child who is in pain from physical or sexual abuse, education and learning is not a priority, so this child will often not be a productive student.

As related to physical health, even for those children who may not have experienced a physical injury from their abuse, their physical health may be compromised. Research suggests that even a child exposed to violence is more at risk for physical ailments.[44] Therefore, a child who is a victim of bullying or intimidation may experience physical symptoms such as stomach-aches, headaches, and dizziness. Those children who are victims of sexual abuse may be left with a sexually transmitted disease or a pregnancy in addition to their history of abuse.[45]

In the short term, children who are victims of violence within the school environment may suffer a variety of physical injuries and conditions, which prohibit them from attending school and being attentive while in attendance. The long-term consequences of such abuse often include a decline in academic success, truancy, delinquency, and even withdrawal from school. Therefore, the physical health of students who are victims of school violence produces negative economic consequences for the school.

Emotional Health

Finally, one cannot discount the effect of school violence on the emotional health of a child. Although most research examines emotional abuse from a family perspective, peers do emotionally abuse each other.[46] In today's world that emotional abuse may also occur online.[47] Just as in cases of physical and sexual abuse, there are no clear indicators of emotional abuse. However, some of those indicators include personality changes of the child, such as extreme behaviors from very happy to manically depressed, eating disorders, substance abuse, and a compulsion toward details in order to maintain some semblance of control and order in their lives.[48] Oftentimes, emotionally abused children will interact cruelly with others; and so, just as with the cycle of abuse, the emotional abuse of one child may lead to the emotional abuse of others or an incident of severe violence within the school environment. Other times, children who are victims of emotional abuse will continue to abuse themselves. In some cases, the emotional abuse of children leads to a heightened action of violence against themselves such as a suicide.

Accordingly, school violence as related to the emotional health of students is a costly consequence for victims and the school. For the victims, the costs include counseling services, prescribed medicines, and substance abuse treatment. For the school, the victim is disconnected, without a social bond to the school or those involved in the school setting. This lack of a social bond, in some cases, may lead to truancy, delinquency, and severe violence, the most negative of outcomes for all.

CYCLE OF VIOLENCE

The term *cycle of violence* refers to repeated and dangerous violent actions that are associated with high emotional levels and retribution. This pattern or cycle is most often applied to intimate partner violence; however, research supports its application to child abuse.

Social Capital

The phrase "social capital" refers generally to the components of society that allow a society to function. School violence results in an erosion of trust in the schools and in the educational system.[49] Students with little attachment to their educational systems are more likely to be involved in delinquency. With this mistrust in the schools also comes a mistrust of other parts of society, such as the criminal justice system.

The cost of addressing youth crime (i.e., arrests and prosecutions) is one outcome of school violence. The cost of repairs to vandalisms and other destructions of property is another outcome of school violence. Finally, the loss of value of properties within the proximity of the school is another consequence of school violence.[50] Therefore, school violence affects not only the school but also the community. As a result of school violence, students are not as productive; hence, they are not invested in their school. Therefore, these students are not invested in their communities.

Overall Economy

When children do not complete their education, they are less likely to be successful contributing members of society.[51] In the majority of the cases, the students who were unable to complete their education are left with their wages lower than those who completed school. In addition, they experience extended periods of unemployment, and they often engage in risky activities. In some instances the risky behaviors by these students include criminal behavior and substance abuse. These choices of lifestyle result in different demands for services such as substance abuse counseling and judicial interventions across communities. Therefore, the indirect results of school violence include an increase in community expenses and a decrease in economic growth. Thus, school violence, often thought of as a problem for students and their parents, produces costs that are paid by all members of a society.

PROACTIVE APPROACHES

Despite legal actions to address school violence across the globe, incidents of school violence continue to occur. In 2018, in Brazil, two teens shot several of their classmates. Also in 2018, in Mexico's Victoria School, another shooting occurred. Ergo, efforts to reduce school violence must go beyond the legislative reactive efforts and include the proactive efforts of the schools and their surrounding communities. Many of these efforts within the schools involve policies to address violence and teacher training.

In addition, many of these efforts within the community involve law enforcement and security officers assigned to the schools and youth programs, which attempt to provide social bonds between the students and their local settings. Regardless of its origin—the school or the community, there are proactive approaches to address school violence. Those approaches within the schools include school safety policies, counselor training, teacher training, and school programs.

School Safety Policies

In the United States during the 1980s and 1990s, the fear of victimization within the school setting led to the implementation of "no non-sense" approaches to infractions on school discipline policies.[52] As mentioned previously, one such policy was zero tolerance. The phrase "zero tolerance" refers to a widely accepted and enforced policy imposed upon schools in which students are notified prior to entering the school that there will be no acceptance of violence in terms of behaviors, weapons, or drugs within the school environment.[53]

Globally initiated in the latter part of the twentieth century, in reaction to the suddenly documented increased incidents of severe violence within the schools, the policy of zero tolerance has been the topic of numerous debates on its effectiveness in reducing or controlling violence within the school.[54] Zero tolerance, once promoted as the solution to youth violence, gets mixed reviews. In the United Kingdom, zero tolerance policies regarding teenage drinking have been known to reduce the incidents.[55]

In Canada, zero tolerance policies have been found to be in conflict with an all-inclusive educational system.[56] For many, zero tolerance is perceived as an effective method for reducing incidents of school violence, for others it is a policy based upon fear, frustration, and the perception that the United States has been "soft" on crime;[57] for others it is only a small part of reducing school violence.[58]

The recognized institutionalization of policies regarding school safety demonstrates a dedication to the subject. Although zero tolerance was originally designed to prohibit weapons and then drugs, it is now being adopted to address a wide range of behaviors within the United States and Canada to include violence toward teachers and dress regulation.[59] Research suggests that zero tolerance in the area of violence toward teachers helps to support the missions of most schools to maintain a safe learning environment.[60] From this perspective, especially in grades K–12, zero tolerance provides teachers the opportunities to focus their efforts on student learning without the fear of victimization.

In regard to dress codes, zero tolerance prohibits clothing that may be too revealing or associated with gang memberships. From this perspective, by not allowing gang members to "advertise" their affiliations and subgroup conflicts, there is a reduced likelihood of gang violence within the school setting.[61]

Zero tolerance is a prevention strategy based upon theories of delinquency and the result of our country's history to endure harsher punishments for juveniles in an effort to deter crime.[62] From the classic free will perspective, which was reintroduced in the 1960s under the philosophy of rational choice theory, crime will occur when the individual decides, after weighing the cost and benefits of the action, that the benefit of illegal activities outweigh the costs. Under this philosophy of a rational thought process for those who commit crimes, crimes with strict punishments for violating policies of zero tolerance will be less likely to occur within the school setting. With a policy such as zero tolerance, any infraction of the school's policy warrants action; these actions are typically either suspension or expulsion.[63] Zero tolerance supports the responsibility for the infractions of school policy on the student.[64] Unfortunately, although theoretically zero tolerance appears to address many of the preconditions to school violence, reviews are not as positive as approximately 40 percent of those students in the United States who were expelled through zero tolerance were from elementary and middle schools.[65] Early on in practice, the overwhelming violators of the zero tolerance policies were those young minorities from lower socioeconomic areas.[66] In addition, more recent evaluations conclude that disparities in the application of zero tolerance have increased with gaps in the applications occurring most often along racial lines and socioeconomic strata.[67]

However, although the evidence of zero tolerance evaluations conflicts in support of the effectiveness of zero tolerance policies, they continue to be applied and perceived as a positive approach to reducing school violence.[68] And so, zero tolerance is an appealing policy in the eyes of public officials to reduce school violence.

Other approaches to reduce incidents of violence within the school setting include programs based around the concept of conflict resolution. For clarity, conflict resolution is a concept similar to mediation, which facilitates a peaceful end to a conflict among parties. For school-based programs founded on conflict resolution, the goal is to instill students with the problem-solving skills in order to determine an acceptable resolution to a problem. For most conflict resolution programs, a five-step process is involved. Those five steps include: (1) identifying the source of the conflict; (2) thinking beyond the incident; (3) requesting solutions from all parties; (4) identifying solutions that all can support; and (5) resolving the conflict through an agreement. For those individuals familiar with the concept of restorative justice in criminal justice, restorative justice is built upon conflict resolution.[69] In the school system wishing to apply conflict management programs designed to reduce school violence, the principal is often the leader.[70]

In the United States, two of these conflict resolution programs include Resolving Conflict Creativity Program and Positive Ways Program. The Positive Ways Program attempts to provide students the power of productive communication to de-escalate incidents of violence toward them by their peers, and the Resolving Conflict Creativity Program utilizes workshops and one-on-one communications practices for provided victimization scenarios.[71] Both programs have appeared to lessen the incidents of bullying within the schools. Other US programs that apply positive reinforcement to reduce school violence include Positive Action, a K–12 program for character development; Too Good for Violence, an elementary and middle school effort to emphasize positive character traits; Connect with Kids, a program that promotes positive social attitudes in grades three through twelve; and Peace-Builders, designed to reward positive behaviors.[72]

Programs that apply the foundations of conflict management to reduce school violence are global. From the perspective of UNICEF's Child Friendly Schools initiative within several African counties, the link between the school environment and the wider community is recognized as it suggests that the protection of children in their homes has a direct impact on their behaviors in school.[73] Learners in child-friendly schools, who felt safe and secure in their homes and communities, were better prepared to learn and less likely to participate in policy-forbidden activities while in the school environment.

In addition, Norway's Anti-Bullying Manifesto and Olweus Bullying Prevention Programme, both implemented in elementary and middle schools, involve parents, education staff, students, and the community and have been implemented in over a dozen counties, including Australia and the United Kingdom.[74] These programs emphasize children's rights and positive communications among all parties. Results indicate fewer incidents of school bullying.

In the United Kingdom, conflict resolution is taught though drama and role play in a program called Win-Win Resolutions.[75] The standard curriculum for this program includes strategies for self-control, self-management of feelings, and interpersonal problem-solving. Results of this program indicate a decrease in incidents of physical aggression within the school environment.

In Australia, the Responsible Citizenship Program is grounded in the principles of restorative justice and applied to bullying within the school environment.[76] The core principles are respect, consideration, and participation with an emphasis on resolving conflicts productively. Through workshops with students, conducted at the primary/middle school level (i.e., ages ten and eleven), students reported feeling safer at schools and able to utilize strategies discussed to address their victimization by bullying.

Teacher Involvement

As discussed in a previous chapter, teachers occupy unique positions that enable them to recognize the risk factors for violence and victimization within their students. In the majority of schools, teachers assume the roles of police officer, therapist, and babysitter. It is in the function of those capacities that teachers are often most aware of a student's propensity toward violence or victimization. Through training teachers are able to identify those students at risk for committing acts of violence.

Historical research suggests that students who become involved in delinquent activities are more likely to report that they dislike their teachers.[77] Teachers have acknowledged that students who engage in violent writings or drawings that threaten violence to others, who have experienced a recent relationship break, and who have begun to isolate themselves socially from others are at risk for actions of violence.[78] In the United States, teacher training includes not only the identification of risk factors but also training in what actions are most productive in the event of an incident of school violence. This training, conducted by local law enforcement and school resource officers, provides teachers the necessary skills they may someday require for survival.

To address lesser incidents of severe violence, the Council on Europe's Violence Reduction in School Teachers training since 2008 has focused on making the school environment safer by helping teachers to understand and influence gender relations in a positive manner and ensuring that they receive adequate training in preventing and responding to gender-based violence.[79] Results of this have indicated fewer incidents of gender violence and a lower rate of pregnancy.[80]

Counselor Involvement

The role and power of the school counselor should not be minimized. Counselors, because of their positions within the school and the community, are wonderful sources of outreach for parents and criminal justice personnel. Counselors are often aware of the social ability, social networks, and cliques within the school setting. As discussed with the consequences of victimization, exposure to violence (both direct and indirect) may have a significant impact on students.[81] Students who are victims of school violence may be angry, anxious, depressed, or disassociated with others.[82] A school counselor is the person to help in these situations as counselors are trained to help. Their educational background includes courses in communications and the recognition of the symptoms of trauma.[83] In addition, a counselor may gauge the student's potential for violence as well as help to implement various programs of anti-violence.[84] Counselors, with the help of criminal justice practitioners, may be trained in identifying and diffusing situations of violence as well as conflict resolution. Also, counselors are most often aware of the concerns embedded in the social relationship formed within the schools. In fact, one of the first steps in most school crisis plans involves the employment and training of counselors for the school.[85] Finally, counselors may not only offer students help with the academic side of their lives, but they also lend a sympathetic ear to a student discussing the stresses or problems of his or her life as well as the parents with concerns about their child, and they provide a source and referral for additional counseling outside of the school.[86]

Criminal justice practitioners will acknowledge that when it comes to reducing any sort of victimization or acts of delinquency that involve young people, there must be more proponents than simply law enforcement and court personnel.[87] Academics will also recognize that in reducing youth violence, there is a need for a systematic approach with collaborative actions involving the staff at the school, the families, and the community.[88] By involving teachers, and in particular school counselors, criminal justice efforts are more likely to succeed.

School Resource Officers and Security

Today, in reaction to the incidents of school violence and the public's fear of the victimization of children while attending school, it is rare to find a high school in the United States that does not have its own law enforcement officer or school resource officers (SROs) monitoring the student body.[89] Initiated in the United States within the 1980s through the program of DARE, or Drug Abuse Resistance Education, the presence of law enforcement officers within the school environment has become common. These SROs, who are employed by the local police agencies, serve not only their agencies but also the school system by promoting a visibility of law enforcement and suggesting that law enforcement officers deter incidents of violence.[90] Law enforcement officers who serve as SROs are trained to recognize problems.

Also present in the schools today, and in direct response to incidents of violence, are school security measures beyond police presence. As mentioned, current funding in the United States through STOP supports the purchase of security equipment. Metal detectors, random searches, drug screeners, and the presence of non–law enforcement criminal justice officials such as probation officers are visible within schools today. Just as security has increased in US airports following 9-11 and the majority of global travelers have accepted the measures of safety, parents, students, and school personnel have accepted these measures as a means by which to reduce the incidents of severe school violence. Accordingly, school officials will often welcome the opportunity to create a culture of safety, to increase tactical options and training for teachers, to discuss school violence with students, and to improve communications throughout the community.

In addition, another avenue of response by criminal justice agencies in response to school violence is in the area of police training or crisis training. Since the inception of various laws and policies across the globe to target violence in the schools, there have also been consistent efforts made to train law enforcement in the area of combating violence in the school setting.[91] In the United States, whether it be adjustments made in training procedures for entering a building or policies of radio communications, there are nationally accrediting agencies that mandate that all accredited law enforcement agencies have in effect a policy to address standards of crisis training.[92] Law enforcement learned from Columbine that emergency services need to be centralized, that current blueprints for the school must be available, and that multi-jurisdictional police efforts require compatible radio communications. Globally, law enforcement has recognized the need for change in combating school violence.[93]

Victimization through the internet also has become more common in today's society, and this increase in victimization extends to children within the schools.[94] In these cases SROs are often the first law enforcement officers aware of the incidents. SROs trained in Internet Crimes against Children (ICAC) often provide programs to the students and provide information to school staff, parents, and children regarding legal actions if they are victimized. This training of SROs not only increases the likelihood of an ICAC being detected, it also increases the likelihood that the crime with be reported, investigated, and solved.[95] Results on the evaluation of SROs in the school setting have varied. However, findings do indicate that while the presence of a police officer or security officer may not reduce drug use among students, it does deter incidents of violence.[96]

Prevention Programs

Finally, prevention programs are another avenue in proactively reducing the incidents of school violence. Some of the programs, such as the US program I Can Problem Solve, were originally designed for students in kindergarten and preschool.[97] In addition, there are prevention programs such as those in the United States that exist and are implemented in the elementary school environment to educate young people in the areas of drugs (the DARE program), impulse control, and anger management.

Even more than violence prevention, there are also antigang programs such as GREAT that involve criminal justice and school officials in educating students on the dangers of gangs, the recognition of gangs, and the penalties associated with gang memberships and activities. For many of the GREAT programs and the UK's GANG program, gangs in schools are addressed as these initiatives focus on attempting to engage gang members in school-related activities such as clubs or sports;[98] thus, by providing students an opportunity to succeed at something other than gang activities, they provide them another avenue for success.[99]

Community Programs

The contributions of communities should be acknowledged when it comes to reducing school violence. Communities are responsible for the actions of their citizens—to include the actions of their children. Communities must be engaged in keeping their schools safe. Hence, community members should ask questions on single points of entry into the school, the visitor policies for schools, the management and control of school visitors, and the use of background checks for all staff employed within the school environment.[100]

In addition, community members keep their schools safe by visiting the school and being involved in the activities of the school.[101] Community members should observe practices and procedures within the school. They should ask questions regarding the crime and victimization within the school.[102] Lastly, community members must support policies of discipline and safety, which help to reduce the incidents of school violence.

The mass murders at Dunblane Primary School in Scotland and Columbine High School and Virginia Polytechnic Institute and State University (VA Tech) in the United States are probably the three most traumatic events of school violence today. Each of these events will be remembered forever. Over the last few decades, parents, the communities, criminal justice officials, and education personnel across the globe have worked together to reduce the incidents of violence within the school, and, in part, their efforts have been successful.

Today school violence is addressed not only with the reactive efforts most often present in police work and policies and laws, but also with the proactive efforts of education, training, and observation. There are those who argue that as school sizes grow, incidents of violence will increase. One of the greatest concerns for parents across the globe is the safety of their children. The news of an incident of school violence, particularly a school shooting, produces a fear unlike no other. The school environment was once one of the safest locations for children. The schools are still one of the safest places for children; however, the victimization of children within the school environment is a reality.[103]

By identifying risk factors for school violence, incidents may be reduced. Those students at risk for victimization or for perpetrating acts of violence within the school structure may be identified. Regardless of the opinions on the causes of school violence, it will be as it is today, a topic of concern for all populations.

CHAPTER QUESTIONS

1. In the United States, what program was amended to include SROs and security measures to educational institutions?
2. What are the four components of social bond theory? Give an example of how each may be broken.
3. What act was signed by President Clinton in 1994 mandating one-year expulsions if a student brings a weapon to school?
4. What are the five steps involved in conflict resolutions?
5. What is the purpose of the two conflict resolution programs?

DISCUSSION QUESTIONS

1. In your opinion, what should be a change/policy implemented in schools in an effort to reduce the overall rate of school violence?
2. Do you feel as though perpetrators who are products of their environment is less responsible for their actions because of what they were exposed to throughout their life? Explain.
3. What are your thoughts on the correlation, if any, between the media and policies implemented in schools to reduce violence?

NOTES

1. Daniel Olweus, *Bullying at School: What We Know and What We Can Do* (Malden, MA: Blackwell Publishing, 2004).

2. HM Government, *Ending Gang and Youth Violence: A Cross Government Report* (London: The Stationery Office, 2011).

3. Hannah Smithson, Rob Ralphs, and Patrick Williams, "Used and Abused: The Problematic Usages of the Term Gang and Its Implications for Ethnic Minorities," *British Journal of Criminology*, 53(1) (2013): 113–28.

4. Robin DeAngeles, "This Is a Crisis Now: Survey Finds More Violence in Ontario Schools," CBC News, June 28, 2017, accessed on November 3, 2018, at https://www .cbc.ca/news/canada/sudbury/catholic-teachers-survey-violence-schools-1.4180894.

5. Peter McGuire, "Claim of Regular Student Attacks on Teachers," *Irish Times*, April 25, 2014, accessed on October 23, 2018, at https://www.irishtimes.com/news/ education/claim-of-regular-student-attacks-on-teachers-1.1773090.

6. Hannah Smithson, Rob Ralphs, and Patrick Williams, "Used and Abused: The Problematic Usages of the Term Gang and Its Implications for Ethnic Minorities."

7. North Carolina Department of Juvenile Justice and Delinquency Prevention [NCDJJDP], "Just What Is School Violence?" News Brief, May 2002, p. 1.

8. Lynn Addington, "Cops and Cameras: Public School Security as a Policy Response to Columbine," *American Behavioral Scientist*, 52(10) (2009): 1426–46.

9. Lynn Addington, "Cops and Cameras: Public School Security as a Policy Response to Columbine."

10. Kimberly McCabe and Gregory Martin, *School Violence, the Media and Criminal Justice Responses* (New York: Peter Lang, 2005).

11. Travis Hirschi, *Causes of Delinquency* (Berkeley: University of California Press, 1969).

12. Lawrence Cohen and Marcus Felson, "Social Change and Crime Rate Trends: A Routine Activities Approach," *American Sociological Review*, 44(4) (1978): 588–608.

13. Jackson Toby, "Social Disorganization and Stake in Conformity: Complementary Factors in the Predatory Behavior of Hoodlums," *Journal of Criminal Law, Criminology and Police Science*, 48(1) (1957): 12–17.

14. F. Ivan Nye, *Family Relationships and Delinquent Behavior* (New York: John Wiley, 1958).

15. Kimberly McCabe and Gregory Martin, *School Violence, the Media and Criminal Justice Responses.*

16. Travis Hirschi, *Causes of Delinquency.*

17. Travis Hirschi, *Causes of Delinquency.*

18. Daniel Curran and Claire Renzetti, *Theories of Crime*, second edition (Boston: Allyn and Bacon, 2001).

19. Travis Hirschi, *Causes of Delinquency.*

20. Lawrence Cohen and Marcus Felson, "Social Change and Crime Rate Trends: A Routine Activities Approach."

21. Kimberly McCabe and Gregory Martin, *School Violence, the Media and Criminal Justice Responses.*

22. Kimberly McCabe and Gregory Martin, *School Violence, the Media and Criminal Justice Responses.*

23. Kimberly McCabe and Gregory Martin, *School Violence, the Media and Criminal Justice Responses.*

24. Everytown for Gun Safety Support Fund, "Mass Shootings in the US 2009–2016," April 11, 2017, accessed on November 23, 2018, at https://everytownresearch.org/wp-content/uploads/2017/03/Analysis_of_Mass_Shooting_033117.pdf.

25. Kimberly McCabe and Gregory Martin, *School Violence, the Media and Criminal Justice Responses.*

26. Kimberly McCabe, *Protecting Your Children in Cyberspace: What Parents Need to Know* (Lanham, MD: Rowman and Littlefield Publishers, Inc., 2017).

27. Kimberly McCabe, *Protecting Your Children in Cyberspace: What Parents Need to Know.*

28. Peter Smith, *Violence in Schools: The Response in Europe* (London: Routledge, 2003).

29. Thomas Gabor, *School Violence and Zero Tolerance Alternatives. Some Principles and Policies* (Ottawa, Canada: Canada Ministry of Supply and Services, 1995).

30. Kimberly McCabe and Gregory Martin, *School Violence, the Media and Criminal Justice Responses.*

31. Paola Pereznieto, Caroline Harper, B. Clench, and J. Coarasa, *The Economic Impact of School Violence: A Report for Plan International* (London: Plan International and Overseas Development Institute, 2010).

32. Kimberly McCabe, *Protecting Your Children in Cyberspace: What Parents Need to Know.*

33. Kimberly McCabe and Daniel Murphy, *Child Abuse—Today's Issues* (New York: Taylor and Francis Publishing, 2016).

34. Kimberly McCabe and Gregory Martin, *School Violence, the Media and Criminal Justice Responses.*

35. Kimberly McCabe, *Child Abuse and the Criminal Justice System* (New York: Peter Lang, 2003).

36. Ronald Stephens, "National Trends in School Violence: Statistics and Prevention Strategies." In A. P. Goldstein and J. C. Conoleys (eds.), *School Violence Intervention: A Practical Handbook* (New York: Guilford Press, 1997), 72–90.

37. Kimberly McCabe, *Protecting Your Children in Cyberspace: What Parents Need to Know.*

38. Billie Gastie, "Truancy, Disaffection and Anti-Social Behaviour," *Educational Review*, 4 (2008): 391–404.

39. Kimberly McCabe and Gregory Martin, *School Violence, the Media and Criminal Justice Responses.*

40. Kimberly McCabe, *Protecting Your Children in Cyberspace: What Parents Need to Know.*

41. Kimberly McCabe and Daniel Murphy, *Child Abuse—Today's Issues.*

42. William DeJong, "Resolving Conflict Creativity Program," 1993, accessed on November 3, 2018, at https://eric.ed.gov/?id=ED379562.

43. Kimberly McCabe, *Child Abuse and the Criminal Justice System.*

44. B. Rosenthal, "Exposure to Community Violence in Adolescence: Trauma Symptoms," *Roslyn Heights,* 35(138) (2000): 271–84.

45. Kimberly McCabe, *Child Abuse and the Criminal Justice System.*

46. Kimberly McCabe and Daniel Murphy, *Child Abuse—Today's Issues.*

47. Kimberly McCabe, *Protecting Your Children in Cyberspace: What Parents Need to Know.*

48. Cynthia Crosson-Tower, *Understanding Child Abuse and Neglect*, eighth edition (Boston: Allyn and Bacon, 2010).

49. Paola Pereznieto, Caroline Harper, B. Clench, and J. Coarasa, *The Economic Impact of School Violence: A Report for Plan International.*

50. Paola Pereznieto, Caroline Harper, B. Clench, and J. Coarasa, *The Economic Impact of School Violence: A Report for Plan International.*

51. Kimberly McCabe and Gregory Martin, *School Violence, the Media and Criminal Justice Responses.*

52. Russell Skiba, "The Failure of Zero Tolerance," *Journal of Reclaiming Children and Youth*, 22(4) (2014): 27–33.

53. Kimberly McCabe and Gregory Martin, *School Violence, the Media and Criminal Justice Responses.*

54. Russell Skiba, "The Failure of Zero Tolerance."

55. Joel Grube and Peter Nygaard, "Adolescent Drinking and Alcohol Policy," *Contemporary Drug Problems*, 28(1) (2001): 87–131.

56. Zachary Levinsky, "Not Bad Kids, Just Bad Choices: Governing School Safety through Choice," *Canadian Journal of Law and Society*, 31(3) (2016): 359–81.

57. Pedro Noguera, "Preventing and Producing Violence: A Critical Analysis of Responses to School Violence," *Harvard Educational Review*, 65 (1995): 190–96.

58. Paul Kingery, Mark Coggeshall, and Aaron Alford, "Weapon Carrying by Youth: Risk Factors and Prevention," *Education and Urban Society*, 31(2) (1999): 309–33.

59. Catherine Kim, Daniel Losen, and Damon Hewitt, *The School-to-Prison Pipeline: Structuring Legal Reform* (New York: New York University Press, 2010).

60. Tary Tobin, Georgo Sugai, and Geoff Colvin, "Patterns in Middle School Discipline Records," *Journal of Emotional and Behavioral Disorders*, 4 (1996): 82–94.

61. Wendy Schwartz, *An Overview of Strategies to Reduce School Violence* (New York: Teachers College, ERIC Clearinghouse of Urban Education, and Washington, DC: National Education Association, 1996).

62. Ronnie Casella, *Zero Tolerance. Punishment, Prevention, and School Violence* (New York: Peter Lang, 2001).

63. Kimberly McCabe and Gregory Martin, *School Violence, the Media and Criminal Justice Responses*.

64. Ronnie Casella, *Zero Tolerance. Punishment, Prevention, and School Violence*.

65. Christopher Boccanfuso and Megan Kuhdeld, "Multiple Responses, Promising Results: Evidence-Based Nonpunitive Alternatives to Zero Tolerance," Child Trends, March 1, 2011, https://www.childtrends.org/publications/multiple-responses -promising-results-evidence-based-nonpunitive-alternatives-to-zero-tolerance. Accessed on December 1, 2018.

66. Michael Tonry, *Malign Neglect: Race, Crime, and Punishment in America* (New York: Oxford University Press, 1995).

67. John Wallace, Sara Goodkind, Cynthia Wallace, and Jerald Bachman, "Racial/ Ethnic and Gender Differences in School Discipline among High School Students: 1991–2005," *Negro Educational Review*, 59 (2008): 47–62.

68. Kimberly McCabe and Gregory Martin, *School Violence, the Media and Criminal Justice Responses*.

69. Kimberly McCabe and Gregory Martin, *School Violence, the Media and Criminal Justice Responses*.

70. J. Patti and James Tobin, "Leading the Way: Reflections on Creating Peaceable Schools," *Reclaiming Children and Youth*, 10(1) (2001): 41–46.

71. William DeJong, "Resolving Conflict Creativity Program."

72. Christopher Boccanfuso and Megan Kuhdeld, "Multiple Responses, Promising Results: Evidence-Based Nonpunitive Alternatives to Zero Tolerance."

73. United Nations, *Tackling Violence in Schools: A Global Perspective* (Nairobi: Office of the Special Representative of the Secretary-General on Violence against Children, 2016).

74. Belinda Basca and Amy Brinkman, "Adapting the Olweus Bullying Prevention Program," accessed on December 31, 2018, at http://www.olweus.org/public/ case_studies.page.

75. Kelly Graves, James Frabutt, Debra Vigliano, "Teaching Conflict Resolution Skills to Middle and High School Students through Interactive Drama and Role Play," *Journal of School Violence*, 6(4) (2007): 57–70.

76. Brenda Morrison, "Bullying and Victimisation in Schools: A Restorative Justice Approach," *Trend and Issues in Crime and Criminal Justice*, 219 (2002): 1–6.

77. Robert Agnew, "Foundation for a General Strain Theory of Crime and Delinquency," *Criminology*, 30(1) (1992): 47–88.

78. Kimberly McCabe and Gregory Martin, *School Violence, the Media and Criminal Justice Responses*.

79. United Nations, *Tackling Violence in Schools: A Global Perspective*.

80. United Nations, *Tackling Violence in Schools: A Global Perspective.*

81. B. Rosenthal, "Exposure to Community Violence in Adolescence: Trauma Symptoms."

82. John Briere, *Trauma Symptom Inventory: Professional Manual* (Rockville, MD: Center for Substance Abuse Treatment [US]. Trauma-Informed Care in Behavioral Health Services, 1995).

83. David Foy and Carole Goguen, "Community Violence-Related PTSD in Children and Adolescence," *Psychiatry*, 32 (1998): 424–30.

84. Marlowe Smaby and R. Daugherty, "The School Counselor as a Leader of Efforts to Have Schools Free of Drugs and Violence," *Education*, 115(4) (1995): 612–23.

85. Steve Abrecht, "The 10 Best Security Tools for School Violence Prevention," *Psychology Today*, January 28, 2013, accessed on October 22, 2018, at https://www.psychologytoday.com/us/blog/the-act-violence/201301/the-10-best-security-tools-school-violence-prevention.

86. C. Archer, *Gang Control of Violence in the Schools* (New York: Teachers College, ERIC Clearinghouse of Urban Education, and Washington, DC: National Education Association, 1994) (ED-377-256).

87. Kimberly McCabe, *Child Abuse and the Criminal Justice System.*

88. Norris Haynes, "Creating Safe and Caring School Communities: Comer School Development Program Schools," *Journal of Negro Education*, 65(3) (1998): 308–14.

89. Kimberly McCabe and Gregory Martin, *School Violence, the Media and Criminal Justice Responses.*

90. Kimberly McCabe and Gregory Martin, *School Violence, the Media and Criminal Justice Responses.*

91. Kimberly McCabe and Gregory Martin, *School Violence, the Media and Criminal Justice Responses.*

92. Kimberly McCabe and Robin Fajardo, "Law Enforcement Accreditation: A National Comparison of Accredited Versus Non-Accredited Agencies," *Journal of Criminal Justice*, 29(1) (2001): 127–35.

93. Hannah Smithson and Robert Ralphs, "Youth in the UK: 99 Problems but Gangs Ain't One," *Safe Communities Brighton*, 15(1) (2016): 11–23.

94. Kimberly McCabe and Daniel Murphy, *Child Abuse—Today's Issues.*

95. Kimberly McCabe, *Protecting Your Children in Cyberspace: What Parents Need to Know.*

96. Gary Zhang, "The Effects of School Policing Programs on Crime, Discipline, and Disorder: A Quasi-Experimental Evaluation," *American Journal of Criminal Justice*, 44(1) (2019): 45–62.

97. Myrna Shure, *Raising a Thinking Child Workbook* (Champaign, IL: Research Press Publishing, 2000).

98. Robert Linquanti and Beth Ann Berliner, *Rebuilding Schools as Safe Havens: A Typology for Selecting and Integrating Violence Preventive Strategies* (Portland, OR: Western Regional Center for Drug-Free Schools and Communities, 1994).

99. Shirley Lal, *Handbook on Gangs in Schools: Strategies to Reduce Gang-Related Activities* (Newbury Park, CA: Corwin Press, 1993).

100. Nikki Alvarez, "5 Ways to Help Keep Your Schools Safe," November 11, 2015, Hero, accessed on October 23, 2018, at https://www.herok12.com/blog/5-ways-to-help-keep-your-school-safe.

101. Kimberly McCabe, *Protecting Your Children in Cyberspace: What Parents Need to Know*.

102. GreatSchool.org, "Is Your School Safe for Your Child?," April 2, 2015, accessed on December 1, 2018, at https://www.greatschools.org/gk/articles/how-safe-is-your-school/.

103. Kimberly McCabe and Daniel Murphy, *Child Abuse—Today's Issues*.

Index

About the Authors

Kimberly McCabe, PhD, is a professor of Criminology at the University of Lynchburg. McCabe has been an expert witness in law enforcement policies and procedures, child abuse, school violence, human trafficking, internet crimes against children, and equity/parity/discrimination of employment in criminal justice and public safety agencies. She has also acted as a consultant for state and local agencies in the United States, United Kingdom, and Albania for design, implementation, and evaluation of criminal justice and public safety programs. She has authored many books and articles on child abuse, sex trafficking, and violence, including *Child Abuse—Today's Issues* (2016) and *Protecting Your Children Online* (2018).

Brianna Egan, MCJ, graduated from Lynchburg College in 2017 with her BA in Criminology, from the University of Lynchburg in 2019 with her MCJ, and is now a candidate for doctoral programs in Criminology and Criminal Justice. Egan has assisted in many research projects revolving around victims of domestic violence, child abuse, and police management. She has experience within victims' services through work she has done with the YWCA's Domestic Violence Prevention Center as well as local pretrial service agencies. Her research interests include the victimization of women and children, sexual assault, domestic violence, and juvenile delinquency. She has also coauthored the article *Youth Gone Wild: Behavioral Disorder in Virginia High Schools* (2018).

Toy Eagle, MCJ, has worked as an advocate for victims of crime for many years as a court advocate, child advocate, and family advocate for primary and secondary victims of domestic and sexual violence. She has assisted with mass casualties as well as having completed training regarding active-shooter situations, proper firearm precautions, and trauma-informed crisis care for victims. Eagle also serves as a member of the Coalition against Domestic Violence for the 24th Judicial District, hosting annual conferences on various issues surrounding victims of violence and raising awareness to combat the issues raised locally.

Printed in the USA
CPSIA information can be obtained
at www.ICGtesting.com
LVHW011410250823
756180LV00007B/894